Lessons from American History
Abraham Lincoln to Modern China

THE BLACK BOOK

of

Vice President Adlai E. Stevenson, 1836 -1914
Governor Adlai E. Stevenson, 1900 - 1965
Senator Adlai E. Stevenson, 1930 –

Edited, with commentary, by the Senator.
American Values and American Politics

First printed by the Stevenson family for their father,
January, 2009

ISBN 978-0-9823710-0-8

www.adlai3.com

3

Contents

4

Preface

Organizing and editing the Black Book with commentary on its implications for America's politics and future consumed nine years more or less of intermittent effort. It was a high priority but always fell behind the daily chores which could not wait. Events and anecdotes continued to accumulate as I sought intermittently to record them from my family's political archive which begins in central Illinois with great great grand father Jesse Fell, Abraham Lincoln's sponsor. Organizing the Black Book for publication threatened to become an endless process, and I was not growing younger. So I closed the Black Book in early 2008. Since then events have continued to over take the Black Book but without undermining its lessons. The chapter on Economics foretells credit crises and menacing global imbalances. Terrorism was foretold with some precision, the futility of war in Iraq - and war in general as a substitute for policy - inter alia, citing Prussian General Carl von Clausewitz - and so it went. The Black Book's improbable ending in China no longer seems so improbable. Tides of history flow in foreseeable directions for those who see the past - citing Confucius and Churchill. I pulled the trigger and have not gone back to record recent events and continue an endless process. The lessons and values of the Black Book are enduring. My few revisions since that indistinct moment of decision in early 2008 are largely editorial, the delay since then occasioned by pursuit of a publisher for a volume which fit no mould. I am grateful to my family, led by son Warwick, for stepping into that breach.

The election of Barack Obama to the U.S. Presidency deserves recognition in the Black Book. It marks a refreshing reengagement of Americans in their politics, notably the youth of America, though Grandmother Nancy Stevenson was back in the precincts, and she was not alone. The election may mark one of the recurring reactions to adverse times and failures of policy which punctuate American history and are cited in the Black Book - a restoration of political energy and idealism. But for all the imagery and exultation, Obama's election reflected an America divided by religion, region, race and gender. The slanders against him were many and venomous. He lost the votes of most American white males. His campaign and inauguration will have cost a billion dollars over more than two years of campaigning and fund raising. He rejected campaign finance limitations and outspent his inept Republican opponents in the general election by two to one. And, still, the election outcome was close, especially considering the failures of George W. Bush and the ideological right.

One election will not restore the political system and values of the Black Book. The internet socializes and personalizes politics, possibly undermining once durable structures of the American past, including what remains of party organization, in a wilderness of electronic messages bereft of the old press. It is dying - as is described in the chapter on Press. Money still reigns. It is pouring into Washington's political coffers from lobbyists, bundlers, corporations and interest groups competing for increased Federal spending and investment. K Street is booming. Roughly half of retiring Members of Congress routinely stay in Washington to multiply their salaries as lobbyists, consultants and lawyers, joining former staffers. Members did not retire to lobbying and consulting in my time and in the Black Book.

Money reigns at all levels of government - debt piles up at all levels. The City of Chicago is leasing its parking meters. In January, 2009, Governor Rod Blagojevich appointed Barack Obama's successor to the U.S. Senate after having been arrested and impeached for his apparent political mercantilism, even seeking a price for the Senate seat.

The election of Barack Obama marks a return of Reason to Washington. He won by appealing to the good sense and decency of the American people after the long years of the Bush Administration and its rule of ideology, religious fundamentalism and ignorance. Obama was eloquent, his intelligence conspicuous. Time and again, I was asked by journalists to respond to complaints and suggestions that he was like Adlai Stevenson, the egghead - too intelligent, eloquent and idealistic to win and govern. For speaking sense to the American people - trusting in their decency and good sense - Adlai II was labeled an elitist, and so was Barack Obama.

The Black Book ended in despair inspired by George Bush, the neoconservatives, their supporters and tactics. That despair has been overtaken by the victory of qualities exemplified by Governor Stevenson, albeit a victory qualified by the historical analogy. In 1952, it was General Eisenhower who ran with a promise of "change" after many years of Democratic rule and against an alleged mess in Washington. As will be recorded, Stevenson lost the election to the returning war hero, but it was he who delivered the change.

President Obama has moved with commendable zeal and speed to organize an administration that includes capable, experienced and rational officials. An ambitious agenda for America and the world is far along as I write in late January, 2009. It is slow to confront challenging life and death issues of terrorism and peace in the Middle East and Central Asia, especially the Palestinian issue, to design a global regime for monetary policy and regulation of financial products and institutions in a global economy. Multilateralism and strengthening the UN, its far flung peace keeping and life saving activities and agencies await action. Massive doses of Keynesian economics wisely, if imprecisely, focus on infrastructure, health, science, education, and the social compact - and with insufficient concern about debt, private and public, including trillion dollar federal deficits and unfunded long term liabilities stretching beyond the horizon, for the dollar, interest rates and the international monetary system - and global economy. Are burst debt bubbles to be cured by larger bubbles? Gas taxes could be raised. Weapons systems could be slashed from the bloated defense budget. Universal service, including a draft, could be established if, indeed, military manpower is to be increased. The tumult and the cheers subside. The stark reality of responsibility has arrived.

The Obama administration is in its infancy. Hope to the Black Book is eternal. It is revived. The presidency of Barack Obama renews the hopes for America of peoples everywhere. The challenges are formidable. The forces of history and the life cycles of nations and empires are relentless. But we can hope again - for a restoration of Reason and American values to American policies. The Black Book remains a reminder of the rich past, its lessons and the demands of service for those who would pick up where America left off and resume leadership of mankind's evolution to a peaceful world order based on cooperation, law and Reason.

Introduction

Anecdotes and maxims are rich treasures to the man of the world, for he
knows how to introduce the former at fit places in conversation, and to
recollect the latter on proper occasions.

Goethe

The Black Book is a compendium of wit, wisdom and whimsy
spanning a century and a half of American public life. It began as a
brown loose-leaf binder in which my great-grandfather, Adlai E.
Stevenson I (1836-1914), collected anecdotes and maxims, stories and
sayings during his life as a county prosecutor, congressman, Assistant
Postmaster General and U.S. Vice President under Grover Cleveland.
His son Lewis, Illinois Secretary of State, added little to the collection,
but Lewis's son Adlai II, known to friends and family as "the Guv,"
expanded the collection in a large black binder during his life as an
official in the Roosevelt and Truman Administrations, Governor of
Illinois, Democratic presidential candidate in 1952 and 1956, and U.S.
Ambassador to the United Nations in the Kennedy and Johnson
Administrations.

This binder was known as the Black Book. It was stuffed with
the Guv's and Adlai I's voluminous notes jotted on menus, place cards,
napkins, whatever was at hand. Supporters and friends contributed as
word of the Black Book spread. The Guv's staff, mine later, edited and
organized this trove as a ready source of jokes, anecdotes, aphorisms,
wise comment, solace and inspiration, often unattributed in the heat of
the moment. I inherited the Black Book, along with the original binder
of Adlai I, and augmented it from my life as a Marine, Illinois Supreme
Court law clerk, partner in a large law firm, State Representative, State
Treasurer, U.S. Senator, two-time Democratic candidate for Illinois
governor, farmer, international investment banker, and ever the
hereditary global sojourner and public policy activist.

I used the burgeoning Black Book as my predecessors had to
enliven speeches. Mine needed it more than theirs. My father, like his
grandfather, was renowned for spontaneous wit and eloquence. I
suffered by comparison. As columnist Mike Royko wrote in the
Chicago Sun-Times:

> The most dangerous element in our politics is charisma.
> It makes people get glassy-eyed and jump and clap
> without a thought in their heads. Adlai Stevenson [III]

never does that. He makes people drowsy. His hair is thinning. He has all the oratorical fire of an algebra teacher. His clothes look like something he bought from the coroner's office. When he feels good, he looks like he has a virus. We need more politicians who make the blood run tepid.

The Black Book helped me only so much.

The Black Book owes much to Abraham Lincoln, a friend of the Guv's maternal great-grandfather, Jesse Fell. Fell was among the first to urge Lincoln to seek the presidential nomination, and it was he who proposed the Lincoln-Douglas debates as a means of bringing Lincoln to the nation's attention. Lincoln had a gift for befriending the audience and making his point with story. His influence and this methodology permeate the Black Book, which reflects a reverence for the politics, warts and all, in which the Stevenson family has participated for generations.

The influence of Woodrow Wilson is less explicit but pervasive. Wilson was a scholar, President of Princeton University, the reform Governor of New Jersey, and President of the U.S. when the Guv entered Princeton, graduating in 1922. He had first met Wilson as a boy in the company of his father, Lewis. Wilson's reformism as Governor and President, his enlightened internationalism, his crusade for a League of Nations, undoubtedly left a mark. The Guv visited the battlefields and military cemeteries of Europe shortly after World War I, and later, as a young newspaper correspondent, saw orphaned "wolf children" of Russia's civil war fighting like animals for scraps of food in the streets. He saw more of war as Assistant to the Secretary of the Navy, among other assignments, during World War II and its aftermath. Like Wilson, Adlai II was an idealist and an intellectual for whom war had no charms. Unlike Wilson, he absorbed the world's history from on the ground. He was an intellectual but not a scholar. The press dubbed him the "egghead," but he was a pragmatic internationalist, a hard-boiled egghead. Following Wilson's failed fight for the League of Nations, he became an architect of the post World War II international order, including the United Nations, which preserved the peace. The Guv was a peace maker.

Our family roots, nourished in politics, farming, the law and journalism, run deep in Central Illinois. But my father's universe, and mine, was the world. From his days as a young newspaper correspondent, the Guv was a peripatetic student of the world, exploring its markets and *favelas* to learn how people lived and suffered, rummaging among ruins and monuments to discover their past, always listening and absorbing history. His perspective came from history and the real world, on the ground and often on the front lines, not from an ivory tower of scholasticism for armchair strategists and polemicists. His thinking was devoid of ideology and religiosity, those facile and convenient substitutes for knowledge and experience. I followed him, sometimes joined him. My global sojourns outside North America began with my father in London in 1945, more than sixty years and eighty countries past. "On the ground and in the real world" becomes a refrain in the Black Book, intended to contrast perspectives of Americans past and now: Reason then; conventional wisdom, ideology and tactics now.

According to the Black Book, politics is the noblest of callings, with more potential for good and for evil than any other. The Black Book reflects a politics all but forgotten in which winning was not the only objective of a campaign. In a democracy one must win well to serve well. The purpose was to inform so the public could make an educated judgment. "Trust the people, trust their good sense, their decency, their fortitude, their faith. Trust them with the facts. Trust them with the great decisions. . . .What wins is more important than who wins," the Guv said. As President Grover Cleveland put it in 1887, "What is the use of being elected or re-elected unless you stand for something?" He was defeated, standing against a protective tariff, but re-elected in 1892 with Adlai I, his vice presidential running mate and my other coauthor.

It was a hard-fought politics, but a politics of humor, wit and the spontaneity made possible by integrity and an ability to trust one's cause—and instincts—and party. As witnessed in the Black Book, politics was barren of sanctimony and deception. Campaign managers asked what the message was. Now pollsters and consultants tell the candidate what the message is.

> I am sometimes very much interested when I see gentlemen supposing that popularity is the way to success in America. The way to success in this great country with its fair judgments is to show that you are not afraid of anybody except God and his final judgment.
> *Woodrow Wilson*, July 4, 1914

Today's politics tends to focus on popularity and the game: who is supporting whom, the polls and the money, personalities over truth, images over policy. Ideology, even religious fundamentalism, substitutes for Reason. From a process thus corrupted, Americans drop out or divide along lines divorced from the democratic dialogue—the life and death issues and policy formulations. In Adlai I's day, people came on foot and horseback from miles around to cheer their candidates and be a part of their politics. Historian Richard Norton Smith tell us that more Americans turned out in 1896 to hear William Jennings Bryan barnstorm and William McKinley orate from his front porch than heard Bill Clinton, Bob Dole and Ross Perot exactly a century later.

The New York Daily Post headlined a crowd of 350,000 in the streets of New York to hear Adlai II campaign for President late in 1956. In 1960, tens of thousands of his supporters converged on San Francisco, breaking into the Democratic convention to demand a third nomination. In my time thousands marched with posters and banners in the streets of Chicago, late in the campaigns, to their rallies in the old Chicago Coliseum, filling its surrounding streets. The Black Book reflects a robust partisanship. Politics was the stuff of debate and hard work in the precincts, not of daily denigration or entertainment on talk shows, let alone fund raisers and marketing. The people's business was serious and joyful—their participation uncontrived. The Black Book's aphorisms and anecdotes highlight the contrast between the founders' ideals and the realities of politics. The contrast diminishes during bursts of enlightened political activism, as during the Theodore Roosevelt, Wilson, New Deal and early post World War II eras, but it is sharper now than it was in the first Gilded Age when Adlai I was active. In today's Gilded Age, the ideals of politics have faded from the rhetoric which has lost its flourishes and its humor. The old, healthy public skepticism toward politics has become an unhealthy cynicism. Ideals receive lip service in clichés about freedom, democracy, conservatism, change, hope and "values." The political ideals of the Black Book express conscience and personal conviction and propositions, which, however unpopular, are rooted in realism and history. These ideals owe nothing to ideology, poll-tested public opinion, the Nixonian ethic of anything goes—and money. The political process reflected in the Black Book yielded an eloquence born of principle, communicable and capable of arousing public enthusiasm. Before patriotism erupted on the lapels of politicians it was what the Guv described as the "tranquil steady dedication of a lifetime."

One of my purposes in publishing the Black Book and augmenting it with comment is to remind readers what our politics was, what it can be, and what it is. Memories are short. Generations are disconnected from one another and the rich American past. Some will say it was always thus and, of course, American politics never was "beanbag," as Mr. Dooley reminded us.

As I try to make clear through some of my recollections, no veteran of Illinois politics is unaware of the demands of party discipline and the underside of American politics. The Black Book weathered the 1870's and the 1920's. But the corruption to which we were accustomed was of an old-fashioned, universal variety. Votes and favors could be traded and bought, but never were the nation's security interests corrupted by foreign interests, religious fundamentalism or the delusions of ideologues with little experience in the real world, none in war. Party organization and discipline were strong, at times abusive, but parties had a purpose which transcended patronage and raw power. Reason, not ideology or religiosity, informed policy. Policy was not for sale. The Black Book spans an Age of Reason in America.

In preparing the Black Book for publication, I have included a chapter on our family origins and background in Illinois, added quotes from my father, weeded out some of the more familiar material, including much from the Bible, and retained materials which, even though they are politically incorrect today, nonetheless reflect public attitudes at the time, some of them racially insensitive. I have added comments from experience to contrast contemporary politics with the more traditional politics reflected by the Black Book, and defined challenges facing America while sketching means of meeting them.

These disparate materials are uneasily organized in two Parts. Part I is a narrative with excerpts from the Black Book focusing on politics, policy making and related abstractions such as freedom, law and justice, money and economics, the press, also Lincoln and the family ties. It reflects the environment within which politics and politicians functioned during an earlier era, and contains comments on the implications of the past for the future.

Part II pulls together excerpts—sayings, anecdotes and "humorous recitations and laugh lines"—from a wider range of subject matter. They lack easy categorization but reflect influences on the thinking and motivation of our generations, and may be of value to readers as they were to us. These Afterwords are often of inspiration, courage, crime and justice and friendship: a universe of diverse comment and wisdom for politicians who carry on, and a reminder for us all.

The Epilogue in Part I raises fundamental issues about America's viability in a new world, its stage in the life cycle of nations and empires. In the chapter "China and Eight Immortals Crossing the Sea," I detect traces of the old America in today's China—a rule of Reason; and in today's America, signs of the former China — a rule of ideology. In East Asia, I have experienced for more than half a century the development of the world's largest regional economy, and in recent years, America's descent and China's rise.

Throughout the Black Book, parables, aphorisms and anecdotes reappear in different versions in different times, but with the same enduring themes. Our own times seem bereft of both the timely anecdote and its enduring message. Political fodder for the Black Book has become scarce.

Despite the metamorphosis of American politics, there still are many courageous and sensible men and women prepared to lay down their political lives for their country. The Black Book is for them. May they gain some amusement, nourishment and strength from its bits of wisdom.

Part I

1: America and Americans

I confess that in America I saw more than America; I sought there the image of democracy itself, with its inclinations, its character, its prejudices, and its passions, in order to learn what we have to fear or to hope from its progress.

Alexis de Tocqueville,
Democracy in America

When an American says that he loves his country, he
means not only that he loves the New England hills, the
prairies glistening in the sun, the wide and rising plains,
the great mountains and the sea. He means that he loves
an inner air, an inner light in which freedom lives and in
which a man can draw the breath of self respect.
Adlai Stevenson II

The Black Book depicts a boundlessly confident, proud and generous people and a rational, at times exuberant, politics. The first to arrive from the Old World were often fleeing intolerance. In the New World they found tolerance—and intolerance. They also found hope. America was built by immigrants. They labored in its fields, mines, and laboratories. Amy Chua, a Yale law school professor and a Chinese American married to an American Jew, is no stranger to America's intolerances and prejudices. In the span of the Black Book, no newcomers to America were more discriminated against, even brutalized, than the Chinese of the late 19th century. Chua explains this seeming paradox of tolerance and intolerance in *Day of Empire: How Hyperpowers Rise to Global Dominance—And How They Fall.* She explores great empires, from the Achaemenid of the Persians and Alexander of Macedon's to the American "hyperpower" of recent times, and concludes that they all owed the sweep of their domains and their longevity to what she terms "tolerance."

The prejudices of many peoples and cultures were transcended by a mutual inclusivity. Rome granted subjects of its domains citizenship, at least free males. Through trade, security, privileges, economic and intellectual opportunities empires by one means and another incorporated their subjects in an overarching political reality made dynamic by its diversity. As intolerance mounted and loyalties of their peoples were divided by religion or nativism, empires declined. Amy Chua's is a scholarly, credible and original analysis but singular in its focus on "tolerance.

The Black Book is not a scholarly exercise. It absorbs history from on the ground and over the years that it spans. History is discovered and interpreted on the ground, as it were. No one phenomenon accounts for the life cycle of nations and empires, but the phenomena which do include the "tolerance" and intolerance of which Amy Chua speaks. The America of the Black Book was a nation of immigrants joined together in an allegiance to their America.

When the Pilgrims aboard the *Mayflower* were approaching shore, they drew up an agreement which read:

> We...do by these presents solemnly and mutually in the presence of God, and of one another, covenant and combine ourselves together in a civil body politic, for our better ordering and preservation and furtherance of the ends aforesaid; and by virtue hereof to enact, constitute and frame such just and equal laws, ordinances, acts, constitutions and offices, from time to time, as shall be thought most meet and convenient for the general good of the colony.

This covenant, dated November 11, 1620, was the Mayflower Compact. It is the seed of the Constitution, a root of our experience as one people and a nation. America is a product of the Enlightenment— and Reason. In a letter to Peter Carr, Thomas Jefferson wrote: "Shake off all the fears of servile prejudices, under which weak minds are serviley crouched. Fix reason firmly in her seat, and call on tribunal for every fact, every opinion. Question with boldness even the existence of a God; because if there be one, he must more approve the homage of reason than that of blindfolded fear."

The cause of America is the cause of all mankind.
Thomas Paine

Methought I saw a nation arise in the world
And the strength thereof was the strength of right.
Her bulwarks were noble spirits and ready arms
Her war was in the cause of all mankind.
Unknown

America: The home of freedom, and the hope of the
down-trodden and oppressed among the nations of the
earth.

Daniel Webster

America is another name for opportunity. Our whole
history appears like a last effort of divine providence in
behalf of the human race.

Ralph Waldo Emerson

The Black Book reminds us of what America stood for in
principle if not always in practice, of what motivated Americans to
serve their country and community in all walks of life. Service to
community and country was a welcome duty. The human spirit
triumphed over matter. The people were religious. Their government
was secular. Americans of the Black Book rejected the Protestant
fundamentalism and witch hunting of the 17th century, the anti-Papism
and anti-Semitism which followed. A bloody war was waged over
slavery. In the Black Book, America exemplified the Enlightenment and
defeat for the age-old scourges of intolerance and ignorance. Americans
sought not to exclude but to Americanize the foreigners within their
shores. Central Europeans and the Irish created neighborhoods in
America's cities. Chicago is a city of ethnic neighborhoods. Newcomers
with yellow and brown skins encountered discrimination. African-
Americans were confined to urban ghettos. But all were Americans and
proudly so.

The Know Nothings of the 1850's were followed by the
Republican Party of Abraham Lincoln. Diversity was a strength of
America—and still is. As of 2007, an estimated 48 percent of the
workers in Silicon Valley, a synonym for technological innovation,
spoke a foreign tongue. Americans were proud of their "melting pot."

Keep, ancient lands, your storied pomp! Give me your
tired, your poor, Your huddled masses yearning to
breathe free, The wretched refuse of your teeming shore.
Send these, the homeless, tempest-tost to me, I lift my
lamp beside the Golden door.

Emma Lazarus, Inscription on the
Statue of Liberty, a gift of France,
1883

The Anglo Saxon and Scotch Irish roots of American nativism and intolerance are explored by British journalist Anatol Lieven in *America Right Or Wrong*, but in the Black Book the harsh Jacksonian democracy of the frontier he describes, including its brutality toward native Americans, had passed. In the Black Book, demagogues, fools and ideologues could exploit the patriotism of Americans by stirring up fears of a Yellow Peril, of Chinese and Soviet communism in Joe McCarthy's time. The Guv was vilified as a member of the Dean Acheson "cowardly school of communist containment." Demagogues could impugn the patriotism of "radilibs" like me, for opposing a putative war against communism in Indo-China. And they could win. Nixon defeated George McGovern, the war hero and peace maker. John Kerry, the vilified war hero, lost to George W. Bush, the ne'er-do-well and draft dodger. But the demagogues never won for long.

The fight to end racial and religious discrimination persevered. The Guv was criticized by Eleanor Roosevelt and others of his supporters for acknowledging it would be a "gradual" struggle. There could be no gradualism, they charged. Policy in the main pursued economic justice as well as economic vitality. America's was a mixed economy managed by realists. Foreign interests from time to time influenced public policy. The China lobby delayed recognition of reality on the China mainland. But alien influences were at the edges in the politics of the Black Book.

As I close the Black Book, candidates for President of the United States inflame hostility toward immigrants. Muslims are objects of distrust and discrimination. The embargo of Cuba has been tightened by the Bush Administration to prevent family reunions. Intolerance, nativism and war fevers are often not far beneath the surface. In the Black Book, in the main they were contained and tempered. America was an inspiration, an architect of a world order based on law and diplomacy. It waged peace, practiced tolerance and stood tall. For President Bush, the aspirations of Americans are more modest.

The American dream, he said, was not limited to owning a home or a business but also could be summarized by the words: "I could own and manage my own health care account or my own retirement account."
George W. Bush, Chicago Tribune, March 27, 2004

The uniqueness of America, from the beginning, was in its founding principles and values rooted in a representative, increasingly inclusive democracy, Reason, equality of opportunity, a rule of law and in time, an enlightened internationalism. Americans of all faiths and colors had reason to believe in themselves, their America and the ultimate triumph of reason and justice.

> I sought for the greatness and genius of America in her commodious harbors and her ample rivers, and it was not there; in the fertile fields and boundless prairies, and it was not there; in her rich mines and her vast world commerce, and it was not there. Not until I went into the churches of America, and heard her pulpits aflame with righteousness, did I understand the secret of her genius and power. America is great because she is good, and if America ever ceases to be good, America will cease to be great.
>
> *Unknown 19th-century French writer,* as quoted by Dwight Eisenhower on election eve, 1952

> The distinctive characteristics of this people [Americans], marking them off from all other nations, included a determined faith in the democratic organization of society and the representative form of government; a taboo against kings and aristocracy; separation of church and state; zeal for universal education; an indisposition to maintain a large standing army; a prevailing and growing trend to the abolition of alcoholic drinks.
>
> *Mark Sullivan*, Our Times, Vol. I, 1927

> With the supermarket as our temple and the commercial as our litany, are we likely to fire the world with the irresistible vision of America's exalted purposes and inspiring way of life?
>
> *Adlai II*

The American compact was rooted in a decent opinion of one's fellow citizen and man. Love of one's country and a desire for its improvement are characteristics of American patriotism. America's wars of national defense were won by the citizen soldier, not the mercenary, not the contractor, not a standing army. Americans willingly served in war and peace.

> The real patriots are those who love America as she is, but who want the beloved to be more lovable. This is not treachery. This, as every parent, every teacher, every friend must know, is the truest and noblest affection.
> *Adlai II*

> Men who offered their lives for their country know that patriotism is not the fear of something; it is the love of something. Patriotism. . .is the love of this Republic and of the ideal of liberty of man and mind in which it is born, and to which the Republic is dedicated....With this patriotism – patriotism in its large and wholesome meaning – America can master its power and turn to the noble cause of peace. We can maintain military power without militarism; political power without oppression; and moral power without compulsion or complacency.
> *Adlai II, 1952*

Today political values of the old America are more evident in secular, rational "old" Europe to which some Americans, having lost the optimism which permeates the Black Book, return, seeking a more civil society. It was not so in the Black Book. From his perch in an Old World forever haunted by war and pestilence of all kinds, Otto von Bismarck, Germany's Iron Chancellor, expressed envy of the young republic beyond the seas: "God holds his hand quite particularly over fools, drunkards and the United States of America."

> Safe from attack, safe even from menace, she hears from afar the warring cries of European nations and faiths. For the present at least—it may not always be so—America sails upon a summer sea.
> *Lord James Bryce*

In the Black Book, the rights and opportunities to which America gave rise were associated with duty and service. The love of the Republic and faith in it inspired Americans to preserve its ideals by fulfilling their duties as citizens. The politics idealized, at times realized, in the Black Book, reflects this love and those ideals.

> ....when the will to power would replace the will to serve and beauty would be well nigh forgotten in the terrible headlong rush of mankind toward acquiring possessions.
> *Sherwood Anderson,*
> Winesburg, Ohio

2: Illinois and Family

Here, my friends, on the prairies of Illinois and of the Middle West, we can see a long way in all directions. Here there are no barriers, no defenses to ideas and aspirations. We want none; we want no shackles of the mind or the spirit, no rigid patterns of thought, and no iron conformity. We want only the faith and conviction that triumph in fair and free contest.

Adlai II, Welcoming Address, Democratic
National Convention, Chicago, 1952

Illinois is a cross section of America, from its industrial northeast around Chicago to its rural south in the Bible Belt. It is north and south, urban, suburban, and rural. Its economy is broad-based, a center of finance, agriculture, heavy industry, transportation and other services. Historically, Illinois voting patterns tended to mirror the nation's. Within Illinois a familiar political cleavage developed between Democratic Chicago and a hostile Republican "downstate," though in recent years this division of political labor has been transformed by the growth of suburbs. Chicago still votes Democratic. The suburbs for the most part vote Republican but are becoming more independent. Downstate has become increasingly mixed in its voting. Illinois goes both ways, Republican and Democratic. Though now labeled "blue," Illinois remains a political swing state near the nation's demographic center. Measured by a host of demographic factors—race, age, income, education, industry, immigration, rural-urban mix—Illinois remains the country's most representative state, according to the Census Bureau.

As a boy of sixteen in 1852, the first Adlai E. Stevenson trudged into Illinois from Kentucky, a speck in the stream of Scotch (Scots) Irish migrating from the Carolinas. He led the horses which brought his family to what was then frontier country. An admirable human being by all accounts, he was elected Woodford county prosecutor in 1864 and served in Congress during the late 1870s where he was an advocate for Samuel Tilden, the Democratic popular vote winner in the disputed 1876 presidential election. The issue was stolen votes in Florida and three other states.

Fortunate, indeed, will it be for this country if people lose not faith in popular institutions; fortunate, indeed, if they abate not their confidence in the integrity of that high tribunal, for a century the bulwark of our liberties. In all times of popular commotion and peril, the Supreme

Court of the United Sates has been looked to as final arbiter, its decrees heeded as the voice of God. How disastrous may be the result of decisions so manifestly partisan, I will not attempt to forecast.

> *Adlai I*, during the House of
> Representative debate on the
> election of 1876

As first Assistant Postmaster General in Grover Cleveland's first Administration (1883-87), Adlai I fired 40,000 Republican postmasters and replaced them with something more than 40,000 good Democrats, according to a legend no doubt embellished by generations of storytelling Stevensons. For that public service, and for his eloquence and affable ways, his grateful party rewarded him with its nomination for Vice President, an election he won with Cleveland in 1892. His vice presidential staff consisted of a messenger, a stenographer and personal secretary—his son, Lewis Green Stevenson, hired at an annual salary of $2,500. A great raconteur and humorist, Adlai I was also known for his amiable and unaffected manners.

Mr. Stevenson never rides in a carriage of his own, but goes to the Capitol and returns from it generally on foot. His greatest dissipation is an occasional ride in one of the slow moving, public herdic coaches that crawl up and down the Avenue for the benefit of ladies with bundles. He always wears a silk hat, but it is at least a year old, and is never brushed.

> *Louis Arthur Coolidge and James*
> *Burton Reynolds*, The Show at
> Washington, 1894

The Stevensons were known for their parsimony and aversion to waste; it may have been the predominance of the Scotch in the Scotch Irish, an enduring trait.

Adlai I ran for vice president again in 1900 with William Jennings Bryan. His opponent was Governor Theodore Roosevelt of New York. Senator Thomas Platt, Republican boss of New York, sought to rid the state of a governor with reformist tendencies and persuaded Senator William McKinley, the Republican presidential candidate, that putting Roosevelt on the ticket would attract progressive elements in the West. Senator Mark Hanna of Ohio, the national Republican boss, stalwart spokesman for the rising industrial creditor class and an industrialist himself, protested but was overruled. Thus did Adlai I lose and Roosevelt win the vice presidency. Roosevelt became an enormously popular figure in the country and was reelected with McKinley in 1904. Shortly after the inauguration, McKinley was assassinated, and "that damned cowboy," in Hanna's words, became president of the United States. Fate plays a large hand in American politics.

After working for William Randolph Hearst in California, Adlai I's son Lewis, and his wife, Helen Davis Stevenson, a granddaughter of Jesse Fell, settled in Bloomington, the central Illinois family home. Lewis was a reformer, and served as Illinois Secretary of State from 1914 to 1917. In 1922, the boss of the Cook County Democratic organization, Roger Sullivan, entered several other Lewis Stevensons against him in the Secretary of State primary election. Lewis exposed the fraud. Supported by the press and civic organizations, he won the nomination but was overwhelmed by a Republican landslide in the general election while leading the Democratic ticket. According to the Black Book, "politics is the gizzard of society, full of grit and gravel." Grandfather Lewis was ground up in the gizzard. That was the end of his political career. We were all ground up sooner or later—Adlai I in campaigns for vice president in 1900 and governor in 1912, Adlai II in campaigns for the presidency in 1952 and 1956, and myself in campaigns for governor in 1982 and 1986.

> I am reminded of Lincoln's story about the little boy who stubbed his toe in the dark and said he was too old to cry but it hurt too much too laugh.
> *Adlai II*, after losing the 1952 presidential election

Lewis's son, my father—the Guv—moved from Bloomington to Chicago after graduating from the Northwestern University School of Law, and married Ellen Borden, of a prominent Chicago family. He practiced law with a large Chicago firm, and in the early 1930s moved with his family to a newly built home on seventy acres near Libertyville, about thirty-five miles northwest of Chicago. This became known as "the farm." A rural village in the thirties, Libertyville later became part of the suburban sprawl.

Our home there was something of a museum reflecting the Guv's itinerant life and political antecedents. Mementos from his travels littered the house. The floor of a large room in the basement was covered by a magnificent Arab rug. It seems the Guv was warned by U.S. officials in Riyadh, Saudi Arabia, not to admire objects in the palace because King Ibn Saud would then be obliged by Arab custom to give them to him. The Guv was a tight man with the dollar. He admired the king's rugs selectively, thus furnishing one of his home's bare floors. Many years later I picked up a few rugs from the King of Morocco, but by then Senators were obliged to turn their booty over to the State Department. Ethics was being legislated. And I was the enforcer.

Adlai II said he was a born political compromise, taking his Democratic politics from the paternal side and his religion (Unitarian) from the maternal. With roots downstate, in Chicago and the suburbs, he was also something of a geographical compromise. The Adlais felt at home everywhere in Illinois, knew it like few others, and had better success than most in crossing its political divides, though we were never very successful at persuading downstaters that we were just farmers at heart. In his 1952 presidential campaign, the Guv invited the press and entourage to the family farm near Bloomington. He climbed behind the wheel of a car, shouted, "Follow me," and proceeded to get lost. He could not find the family farm. But there was no denying the roots were downstate, and they ran deep.

Like my father, I would work the county squares, encounter an octogenarian seated on a bench whittling or chewing, and solicit the gentleman's vote. In my first campaign for governor, one of these old gents said, "Why, Ad-lie, where yuh been all these years? Why sure, I'll vote for yuh. I voted for yuh last time you run, didn't I?" Adlai II, running in 1948, had the same experience. Adlai I was the Democratic candidate for governor in 1912.

> Philologists sweat and lexicographers bray,
> Yet the best they can do is to call him Ad-Lay.
> But at longshoremen's picnics, where accents are high,
> Fair Harvard's not present, so they call him Ad-Lie.
> *Mark Twain*

Twain's verse didn't do much to clear up confusion about the pronunciation of the name which is of obscure Biblical origin, reflecting a 19th century practice of picking names for the newborn from the Bible.

King David's shepherd begat an Adlai who begat another, or so the explanation goes. A Chicago politician once admonished me, "It don't matter how they say it, so long as they can read it"—meaning, on the ballot.

It's pronounced Ad-lay, but we answer to most anything.

3: Political Roots

A small boy's prayer in an Irish Chicago ward: "Our Father who art in heaven, O'Halloran be thy name."
O'Halloran was the Democratic ward committeeman

Politics differed upstate and down. Downstate, reporters tended to be generalists and more interested in issues than in the "game" which came to consume big city pundits and political editors. Politics in Chicago was all meat and potatoes. In the days of Adlai I, Chicago was developing the classic American political machine lubricated by patronage and favors which later tried to do in his son, Lewis. The machine flourished in Adlai II's time, churning out the votes of the poor, many of them newly arrived, first from the Old World, then the American South, later from Mexico and Puerto Rico and the Far East.

At the heart of the machine, always known to its members as the "organization," was the ward committeeman, the party dispenser of patronage and discipline, and often on the public payroll. In addition to electing Democrats, the machine served an important purpose. It offered the disadvantaged and newly arrived a route to the middle class—the Irish predominantly, also Germans and Poles, and later African Americans and Hispanics. Chicago was and remains a city of ethnic neighborhoods. These immigrants became firemen, policemen, civil servants of all kinds, and developed businesses through political connections.

1948 was shaping up to be a bad year for the Democrats. They had held the Presidency since 1933. In Illinois the Democratic organization needed "blue ribbon" candidates to dress up the ticket and stem the Republican tide. It endorsed Adlai II for Governor and, for the U.S. Senate, Paul H. Douglas, a reform Chicago alderman (something of an oxymoron), and a distinguished professor of economics at the University of Chicago. Adlai II had sought the Senate nomination and Douglas the nomination for Governor, but the party elders decided it was better to trust the spoils of the governor's office to the unknown quantity rather than to Douglas, the known reformer, in case they did win. What's more, Wayland "Curly" Brooks, the incumbent Republican Senator, was a Marine — and Douglas was a wounded Marine veteran of the Pacific. (I was taught in the Marines that once a Marine always a Marine; Marines never refer to themselves in the past tense.)

At the 1948 Democratic Convention in Philadelphia, I was a seventeen-year-old sergeant at arms stationed beneath the rostrum, with responsibility for maintaining order and clearing the aisles of rumpled, garrulous politicians assembled for serious business. The air was heavy with sweat and tobacco smoke when an unknown young mayor of Minneapolis and U.S. Senate candidate made an impassioned speech challenging those politicians to approve a strong civil rights plank. They rose to Hubert Humphrey's challenge. The South, led by Governor Strom Thurmond of South Carolina, stormed out. President Harry Truman, a product of the Kansas City Pendergast machine, went on to win the presidential nomination. He barnstormed across the country by train, railing against the "do-nothing" Republican Congress. Thurmond would long survive Humphrey and the Guv. When Humphrey took his seat in the Senate in 1971, it was beside my own. He, the former Senator, Vice President and Presidential candidate, was my junior.

Like Truman, Adlai II and Paul Douglas were given little chance of winning. They each headed a caravan of candidates which traversed the state day in and day out, occasionally converging with local candidates to exhort the faithful at rallies. They took no polls. They had little money and no consultants. The Guv's campaign cost $157,000. My cousin, Tim Ives, and I were his drivers.

At county fairs and courthouses, at factory gates and Chicago ward meetings, up and down the streets of Illinois towns, the candidates exhorted the people and pressed the flesh. I learned early to preempt the calloused hand of the farmer by going in deep for his or grabbing the fingers before they could crunch mine, already swollen and tender from countless embraces. The candidates denounced the corrupt Republican Administration in Illinois and that do-nothing Republican Congress in Washington, and urged the people to vote the straight Democratic ticket. People responded. Even Republican Bloomington staged a torchlight parade. (We always had more friends than votes in Bloomington and Libertyville.) Politics and political parties were obligations of citizens. Political organizations and volunteers got out the vote. The Guv won by the largest plurality in Illinois history to that time and, with Douglas, helped Harry Truman narrowly carry Illinois and win the presidency. Hubert Humphrey won in Minnesota.

> There are only three rules of sound administration: pick good men, tell them not to cut corners, and back them to the limit; and picking good men is the most important.
> *Adlai II*

Adlai II recruited professionals and academics from outside the sphere of politicians and their allies in labor and business. Citizens doing their duty poured into state government, as they had during the New Deal and would during the New Frontier of John F. Kennedy. Few bore the endorsements of campaign contributors and political leaders. Professor Willard Wirtz of the Northwestern University law school recalls receiving a telephone call from the governor-elect, asking him to become chairman of the Liquor Control Commission. "The what?" Wirtz asked. "I know nothing about liquor control." To which Adlai II replied, "You know how to keep your fingers out of other people's pockets, don't you? That's all you need to know." State Senator Richard J. Daley of Chicago, appointed director of the Department of Revenue, was something of an exception to the reformist pattern, though he was a fine director and would become the legendary mayor of Chicago and a steadfast supporter of Adlais II and III.

The Guv was a realist, attuned to politics since childhood, experienced in law and national government and unencumbered in Illinois. The issues in state government are of nuts and bolts and priorities, fiscal rectitude and resistance to special pleading. The job of governor requires discipline and, as Governor John Peter Altgeld put it in the 1890s, the "courage to be right," and an ability to say "no." But with 30,000 jobs to fill with hungry Democrats, the Guv was also in a position to say "yes," and reward the faithful. One grateful beneficiary assured him he had been a lifelong Democrat ever since he got his state job. Patronage was employed to good effect. That old patronage of menial jobs for the Party's foot soldiers was subsequently outlawed, leaving it to compete with Republicans on Republican terms, with money. "Pin stripe patronage" followed, including government contracts, appointments to boards and agencies, all on a scale never known to the Black Book.

When the Guv's reforms were blocked in the legislature, he appealed directly to the people through weekly radio programs, winning support for a gas tax increase and better roads. Regular Democrats developed respect and affection for the Governor. Senator "Botchy" Connors of Chicago, the Democratic floor leader, referred to him as the "little fella." Bill Wirtz called Adlai II's approach to governing "idealism with muscle." Paul Powell, Speaker of the House, was forced to go along with increased truck license fees. The Guv thanked him for the support, to which Powell replied that he was sure glad to have the thanks because it cost him $50,000. The Guv explained that "cleanliness is next to godliness, except in the Illinois legislature, where it is next to impossible."

The Guv worked sixteen- and seventeen-hour days in Springfield, the state capitol. The home in Libertyville was rented out. The airy, slightly worn, but comfortable old executive mansion became home and office. State aid for education was doubled, municipal government modernized. Mine safety was improved. Appalling conditions in mental institutions were corrected, a state reformatory established. The way was prepared for a fair employment practices commission and a constitutional convention. The civil service was strengthened, and the state police were put under a merit system. Gambling was shut down. It was a long litany of achievement. The Guv was a tight man with the people's money, and the state budget reflected his parsimony. At night he went about the mansion turning out the lights, and would sometimes walk alone to Lincoln's home nearby, to commune in the darkness and seek wisdom from the martyred president. By day he often answered the doorbell at the mansion.

The mansion became a destination for artists, authors, newsmen, and political leaders: Carl Sandburg, John Steinbeck, John Gunther, Bernard DeVoto, Allan Nevins, Arthur Schlesinger Jr., James "Scotty" Reston, Edward R. Murrow, Walter Lippmann, Ralph Bunche, and cousin Vice President Alben Barkley. From Arthur Rubenstein to Bob Hope, a spectrum of the creative, curious and influential trekked to Springfield to meet this improbable product of the world, the prairies and Illinois politics.

At the height of McCarthyism, the Guv vetoed loyalty oath bills then in fashion. He also vetoed a bill requiring that cats be kept on leashes.

> I cannot agree that it should be the declared public policy of Illinois that a cat visiting a neighbor's yard or crossing the highway is a public nuisance. It is in the nature of cats to do a certain amount of unescorted roaming…to escort a cat abroad on a leash is against the nature of the owner. Moreover, cats perform useful service, particularly in the rural areas, in combating rodents—work they necessarily perform alone and without regard for party lines….The problem of the cat versus the bird is as old as time. If we attempt to resolve it by legislation, who knows but what we may be called upon to take sides as well in the age-old problems of dog versus cat, bird

versus bird, or even bird versus worm. In my opinion, the State of Illinois and its local governing bodies already have enough to do without trying to control feline delinquency.

Adlai II, Veto Message to the
Illinois General Assembly, 1949

The Guv was never known as a man of the people. He was an egghead and not given to gimmickry. But he was unaffected by his station. He loved retail politics and people, was a good listener and a great stump speaker. With old Captain van Diver of the state police behind the wheel, he traveled around Illinois in an ancient Cadillac limousine, mending fences and inspecting state institutions. At the entrance to one, the limousine, which had clocked more than three hundred thousand miles, broke down. A state trooper arrived on the scene to find the governor's feet protruding from beneath the vehicle he was attempting to repair. Inspecting a mental institution during its social hour, he danced with a woman inmate and was pleased to hear that her late husband, Abraham Lincoln, spoke warmly of him.

1952 was shaping up to be another bad year for the Democrats. They had held the presidency for twenty years, and Republicans were complaining of a "mess" in Washington. War was raging in Korea. Adlai II wanted to finish cleaning house in Springfield, and was well aware it would be next to impossible to win the Presidency, especially if the returning war hero, Dwight Eisenhower, was the Republican candidate. He entered no primaries and disavowed any interest in the presidential nomination, but after his eloquent welcoming address, he was drafted for President by the Democratic National Convention in Chicago. He addressed two of the contenders for the presidential nomination as "cousin": Vice President Alben Barkley and Senator Richard Russell of Georgia. (In November 1970, when I claimed the Senate seat which had been occupied by the deceased Everett Dirksen, Senator Russell greeted me by saying he was glad to have lived long enough to welcome a cousin to the Senate. He died shortly thereafter.)

The Guv began his campaign at that convention with no staff, no money, no program, only a small band of sturdy, talented volunteers. He lost the election, but his vision, humor and eloquence won the hearts and minds of people the world over. He aimed to close the gap between "the haves and the have-nots" in the world, curb the strategic arms race, preserve the global commons, and in all things rely on international law and cooperation to preserve peace. He was a Cold War warrior, but his arsenal included America's democratic values, its economic system, and commitment to human rights and human welfare. He distinguished between support for the military and militarism. The world responded.

> We will not lose faith in the United Nations. We see it as a living thing and we will work and pray for its full growth and development. We want it to become what it was intended to be—a world society of nations under law, not merely law backed by force, but backed by justice and popular consent. We believe the answer to world war can only be world law. This is our hope and our commitment …
>
> *Adlai II*, October 24, 1952

After the election, Dwight Eisenhower confided to Hedley Donovan of the New York Herald Tribune that if he had known Stevenson would be the Democratic candidate he would not have run. The 1952 campaign led to another.

Adlai II's 1956 re-nomination by the Democratic Convention, again held in Chicago, was decided in the California primary, the last of five contested primaries. The convention outcome was in little doubt. To generate excitement on the floor, Adlai II threw open the nomination for vice president, making no recommendation to the convention. The principal contestants were Senator Estes Kefauver of Tennessee and an obscure junior senator from Massachusetts, John F. Kennedy. The Guv, close associates, and family privately supported Kennedy. The balloting seesawed, and at one point Kennedy surged ahead. I raced downstairs to Kennedy's suite at the Stock Yards Inn where he was pulling up his trousers for the trip to the convention floor to accept the nomination. His brother-in-law, Sargent Shriver, was guarding the gate. I barged in, excitedly congratulated "Jack," and returned to the Guv's suite in time to see Kennedy lose the nomination to Kefauver. It was just as well for Kennedy. He was brought to the attention of the country and the party, and he was not implicated in a failed campaign for vice president.

After France, Israel and Great Britain invaded Suez, and the Soviet Union invaded Hungary, the 1956 campaign was hopeless. The country rallied to Ike, its popular president. The Guv lost, but his campaigns and the advisory committees he organized during the Eisenhower interregnum laid much of the programmatic foundation for the New Frontier of John F. Kennedy and the Great Society of Lyndon Johnson. The opposition, under the Democratic Party's titular leader, did more than oppose. Arthur Schlesinger Jr., a veteran of the 1952 campaign and the Kennedy Administration, opined that President Kennedy was "executor of the Stevenson revolution." Stevenson, he added in his Journals published in 2007, "stated most of the leading themes of the New Frontier and Great Society."

Willard Wirtz and many of the good citizens who heeded Adlai II's call to state government went on to serve under Kennedy and Johnson. The Stevenson Administration in Springfield produced two judges of the U.S. Court of Appeals, a Congressman, a renowned Illinois Supreme Court Justice, two cabinet members in addition to the Guv, a Vice Chairman of the Federal Reserve Board, a Chairman of the Federal Communications Commission, an Ambassador, Mayor of Chicago, Richard J. Daley—and not one lobbyist or convict. (Since then three Illinois governors have been convicted of corruption, already.) Some of the Gov's recruits to the Kennedy Administration served in the law firm he set up in Chicago after the 1952 campaign. At his Senate confirmation hearing for UN ambassador in 1961, the Guv said that he regretted he had but one law firm to give to his country.

Like the Guv, I was born with an incurable, hereditary case of politics, though the condition owes something to an environment steeped in service and the world. When I was born in 1930, Adlai II was practicing law in Chicago, but we soon moved to Washington, where he took several posts in the New Deal. We were living there again in 1941 when Pearl Harbor was attacked, and Adlai II was an assistant to the Secretary of the Navy, Frank Knox. In 1945, I crossed the storm tossed Atlantic in the first of several troop ship ocean crossings to war-torn London, where I attended the famous Harrow School and Adlai II represented the United States on the UN Preparatory Commission.

Our little home, on a mews off Grosvenor Square, where he would die twenty years later, became a nightly watering hole for great men enthusiastically rebuilding Europe and laying the foundation for the United Nations. Jan Masaryk of Czechoslovakia, Gladwyn Jebb of Great Britain, Henri Spaak of Belgium, Lester Pearson of Canada were there—and Andrei Gromyko of the Soviet Union. Thirty years later I would cross swords with Gromyko in his Kremlin lair. By then he was the Soviet foreign minister and I was a U.S. senator with special responsibilities for international finance and trade, space policy and intelligence.

Gromyko began the conversation by recalling those evenings in London with warm words for my father. I told of how my mother attributed his longevity to the vitamins she fed him. He saw no humor in the remark, and after he had chastised me for authoring the "Stevenson Amendment" subjecting U.S. credits for the Soviet Union to periodic congressional approval, I chastised his government for developing anti-satellite weapons in secret. He accused me of hallucinating. Later the U.S. developed anti-satellite weapons.

As I close the Black Book, the George W. Bush Administration is developing an apparent nuclear first strike capability, including anti-satellite weapons, a national missile defense system with bases in Eastern Europe, and "bunker busting" nuclear weapons of the "useable" sort. It has withdrawn from the Anti-Ballistic Missile Treaty and effectively declared a pre-emptive war doctrine for outer space. China and Russia seek the demilitarization of space while defending themselves with cost-effective counter measures, including anti-satellite weapons and nuclear deterrents. They are not hallucinating.

During the gubernatorial years I was a student at Harvard, where I concentrated in political theory, figuring it would be my last chance to develop a theoretical grounding for the practical politics bound to follow. The Korean War was raging as graduation approached in 1952. The draft was beckoning, and my roommate and I decided to join officer candidate programs. He chose the Navy, while I chose the Marines, which needed cannon fodder. The life expectancy of a front line second lieutenant in Korea was short. When we reported for our physical exams at the Boston Navy Yard, my roommate failed his blood pressure test, and I failed my eye test. We were invited to return and try again. We did—and exchanged our papers. He passed my eye test with flying colors. While I was seated with the inflatable strap around my arm, taking his blood pressure test, a corpsman approached and inquired if my name was Kerry Lyne, whereupon my blood pressure shot up. I thought our fraud had been discovered. I flunked Kerry's test. He was given a third try and passed without benefit of my assistance, later serving with distinction as executive officer of a landing ship tank (LST). After several months of intense training, I was commissioned a second lieutenant at a ceremony addressed by governor and presidential candidate, Adlai Stevenson.

> You know something about the life of a candidate for high office in this country. You know what happens to him, what is expected of him. He is supposed to have something to say about every sort of issue to every kind of audience. He does his best to put his beliefs, his convictions, into words so that the people who listen to

him can think about them and judge for themselves. His whole concern is to find the right words, the true, faithful, explicit words which will make the issues plain and his positions on those issues clear. . . .

Well, there are times when words are very hard to find and this is one of them....Let me just say that I am proud of my son and each one of you who have achieved the special distinction of a commission in the Marine Corps.... Your job, wherever you are sent, will be the first line of defense or assault to halt aggression before it gains ground and momentum. More than that, you will be ambassadors to men in other lands whose hopes for freedom are dimmer than ours. Understand them and their hopes....

You carry with you not alone the hope, the prayer and the love of the people who gave you birth. You carry the same hope, the same prayer, the same love of people around the world who do not know your names, but who do know you by your cause and your great tradition.

> *Adlai II* at the commissioning
> ceremony for Adlai III and his
> fellow Marines, Quantico,
> Maryland, September 20, 1952

After more officer training, I volunteered for combat in Korea and received orders to report to Fort Knox for tank training, and then to Camp Pendleton, California, for "duty beyond the seas." In Louisville, near Fort Knox, at the home of family friends, I met Nancy Anderson. We knew each other briefly but corresponded daily while I was overseas, became engaged after my return a year later, and were married after another year and her graduation from college. Nancy remains my partner and constant source of strength in all the endeavors which followed our chance meeting in Louisville.

At Camp Pendleton I was assigned command of a tank platoon and shipped out immediately with the Third Marine Division for an unknown destination, my footlocker packed with history books, including all the volumes of Arnold Toynbee's massive *Study of History*. After a brief stint in an old Japanese army camp at the foot of Mt. Fuji, which we used for target practice, I was transferred to the 1st

Marine Division in Korea. There I received command of another tank platoon, and after being promoted to first lieutenant in the spring of 1954, served as the tank battalion assistant operations officer with responsibility for "reconnaissance and liaison." The assignment was accompanied by a jeep driver and used for explorations. (Later, in the reserves, I was promoted to captain.) On my last night in Korea, a group of field officers drove up from Division headquarters to our battalion headquarters and urged me to make a career of the Marine Corps as they had after serving in World War II. They were fine men. I loved the Marines—the "old Corps." But it was time to move on.

Hour by hour, hunched on an aluminum bench, our backs to the fuselage, our packs on the deck before our knees, we were pounded by propellers chopping at the air as our leaky transport hauled its crowded contents from Kimpo air field in Korea, to Atsugi outside Tokyo, to Wake, Guam, a base near Honolulu for the first night between sheets in many months. Then came the long haul to San Francisco where we were discharged from the Marines. My first stop as a civilian was a book store to replenish an exhausted supply of histories. The trip by air from Korea to home in Illinois required more than three days in 1954.

4: The Kosher Nostra

Discharge from active duty in 1954 came just in time for admission to the rigorous academic equivalent of the old Marine Corps, Harvard Law School, for more preparation for politics and a profession to fall back on in the lean years. After emancipation from law school in 1957, Nancy and I settled in Chicago, where I clerked for Walter Schaefer, Justice of the Illinois Supreme Court, a great human and jurist. After a year I joined a major Chicago law firm as an associate. The machine was flourishing. Downstate antipathies for Chicago were strong. We bought a home in the 43rd ward for $17,000 and, as if Harvard wasn't bad enough for the Party regulars, promptly became active in Democratic reform politics.

The 43rd ward committeeman was Paddy Bauler, one of Chicago's last "Lords of the Levee," an old-fashioned ward committeeman and an alderman with an army of precinct captains on the public payroll. His captains delivered their precincts or lost their jobs. Big Bill Thompson, a colorful mayor of Chicago in the 1930s, announced that if the King of England visited Chicago he would punch him in the nose. Asked if he agreed, Paddy said, "Nah, he's a German anyway." Harold Waller, a reformer and an uncle on the maternal side, pooled his resources and beat Paddy for alderman in the thirties, the only time Paddy was ever defeated. Somewhere down the line, Paddy announced, "Chicago ain't ready for reform." He was evidence of the truth of that assertion. He ran a speakeasy during Prohibition and shot two policemen who didn't know enough to mind their own business. Once, in the sixties, a newly elected alderman, replete with briefcase and neatly pressed grey serge suit, accosted Paddy in the Chicago City Council and poked an accusing finger at him. "You're a thief," he charged. "Yeh," Paddy responded, "and the only difference between us is I admit it."

Nancy soon received a lesson in Chicago politics. She was detected by one of Paddy's captains taking thirty-five seconds to vote. What's more, her feet were seen below the curtain at the polling booth moving from left to right along one of the voting machines used in those days, more reliable than the infamous punch-card system which would do me in many years later. It did not take thirty-five seconds to vote the straight Democratic ticket, nor did your feet move laterally. The next day the plumbing inspector arrived at our home, and then the fire marshal and finally the electrical inspector. They each found longstanding violations of city ordinances. Evidently, the prior owner of our home had known to vote the straight Democratic ticket or split his ticket fast.

In spite of my reformist habits and Nancy's irredentism, Richard J. Daley, Mayor of Chicago and, more to the point, chairman of the Cook County Democratic Central Committee, called me in late 1963 and asked me to run for the Illinois House of Representatives. The legislature had deadlocked and failed to redistrict the House as required by the one man, one vote decisions of the U.S. Supreme Court, so the Illinois Supreme Court had ordered an at-large election for all 177 House seats. Each party selected 118 candidates so that neither could win all the seats, and dressed up its slate with blue ribbon candidates. Rumor had reached Daley that the Republicans would lead their slate with Earl Eisenhower, brother of the former president. Daley wanted a Stevenson to dress up the Democratic slate and reach across the upstate-downstate divide. I was eager to work my way up the political ladder and enthusiastically agreed to run.

In what became known famously in Illinois as the "bed-sheet ballot" election—a huge orange ballot carried the names of all 236 candidates—I led them all, and the entire Democratic slate was elected. A Stevenson led an Eisenhower, though Earl was also elected. The Guv lived just long enough to see the line continued, his name victorious. He died on July 14, 1965. Earl Eisenhower proved a friendly, somewhat garrulous old gentleman. He served one term in the House and was later defeated for Cook County clerk. A good name did not assure survival in those days.

The Illinois House was a fertile place for a reformer. Scandals were often breaking out, especially in the regulated horse racing, liquor and currency exchange businesses. Paul Powell, the former speaker of the House, was then secretary of state, a patronage-rich office. He was boss of Southern Illinois, an old-fashioned orator and nemesis of the Guv and me. He caused "fetcher" bills to be introduced whose sole purpose was to fetch money from special interests supporting or opposing them. When he died, a lifetime bachelor, more than $800,000 in cash was found stashed in shoe boxes at his Springfield apartment. Asked by the press for a comment, I said, "His shoe boxes will be hard to fill."

The blue-ribbon candidates from the Democratic and Republican slates became known as the "bluenose representatives" and joined forces across the aisle. I led successful efforts to draft and pass conflict of interest and lobbying reform legislation and an extensive anti-crime program, but most of the political reform bills died in the unreconstructed Senate. Our leaders and mentors, both having served previously in the House, were Tony Scariano, an irrepressible, talented reformer and later an outstanding state appellate judge, and Abner Mikva, a brilliant and principled lawyer, later to become Congressman, White House Counsel and U.S. Appeals Court Judge. Tony dubbed the bluenose Democratic reformers the "Kosher Nostra."

The Mafia and its Cosa Nostra were represented by the "West Side Bloc" from Chicago. We uncomfortably joined forces at times on bills protecting civil liberties. Tony designed a system for detecting who was on the take. At the end of an annual session, he tucked dollar bills around the edge of his attaché case, slapped it on a legislator's desk, and said, "Well, Joe, it's been a good session. See you around." If the legislator laughed, and most did, he was in the clear; if unamused, he was suspect. Tony's test would be unamusing in Congress and the legislature nowadays.

Each morning when the House was in session, Democratic legislators received an "idiot sheet" with instructions on how to vote on the day's measures. Downstate Democrats could escape these edicts with a degree of impunity not enjoyed by their brethren from Chicago, many of whom were on second public payrolls. One of my seatmates was Harold Washington, who became a lifelong friend and ally and the first African-American mayor of Chicago. Harold turned to me one day after I had disobeyed my idiot sheet and remarked wistfully that he wished he could do the same. He gave me a lesson in humility; I could get away with more than he could.

In 1965, another call came from the mayor. The Democrats were facing a Republican year, and Senator Paul Douglas was up for reelection. I had won an Outstanding Legislator award from the Independent Voters of Illinois, and Daley said I was needed to run for state treasurer. He told me you had to take the opportunities in politics as they came. It was sound advice, and I agreed to run.

Paddy Bauler's dark, wood-paneled speakeasy, his ward headquarters over the years, was an obligatory stop on the campaign trail. Democratic candidates, judges included, dutifully trooped from ward office to ward office, night after night paying homage to the ward leaders and precinct captains while exhorting them to get everyone registered and out to vote the straight Democratic ticket. I was again running as Adlai III. Paddy presided at these smoke-filled meetings, often flailing a large, sloppy stein of beer amidst much raucous singing to the accompaniment of a jangling ukelele. After he had introduced me at one such meeting and I had made my short speech, he exclaimed to the crowd, "Why, ya know, da little shit ain't so bad after all, but he oughta drop dat turd." I took the hint, dropped the "Third," and thereafter ran under my unadorned first name, posters and bumper stickers emblazoned with a large red ADLAI against a black background, the "I" topped by a white star and "Stevenson of Illinois" in small white print at the bottom. We often did not mention the office I sought so any surplus campaign materials could be used again, no matter what I ran for. Our bumper stickers were stuck to lamp posts across the state with a mysterious substance which assured they remained in place for succeeding campaigns. An old ward committeeman once told me, "I'll give you a million dollars' worth of free advice. Don't change your name."

That campaign for state treasurer was the only campaign I had no difficulty funding. Illinois bankers had been well trained. Campaign costs were low, and the money flowed in, largely unsolicited, from bankers who were not noted for Democratic proclivities but sought deposits of state funds. I narrowly survived a Republican landslide which swept Douglas out of the Senate and Charles Percy in. (Chuck later became my Senate colleague and remains a good friend.) After the election, as a courtesy, I called my immediate Democratic predecessor, Francis Lorenz, and asked his advice. He said, "Adlai, my advice is to get a good deputy or you will have to be treasurer, and then you won't have time to practice law." I took the first part of the advice and appointed Charles 'Chuck' Woodford, a bright young Chicago banker, deputy treasurer.

Parky Cullerton, a powerful ward committeeman and the assessor of Cook County, wasted no time in calling on the treasurer-elect. He said he represented a prominent casualty company which could post the bond required by law of the state treasurer. I gulped and mumbled something about trying to oblige him, then called a friend at Marsh McLennan, the country's largest insurance brokerage, and asked his firm to review Parky's proposal. He called back a few days later to say that the company was highly rated and that Marsh McLennan could not find a better proposal for the state. Parky got the business—an example of "honest graft," politicians using their influence on the side to secure public business. It was by no means impossible for the public to benefit from honest graft, but the appearance of favoritism eroded public confidence.

I was sworn in as state treasurer by an Illinois Supreme Court Justice, Ray Klingbiel, who was later implicated in ethical improprieties and forced to resign after an investigation led by an obscure lawyer named John Paul Stevens. His reputation for integrity and professional competence established, Stevens was nominated for the U.S. Court of Appeals by President Nixon and later for the Supreme Court by President Gerald Ford in the wake of the Watergate scandal. To this day his reputation for integrity and judicial excellence is uncompromised and undoubted. It was burnished by many principled and learned opinions, including his dissenting opinions in the Supreme Court decisions which ignored judicial precedent and established constitutional law to deprive the people of their choice for President in 2000.

My predecessor as state treasurer, William J. Scott, was later caught evading taxes. I called Scott to offer and invite assistance in the transition, and as a courtesy asked his advice. He replied, "I have not had a good night's sleep since taking this office. My only request and advice is that you fire all my lockbox examiners." The state treasurer had responsibility for examining and inventorying the contents of safety deposit boxes (lock boxes) after the death of their lessees, to prevent concealment of assets subject to taxation. The General Assembly in its wisdom restricted this treasurer's duty to Cook County because that was where all the crooks resided with their lock boxes. A corrupt lockbox examiner could avert his eyes and be rewarded, hence Scott's discomfort. I resisted the entreaties of Paddy and other ward committeemen for patronage appointments and replaced the lockbox examiners with able, honest, mostly part-time staffers.

Box contents often gave rise to uncomfortable, even incriminating moments. Larry Hansen, one of my able assistants, reported that he was in attendance with grieving, expectant survivors when a box was opened and found to contain nothing except an old cheese sandwich wrapped in wax paper, with a note: "This is for all my hungry relatives." On another occasion, Sydney Olson, the Cook County recorder of deeds, a man of Norwegian origin hailed improbably at party rallies as the Fighting Viking, came in and announced that his wife had died. I expressed my sympathy and asked what I could do to be of assistance in his time of grief. He explained that he and his wife had jointly leased a lockbox which had been sealed after her death. I said I would put someone on the case right away. After a fair amount of hemming and hawing, he got to the point. "Adlai," he said, "you still don't seem to understand. That's where the cash is." "Oh, Sydney, sorry to be so slow," I said. "I'll have the right person take care of it immediately." The right person did take care of it, but not as Sydney expected. The contents of the lockbox were carefully inventoried and reported.

After my inauguration as treasurer in January, 1967, I gave a reception which could have been the wake for a Chicago ward committeeman. People crowded in, many of them bankers. Trucks pulled up to disgorge cases of liquor. The walls were piled high with floral pieces. Come the following Christmas, I did not receive so much as a posey from a banker. The state treasurer's books had been made public for the first time. State deposits were awarded to banks for services rendered and for utilizing their assets for the benefit of their communities. We cut the treasurer's office budget every year and quadrupled earnings on the investment of state funds while keeping the funds working in Illinois. The Ford Foundation financed a study which endorsed our system for the management of public funds, and soon we were acting as unofficial advisors to Mayor John Lindsay of New York, a principled public servant and a Republican of the near-extinct moderate, rational stripe.

State treasurer was a great job. I was my own boss. It was an old-fashioned patronage office. Civil service can prevent abuses but can also prevent reformers from cleaning house. I prohibited employees of the office from raising funds and contributing to my campaigns. We cleaned house, put together a first-rate staff, and ran a tight ship in high spirits. From then on, fund raising was increasingly difficult. I was not influenced by money, and according to a Black Book definition, a dishonest politician—one who when bought doesn't stay bought. In those days, elected officials had no time or stomach for "dialing for dollars." Money was a source of discomfort. Nowadays it is publicized, a measure of political viability.

Soon after taking office as state treasurer, I received a torrent of mail demanding the deposit of state funds in African American controlled banks, of which Illinois had two. The mail had been organized by Operation Breadbasket which I learned was headed by a Reverend Jesse Jackson. I arranged to meet with him at his office, and found him holed up in the basement of a church on Chicago's South Side. When I arrived, the door opened, and there was Jesse—with three television cameras. That's Jesse. We deposited funds in the banks (no contributions required or accepted) and prohibited state depositories from discriminating in lending and employment. I would often pass the plate at Jesse's Sunday services. Though I often disagreed with him, Jesse Jackson's loyalty survived all my campaigns. He always supported me, once remarking, "Adlai, there's just two things wrong with you as a politician. You're too honest, and you don't know how to talk in parables."

I sought the 1968 Democratic nomination for governor, but that was not for an independent minded, young reformer. Instead, I was offered the party's endorsement for the U.S. Senate, only to be "dumped" from the ticket in the vernacular of a *Chicago Tribune* headline for refusing to pledge support for the war in Indochina, a pledge then required of all Democratic candidates down to and including candidates for the Chicago Metropolitan Sanitary District. Mayor Daley urged me to take the pledge and repudiate it later, if so inclined. I refused. It was too late to mount a primary challenge, but I resolved never to let that happen again, and began organizing for the next round. Bill Clark, the Illinois attorney general, took the pledge, ran for the Senate, repudiated the pledge, and lost to the incumbent, Senate Minority Leader Everett Dirksen.

On a beautiful Indian summer day in 1969, some fifteen thousand Democrats gathered at the Libertyville farm to celebrate and support reform of the national and state parties, contribute money, cheer the speakers, and be a part of the democratic process. Smoke wafted into the blue sky from hotdog and hamburger stands. Children rode ponies and floated balloons. The ancient maples, beloved by Adlai II, were ablaze with orange and gold. The movement for party reform had gathered strength in the wake of the 1968 Democratic Convention in Chicago, which was engulfed by riots stemming from Vietnam War protests, and followed by the victory of Richard Nixon over Hubert Humphrey—a victory for prolonged war and American defeat. At the national level the movement was led by the McGovern Commission, named for its chairman, Senator George McGovern. It formulated rules which led to a more democratic Democratic Party. At the state level, the reform effort was led by the Committee on Illinois Government formed by idealistic young supporters of Adlai II. It compiled the record of the Republicans and formulated policy recommendations for candidates of the Democratic Party. The candidates listened in those days. I was a member of the Committee and Commission, and brought the two groups together at what became known as the Libertyville Rally, a celebration of reform and a fundraiser for reform.

As the program was about to start, a caravan pulled up and disgorged Mayor Richard J. Daley, the Boss, and his entourage led by Dan Rostenkowski, ward committeeman and congressman (the proper order of salutation in Cook County political etiquette). These were not exactly reformers. Rostenkowski later went to jail. But they were politely received by the multitude, and they dutifully joined in pledging support for reform and a united party. During the speeches, someone whispered to me that Senator Dirksen had died. I suggested to Senator McGovern that at the conclusion of the program he announce the death and eulogize Dirksen, which he did with the grace and gentleness that always concealed the steely character of this patriot in war and peace. After Senator McGovern's eulogy, I asked Jesse Jackson to pray for the dead senator's needy soul. Jesse prayed—and prayed. As he did so, the choir he brought from Chicago's South Side began chanting the *Battle Hymn of the Republic*. Senator McGovern, Senators Harold Hughes and Fred Harris, Congressman Rostenkowski, Mayor Daley, everyone on the speaker's platform—reformers and regulars—locked hands, and soon fifteen thousand people were chanting the *Battle Hymn of the Republic* in celebration of reform and the Democratic Party.

After the Libertyville Rally there was little doubt who the 1970 Democratic candidate for U.S. senator would be. Someone came up to me at the rally and said, "Adlai, why don't you walk down there to the Des Plaines River and see if the waters part." I won the nomination with little opposition. My opponent was Ralph Smith, a former Illinois house speaker appointed by Governor Richard Ogilvie to succeed Senator Dirksen.

The campaign was dirty by the standards of the time. President Nixon and Vice President Spiro Agnew were riding high. After the 1968 convention, I had written a "white paper" which praised free speech and condemned the violent overreaction of the Chicago police to war protesters. It was published by the *Chicago Sun-Times*. My campaign chairman, Dan Walker, had headed a commission which investigated the events surrounding the convention and issued a report critical of the city. The Republicans tried to tar me as a hippie and radical. They ran cunning television advertisements featuring riots and one of the Chicago Seven war protesters, David Dellinger, who bore a faint resemblance to me owing partly to his receding hairline. The Republicans coined the term "radilib" for me and others who could not support the war in Vietnam, impugning our patriotism and implying radicalism. As civil libertarians, we were also soft on "law and order." Army intelligence was caught spying on me. My opponent's advisors included Karl Rove, then cutting his political teeth and later an adviser to President George W. Bush, who appropriately nicknamed him "Turd Blossom," a Texas term for flowers that spring from manure.

I appointed Tom Foran, the gruff former U.S. Attorney who had prosecuted the Chicago Seven war protesters, my campaign co-chairman. He took some of the wind out of the Republicans' sails. I campaigned hard on a platform of reordered national priorities (less money for the military) and ignored the accusations and smears until a few weeks before the election. We organized a 99-cent dinner to coincide with a stodgy Republican $100-a-plate dinner to be addressed by Vice President Agnew. At our dinner I poured it on my opponent for the first time, ridiculing him for each of many absences on Senate votes, to which the audience responded with a rollicking refrain, "But where was Ralph Smith?" The press coverage contrasted the two events. We did not let up. Three weeks later we organized another overflowing, uproarious dinner, charging $1.42 a plate, attributing the increased price to Republican inflation. I led the Democratic ticket as I had in 1964 and 1966 and would in 1974, sweeping Democrats into office.

I was sworn into the Senate within days of the election. Soon thereafter, I met with two colleagues—Cyrus Vance, later to be Secretary of State, and George Ball, former Undersecretary of State and Ambassador to the UN—to craft my "maiden" speech in the Senate. It outlined a proposal for U.S. disengagement from Vietnam. Since the ostensible purpose of the engagement was self-determination for the Vietnamese, we proposed supervised free elections, thinking that General Duong Van Minh (Big Minh), an Eisenhower-like figure (though implicated in the assassination of President Diem), might be persuaded to run. If the South Vietnamese could not govern with a popular leader and popular support, they would be unlikely to govern with U.S. support. However the election came out, the U.S. could declare its purpose won and depart with honor. Senator Barry Goldwater responded to my maiden speech by asking what a Cook County boy knew about free elections. A few months later I met with General Minh at his tiny home behind the small rose garden he tended in Saigon. He was noncommittal, which I took as a positive sign, but the Nixon-Kissinger Administration did not accept this formula until the Viet Cong were at the gates of Saigon, and then it was too late.

The Republicans had difficulty finding a candidate to run against me in the 1974 Senate election. A *Chicago Tribune* cartoon depicted a Republican politician saying to a panhandler with outstretched hand, "Dime? Run against Stevenson and I'll make it a buck!" George Burditt, one of the blue ribbon candidates for the Illinois House in 1964, agreed to run. He was a respected legislator and member of a prominent Chicago law firm, a Lincolnesque figure eminently qualified to be a United States senator. He lost by almost two to one. Five days before the election the League of Women voters sponsored the last of several debates between us. It was held in downtown Chicago. The press did not show up: the polls indicated I would win, and we were discussing serious issues seriously. Politics was changing, the media becoming more visual and episodic. George Burditt was, and remains, the kind of man our politics deserves and for whom winning is increasingly difficult. Later, I would be on the losing end.

In 1975, Mayor Daley called again, this time to urge me to run for president and to pledge his support. I decided I wasn't ready. Instead, the Democratic Party of Illinois ran delegate candidates pledged to me as a favorite son, many of whom won. This was a device for holding delegates in reserve. Later Daley and I released them to Jimmy Carter, assuring his nomination. I was one of six finalists for the vice presidential nomination at the 1976 Democratic Convention in New York. Governor Carter called me the morning of the balloting to say he had chosen someone else to recommend to the convention. I promised my support and breathed a sigh of relief, but not without a twinge of regret. He had chosen Walter "Fritz" Mondale, my then Senate seat mate and friend going back to his days as Minnesota Attorney General.

I left the Senate voluntarily in 1981, burnt out and unenthusiastic about the prospects of serving with either Ronald Reagan or Jimmy Carter, an admirable human being with a strong cabinet but limited vision and purpose. It was time to take a breather and reflect on whether to run for the office I had always sought, governor of Illinois, where I could get my hands on levers of government and make it a platform for comment on national and international as well as state issues, as the Guv had. A campaign for governor followed, and was doomed by a new punch card ballot system in Cook County and my efforts in the Senate to prevent terrorism—a campaign to which the Black Book will return.

In 1970, my patriotism impugned by the Nixon-Agnew campaign tactics, I stuck an American flag in my lapel—and was embarrassed. I had volunteered when my time came. The flag is a symbol of America: revered, not flaunted, never exploited. Patriotism was demonstrated by that lifetime of "tranquil, steady dedication" of which the Guv spoke. I took the pin off. As I close the Black Book, another conservative Republican Member of Congress and self-anointed patriot and champion of social values and faith has been caught. The police department's frontal mug shot of Senator Larry Craig of Idaho depicts the flag in his lapel. Evidently the Senator was wearing the flag while soliciting a "lewd act" in a public toilet, for which offense he was charged by the police, arraigned and pleaded guilty.

46

Ever' once in a while some feller with no bad habits gits caught.

Will Rogers

5: Politics and Politicians

Politics is the most hazardous of all professions. There is not another in which a man can hope to do so much good to his fellow creatures—neither is there any in which by a mere loss of nerve he may do so widespread harm—nor is there another in which he may so easily lose his own soul—nor is there another in which a positive and strict veracity is so difficult. But danger is the inseparable companion of honor. With all the temptations and degradations that beset it, politics is still the noblest career any man can choose.

Andrew Oliver, ca.1810

In coping with the exercise of political power and the nature of government, the Black Book swings between the solemn and the humorous, between the utopian and reality, between political theory and practice, between abstractions like freedom and democracy and anecdotes about the mundane politics of getting elected to, and serving in, public office. For some politicians the purpose of political power is its acquisition and perpetuation. Thus do means become ends.

In 1956, Adlai II warned of the nation becoming "a land of slander and scare, the land of sly innuendo, the poison pen, the anonymous phone call and hustling, pushing, shoving; the land of smash and grab and anything to win. This is Nixonland." It was often said of Adlai II that he was before his time.

In the Black Book the democratic process, including the deliberations of a free and informed people and their elected representatives, is an end in itself. As Adlai II put it, "We mean by politics the people's business—the most important business there is. We mean the conduct of the people's business by all the people, in open meetings where we can say what we think, and what we think should be done about what we think."

The Black Book comments, as in all things, reflect an omnivorous appetite for disparate, even contrarian, perspectives.

Politics is a strong and slow boring of hard boards. It takes both passion and perspective. Certainly all historical experience confirms the truth—that man would not have attained the possible unless time and again he had reached out for the impossible. But to do that a man must be a leader, and not only a leader but a hero as well, in a very sober sense of the word. And even those who

48

are neither leaders nor heroes must arm themselves with that steadfastness of heart which can brave even the crumbling of all hopes. This is necessary right now, or else men will not be able to attain even that which is possible today. Only he has the calling for politics who is sure that he shall not crumble when the world from his point of view is too stupid or too base for what he wants to offer. Only he who in the face of all this can say "In spite of all!" has the calling for politics.

Max Weber, "Politics as a
Vocation"

Politics is applied religion.

Reverend Kenneth Walker of
Bloomington, Illinois, ca. 1950

Politics is not a game between two clubs, but the way in which people make moral decisions that affect the public welfare.

Bishop McConnell

In his address to the electors of Bristol in 1774, Edmund Burke pronounced the much neglected cardinal rule of politics in a self-governing country. A politician, Burke said, owes the public his conscience and his best opinion, ". . . not his industry only, but his judgment; and he betrays instead of serving you if he sacrifices it to your opinion."

Those who hold in their hands the power of government must themselves be independent—and this kind of independence means the wisdom, the experience, the courage to identify the special interests and the pressures that are always at work, to see the public interest steadily, to resist its subordination no matter what political hazards.

Adlai II

It is as hard and severe a thing to be a true politician as to be truly moral.

Sir Francis Bacon

For a man is justly despised who has one opinion in history and another in politics, one for abroad and another at home, one for opposition and another for office. History compels us to fasten on abiding issues, and rescues us from the temporary and transient....It is our function to keep in view and to command the movement of ideas, which are not the effect but the cause of public events.

Lord Acton, Inaugural Lecture on
the Study of History, 1895

I have come across men of letters who have written history without taking part in public life, and politicians who have concerned themselves with producing events without thinking about them. I have observed that the first are always inclined to find general causes, whereas the second, living in the midst of disconnected daily facts, are prone to imagine that the wires they pull are the same as those that move the world. It is to be presumed that both are deceived.

Alexis de Tocqueville

In the 1970's, episodic television and money, the crafts of the pollsters and campaign consultants, Watergate, Vietnam, public cynicism, and political reforms converged. Candidates were cut loose from withering party organizations to raise money and fend for themselves. Some of the best began to drop out. Party organizations focused on raising money. Office holders were cut off from the public by the new big business mass media. News reporting symbolized by Edward R. Murrow turned into sound bites. Civility began its slow death. Senators did not campaign against one another in the old politics. In early 2007, the *Chicago Tribune* ran a front page news report of a partisan Democratic congressman having dinner with Republicans. That was news. Arm chair polemicists, consultants, lobbyists and ideologues moved into the void. The dialogue between public and public official all but ceased. In earlier days I could go to a high school and classes would be adjourned. Students would assemble in the gym, ready to bombard me with questions or berate me, as during the 1968 campaign when the draft was on and I was supporting Hubert Humphrey. No more. The young people were dropping out, too. And so were the candidates. Instead of pounding the pavements, pressing the flesh at court house squares, fairs, bowling allies, factory gates and restaurants, elaborating positions and policies in speeches and papers, candidates were increasingly dialing for dollars, massaging reporters and editors and doing "fly arounds"— flying from one media event and fundraiser to the next, each public appearance carefully staged for effect, not for democratic dialogue.

The Vietnam War and the Watergate scandal led to political reforms intended to make government more accountable by making it more democratic. I served on the McGovern Commission of the Democratic party, organized after the 1968 Democratic Convention was disrupted by protests over the war in Vietnam. The convention had nominated Vice President Hubert Humphrey, a peacemaker but compromised on Vietnam by his ties to President Johnson. The commission's well-intentioned recommendations for reform and the opening up of the party contributed to the death of the national convention as a deliberative body. Primary elections spread. Except for the ex-officio delegates, they ran as candidates pledged to support presidential candidates, and were selected by the candidates for reasons of race, religion, gender and "expressed sexual preference" in the Democratic Party—no thought to the deliberations of a party's leaders assembled quadrennially to debate issues and establish policy, as well as nominate its candidates.

Our efforts to make the democratic process more democratic made it more plutocratic. The U.S. presidential election cycle became a multi-year, billion dollar exercise in money raising, polling and marketing on commercial television which is increasingly consolidated. Presidential candidates pander to special interests in fifty states. They dare not compete in the Iowa caucuses without pledging subsidies for ethanol made from corn. Selection of presidential candidates was left to the investors in politics and activists in early caucuses and primaries. The national nominating conventions which nominated all the great Democratic candidates (and the first and last great Republican, Abraham Lincoln), became media events. Delegates wave flags and cheer on cue amidst cascading balloons.

The eloquent, informed speech on vital issues all but vanished from the discourse—or at least from the reportage, the old rallies and torch light parades with it. The Illinois Democratic organization "slate making" sessions which produced Paul Douglas and Adlai II died. Today candidates stagger from one media event and fund raiser to the next, courting interest groups, solidifying their "bases," uttering poll-tested news bites and jokes while raising money to keep themselves up in the polls which keeps the money flowing to keep them up in the polls, month after month.

The *demos* has been dropping out of this democracy. The percentage of eligible Americans who exercise their right to register and vote in Presidential elections is at one of the lowest levels of participation in the developed world. Political power was steadily removed from party leaders who had knowledge of issues, the candidates and the demands of public office. Ronald Reagan was an impossible presidential nominee as late as 1976, an eccentric fringe figure with simplistic ideas and a celluloid experience in life. The impossibility of 1976 became the telegenic inevitability of the reformed, more democratic presidential selection process in 1980. In a general election contest between a movie actor with simplistic ideas and a naval engineer/farmer, albeit honorable, incumbent President of the United States, there was never much doubt about the outcome, at least not among Senators meeting regularly with our Leader to compare notes from our states. When Republicans began advertising on television in 1952, Adlai II complained that a presidential election was not a contest between Palmolive and Colgate, and an alarmed George Ball, the Guv's lifetime companion in arms, complained that some day movie actors would run for President of the United States!

Political decadence is not confined to the national government. Between the time I, as State Treasurer, left Springfield in 1970 for the Senate and returned in 1982 as the Democratic candidate for governor, the Illinois state government had been transformed. The capitol's growth industry had become lobbying and special interest pleading by proliferating interest groups and associations. State government was on the block. The treasury was used by the Democratic treasurer and Republican governor to finance real estate projects of a power broker. Agencies of state government hired lobbyists to lobby other agencies of government. Lawyers who once donated their services were bidding for state retainers and receiverships for insolvent insurance companies with political contributions.

I railed against the "pin-stripe patronage" of the Republican Administration. Today the practice of awarding high level appointments and contracts to contributors and money raisers flourishes in Illinois under a Democratic governor and is known as "pay to play." Governor Blagojevich's Administration is under investigation by the U.S. Attorney. His Republican predecessor, Governor George Ryan, has been convicted of playing the "pay to play" game to excess. Members of the State Legislature appropriate money to themselves for pork projects euphemistically called "Member Initiatives," which are similar to "earmarks" in Congress. (Ironically, one $2 million Member Initiative is for restoring the Adlai II home near Libertyville, now owned by the Lake County Forest Preserve District. Plans are afoot to house the International Adlai Stevenson Center on Democracy at the home and bring practitioners together with scholars to address challenges to democratic systems of government in the world, including the empowerment of citizens with information and truth in the information age.)

The contagion spreads to the Judicial branch. A recent campaign for a seat on the Illinois Supreme Court fetched more than $4 million from business interests seeking to limit recovery of damages in cases for negligence which trial lawyers opposed —about the total I spent in four campaigns for senator and governor, primary elections included. New studies draw a rough correlation between decisions of elected judges in America and the interests of their campaign contributors. No other democracy elects judges.

The demoralization of Illinois state government was not occasioned by counterproductive reforms as in the Presidential selection process. Illinois awaits reform. It was driven by money— the sheer cost of competing in the new politics—and the breakdown of Party organization and media responsibility. With opportunities in politics limited by money, and a media which restricts comments to one or two minutes and focuses on the game, the trivial and the sensational, qualified volunteers for elective office at the higher and more costly levels of politics are dwindling, except for those with large personal fortunes to invest. Some of the best are getting out. A few, including Barack Obama, win at first by accident. Fate plays a large hand in American politics. In 2004, Obama's independently wealthy, better funded Democratic Primary candidate's campaign was self-destructed by marital indiscretions. The same fate befell the Republican candidate, leaving Obama to face an eccentric Republican replacement, Alan Keyes, in the general election.

A contest for rural township road commissioner can still attract strong contenders who excite local interest with some knowledge and commitment to the subject matter. But with the demise of democratic dialogue and Party responsibility, Americans tend to divide by race, gender, religion, age and education. In a field of black and white male candidates in the 2008 Democratic primary for Cook County State's Attorney, the lone brown female won hands down. She was financed by a loan from her well-to-do husband. A savvy televangelist and former

Arkansas governor locks up a large constituency which he may be able to trade for a place on the 2008 Republican presidential ticket—or in a Republican president's cabinet. In 2007, Republican candidates for the American presidency lined up in "debates" and raised their hands like school children to answer simplistic questions. Three of the ten Republican candidates raised their hands to assure the American people (and a watching world) that they rejected Darwin's theory of evolution. All ten chanted "Reagan."

The first Democratic presidential product of the new politics was Governor Bill Clinton. He was the first Democratic president in modern history without a New Freedom, Great Society, New Frontier, New America of Adlai II, New Deal, Fair Deal or even a New Foundation of President Carter. He gave the country a now unfamiliar taste of fiscal responsibility and a bold effort to denuclearize the Korean peninsula (later repudiated by the Bush II Administration). But he was both a product and cause of the new politics. President Clinton's modest but complicated compromise for reform of health care bogged down in the pulling and hauling of myriad interests. Aid for dependent children was repealed in the name of welfare reform. Derivatives were de regulated, and the New Deal firewalls in the financial sector repealed - under Clinton, the Democrat.

Politics had become tactics, money and imagery. For some, ideology and religiosity replaced visions like Adlai II's New America, which rested on science, reason, one world and the American compact. The tactics of ideologues were uncompromising. Their purpose was messianic, their methods often corrupt. Instead of crusading in the tradition of a Democratic President against Republican radicals controlling Congress, as I once suggested to him, Clinton tried to co-opt them. For the new radical, ideological breed of politician, presidential lying to cover up a marital indiscretion was an impeachable "high crime and misdemeanor." The Bush Administration's lies to take the country to war were justified by their purpose: war.

> Every citizen is obliged to die for his country but not to
> lie for it.
> *Montesquieu*

In the new politics, money raising no longer ends with the campaign and discharge of any campaign debt. One critical former confidante of President Clinton, Richard Morris, estimates he spent one third of his scheduled public time in the U.S. on fund raising. Adlai II would not have been possible in this politics where truth, never mind all the truth, is mostly incommunicable, and winning is the purpose. For him the purpose was governing. As I write, Presidential candidates have raised as much as $130 million nine months before the Presidential election, $50 million in one month alone. As of early February, 2008, delegates were costing Barack Obama an average of $130,000 each. With the dialogue all but dead, his public meetings acquire a revivalist fervor well known to the Black Book, as if the Second Coming were at hand for secular Americans deprived of hope in their politics and desperate for change.

The Internet creates vehicles for public activism, but a credible response to the world's instabilities and insecurities, America's negative savings and unsustainable debt, climate change, a crisis in credit markets and a sinking dollar, strategic arms control and a military stretched thin by small wars, has not been forthcoming in this politics. If response requires a Great Depression or a nuclear attack, how rational would it be from within America's new politics? No one can predict with equanimity. The government's response to 9/11 is not reassuring. Eloquent incantations of change, hope and faith, or proposals for health insurance, reflect no overarching framework for policy in a disarrayed world. Of the transcendent issues of multilateralism and the UN, strategic arms control, diplomacy as an alternative to militarism, the international monetary system, little is heard to inform and inspire with hard truths. The American dialogue was intended to inform and lead.

Few will appreciate the enormity of the difference between the representative politics of the old empirical America, for all its warts, and the more democratic politics of the new, except the few survivors who were there and remember.

> Let's talk sense to the American people. Let's tell them that there are no gains without pains, that we are now on the eve of great decisions, not easy decisions, like resistance when you are attacked, but a long, patient, costly struggle which alone can assure triumph over the enemies of men—war, poverty and tyranny—and the assaults upon human dignity which are the most grievous consequences of each.
>
> *Adlai II*, Democratic National
> Convention, Chicago, July 1952

The Black Book, which was a source of inspiration and humor, becomes a reminder of what was.

I'm not an experienced hand at politics. But I am seasoned enough to have learned that the hardest thing about any campaign is how to win without proving that you are unworthy of winning.

Adlai II

A campaign addressed not to men's minds and to their best instincts, but to their passions, emotions and prejudices is unworthy at best. Now with the fate of the nation at stake, it is unbearable.

Adlai II

If a man today wants to find out the real defects in his character, the quickest and easiest way is to run for public office. He'll learn more about what's wrong with him in a five-week campaign than a psychiatrist could discover in a lifetime on the couch.

Adlai II

Untruthful accusation and reckless denunciation are an injury not simply to the individuals who may suffer from them but to the government itself.

Charles Evans Hughes, 1910

He who strikes the first blow confesses that he has run out of ideas. The mere proposal to set the politician to watch the capitalist has been disturbed by the rather disconcerting discovery that they are both the same man. We are past the point where being a capitalist is the only way of becoming a politician, and we are dangerously near the point where being a politician is much the quickest way of becoming a capitalist.

G. K. Chesterton

A statesman is a dead politician.

A statesman accepts responsibility. A politician blames someone else.

"To err is human; to blame it on someone else is politics."

Present day politics tends to take the form of a continual attempt to patch up temporary compromises between the rigidly organized interests and rigidly limited minds.

Lord Eustace Percy

If you try to set forth in a catalogue what will be the exact settlement to the problem of political life, you will find that the moment you leave the area of pious platitude you will descend into the arena of heated controversy.

Winston Churchill

The choice of a successor to a titled position in Vanua Leva, Fiji, has the appearance of being done by surprise. The leading men have assembled and consulted. One of their number advances to the person chosen, and makes him their Mata by binding a blade of the red Ti-tree leaf around his arm between the shoulder and elbow. It is the fashion for the man thus bandaged to weep and protest against his election, asserting his incompetency, and pleading low birth, poverty, indolence, ignorance of official phraseology, etc.; all of which objections are met by others declaring their choice to be good.

Buell Quain, Fijian Village
(writing of observations by
missionary Thomas Williams ca.
1850)

The partisan, when he is engaged in a dispute, cares nothing about the rights of the question, but is anxious only to convince his hearers of his own assertions.

Socrates, The Phaedo, Dialogues
of Plato

His weapons were those of the warrior, never those of the assassin.

Said of Lord Henry Brougham

He took counsel ever of his courage—never of his fears.
Adlai I on Sterling Morton

In a virtuous government, and more especially in times like these, public offices are, what they should be, burthens to those appointed to them which it would be wrong to decline, though foreseen to bring with them intense labor and great private loss.
Thomas Jefferson in a letter to Richard Henry Lee

He is a man of splendid abilities, but utterly corrupt. Like a rotten mackerel by moonlight, he shines and stinks.
John Randolph on Edward Livingston

The right honorable gentleman uses two languages: one during the hour of courtship, another for his years of possession.
Disraeli on Robert Peel

The sweetest incense that ever greeted the nostrils of a public man is the applause of the people.
Thomas Brackett Reed

6: Freedom and Human Rights

Liberty does not consist in mere general declarations of the rights of men. It consists in the translation of those declarations into definite actions. The philosophy of conduct is what every wise man should wish to derive from his knowledge of the thoughts and the affairs of the generations that have gone before him. We are not put into this world to sit still and know; we are put into it to act.

Woodrow Wilson

Freedom, as advertised in the new politics, implies freedom of speech and religion, arguably freedom to choose one's government in "free" elections. It lacks definition, but in practice can mean freedom of economic enterprise, the free market and a consequent sacrifice of freedom for exploited common people. "A hungry man is not a free man," said Adlai II. In January, 1941, near the beginning of an heroic war of national defense, President Franklin Roosevelt gave freedom definition:

> In the future days which we seek to make secure, we look forward to a world founded upon four essential human freedoms: The first is freedom of speech and expression—everywhere in the world. The second is the freedom of every person to worship God in his own way. The third is freedom from want. The fourth is freedom from fear—which, translated into world terms, means a world-wide reduction of armaments to such a point and in such a thorough fashion that no nation will be in a position to commit an act of physical aggression against any neighbor—anywhere in the world. That is no vision of a distant millennium. It is a definite basis for a kind of world attainable in our own time and generation.
>
> *Franklin D. Roosevelt,*
> January 6, 1941

Civil servants were martyred for telling the truth about civil war in China during the McCarthy era when demagogues inflamed and exploited fears of Soviet and Chinese communism. Fears are easily cultivated and exploited by demagogues with forcible ideas about the ordering of human affairs. I co-authored the Foreign Intelligence Surveillance Act (FISA). Led by Senator Frank Church, we Senators sought to strike a balance between the protection of American civil liberties and national security by requiring judicial approval for electronic surveillance of Americans. After conducting the first Senate studies of terrorism, I later tried to fine-tune that balance with an amendment to FISA, liberalizing standards for judicial approval of surveillance to facilitate penetration of terrorist cells and prevent terrorism. We feared the reaction to an act of terrorism, but civil libertarians resisted our balancing. The Bush Administration reacted as we feared. It exploited fears to generate support for a "war" against terrorism, a tactic, and resorted to spying, torture, kidnapping and preemptive war in Iraq. It travels a familiar road to autocracy—while preaching democracy and freedom.

> Periods of increasing tensions tend to become periods of increasing repressions. Soon freedom of speech may become only freedom to say acceptable things. Even thinking, except for the orthodox, may become precarious.

> Liberty means responsibility. This is why most men dread it.
> *George Bernard Shaw*

> My definition of a free society is a society where it is safe to be unpopular.
> *Adlai II*

The State Department has been charged by Congress with issuing annual reports on the human rights practices of foreign countries. China is regularly cited as an offender. The Chinese government now responds with an annual report on the human rights record of the "world's human rights police," the United States. The U.S. media covers the State Department's condemnation of China but gives scant attention to China's report based on reports by U.S. government agencies, non-governmental organizations such as Amnesty International, foreign newspapers and other reliable non-Chinese sources.

The Chinese take a comprehensive view of human rights. They fall short of protecting individual rights and liberties, but for them, as for Franklin and Eleanor Roosevelt and the United Nations' Universal Declaration of Human Rights which runs to thirty articles, human rights are defined expansively to also include freedom from fear and war, freedom from poverty and from all the scourges of mankind. In China's response to its annual State Department citation, the Chinese cite the U.S. homicide, incarceration and capital punishment record, the execution of juveniles, the proliferation of offenses related to drugs, mental disease and guns. On political rights and freedom, China cites the Bush-Cheney election by the Supreme Court after their rejection by the American people, the influence of money in American politics, including money from the defense industry, and the abuses of and by the press. China cites the hunger and poverty in America, the homelessness, the growing gap between the very rich and everyone else, the abuses of safety in the workplace, and the forty-three million Americans unable to afford health insurance. It presents evidence of continuing racial discrimination and the disproportionate numbers of African Americans in jail and in poverty and without adequate housing or education. It cites reports on discrimination against and mistreatment of immigrants, domestic violence and abuse of women, children and the elderly.

China moves on to cite U.S. unilateralism in the world, U.S. military aggressions fueled by a defense budget of more than $500 billion, and U.S. responsibility for almost half the world's exports of conventional arms. Relying on Western sources, the Chinese report complains of forty U.S. uses of force against other countries since the beginning of the 1990s, more than forty attempts to overthrow foreign governments since 1945, and the repeated use of mines, cluster bombs and depleted uranium, with endless civilian casualties.

The United States is described as maintaining 364,000 troops in more than 130 "countries and regions"; also mentioned are the assaults, rapes, and other crimes committed by U.S. troops against foreign civilians. In 2005, China underscored its response to its annual State Department citation by issuing it from the office of the premier and expanding it to cite the United States for "wanton slaughter" of civilians in Iraq and the torture of prisoners, echoing complaints from Amnesty International and other observers.

The reports have grown longer year by year. In 2007, Russia began weighing in with similar complaints and charges of American hypocrisy. One can quarrel with particulars of China's reports. Some Western observers would suggest that the particulars are understated in respects (for example, see Chalmers Johnson's *The Sorrows of Empire: Militarism, Secrecy and the End of the Republic*). China is underdeveloped. Huge wealth and income disparities are developing. At the provincial and municipal levels, corruption intrudes. But it is lifting people, including its minorities, out of poverty and oppression, its economy replacing the U.S. economy as a source of growth for the world. It ranks highest in relief of child poverty, according to the UN. (Democratic India ranks lowest.) Global indicia of "human development" reflect immense progress in China—of which more will be said later. Its imperfections are many, but in the Black Book, America is measured against its own values and actions, not the imperfections of others. America spreads freedom and human rights by example and good works.

> I have studied the history of America; I have seen her grow great in the paths of liberty and of progress by following after great ideals. Every concrete thing that she has done has seemed to rise out of some abstract principle, some vision of the mind. Her greatest victories have been the victories of peace and humanity.
> *Woodrow Wilson*

> The goal of life is more than material advance; it is now, and through all eternity, the triumph of spirit over matter, of love and liberty over force and violence.
> *Adlai II*

7: Politics and Humor

Once a man holds public office he is absolutely no good for honest work.

Will Rogers

The Black Book never neglects wit and humor for long. Skeptical comments reflected the frailties of democracy. But good men flourished in politics—and made light of it. Humor reflected their integrity. Besides, politicians were a gregarious lot. They loved to tell stories and jokes. The Black Book recorded them. They were useful to its authors in their discourse. Today they convey some flavor of the old politics, its spontaneity and good nature, its honesty. Adlai II's humor was spontaneous. He could trust his instincts—and his cause. Humor from the Black Book acquires an edge in the new politics.

Adlai I distinguished between wit and humor. As he put it, the gift of humor is:

> the sure indicator of the humane and sympathetic in our nature; that which blends the pathetic with the ludicrous and by the same stroke moves to laughter and to tears....It is not strange, then, that he who in large degree possesses or is possessed by this subtle quality should be subject to moods, it may be melancholy—'the effect of that humor that sometime hath his hour with every man.'

Or as the poet Thomas Hood wrote, "There's not a string attuned to mirth / But has its chord in melancholy."

The line between humor and wit is shadowy, not easily defined, but Adlai I made a distinction: "While wit is a purely intellectual thing, into every act of the humorous mind there is an influx of the moral nature. Humor springs exuberantly, as from a fountain, and runs on, its perpetual game to look with considerate good nature at every object in existence, and dismiss it with a benison. While wit, the purely intellectual quality, sparkles and stings, humor, 'touched with a feeling of our infirmity,' would 'gently scan thy brother man.'"

Lincoln's humor manifested these sentiments. Examples of his humor are recorded throughout the Black Book. Humor and wit lacking an explicit political context overflow into Part II and the Humorous Recitations and Laugh Lines of the Afterwords. They are scattered throughout the Black Book in most all its contexts.

I have generally found that to do the right thing is the right thing to do.

Lord Grey of Falladon

There were two brothers. One went off to sea, and the other was elected vice president. Neither was heard from again.

Vice President Thomas R. Marshall

Woodrow Wilson, although accustomed to being accosted by office seekers, was particularly annoyed by a persistent politician. "Mr. President," he asked bluntly, "you remember the man you appointed to the Federal Trade Commission last week? Well, he died this morning. Would it be all right with you if I were to take his place?" Wilson nodded. "Certainly, if you can arrange it with the undertaker."

When Winston Churchill switched from the Conservative to the Liberal side of the House, some of his adherents were offended. A snippish young lady complained, "There are two things I do not like about you, Mr. Churchill, your new politics and your mustache." "Madame," he replied, "you are not likely to come into much contact with either."

Lloyd George addressed a meeting of hostile suffragettes, one of whom rose and said, "If you were my husband, I would give you poison." To which Lloyd George replied, "My dear lady, if I were your husband, I would take the poison."

He occasionally stumbles over the truth, but he always hastily picks himself up and hurries on as if nothing had happened.

Said of Stanley Baldwin

Of Senator John F. Kerry's gaunt visage an aide inquired hopefully, "Lincolnesque, don't you think?" The unwanted reply: "Yeah, like after the assassination."

A farmer said he supposed he'd have to vote for one of the candidates but didn't like either. He'd vote for the candidate if he would make one promise. He'd have to promise he wouldn't do anything for the farmer if he were elected —the farmer couldn't afford it otherwise.

They have such refined and delicate palates
That they can discover no one worthy of their ballots.
And then when someone terrible gets elected
They say, there that's just what I expected.
Ogden Nash

An infuriated opponent rushed up to Al Smith and yelled: "I hear you're going around telling lies about me!" Replied Smith, "You should thank me. If I told the truth about you, they'd run you out of town!"

Adlai II told with relish of addressing a gathering of cheering Democrats which included a pregnant woman, at least ten months pregnant, he reported, who bore across her ample front a sign that read: "ADLAI IS THE MAN."

In the 1948 campaign, crowds exhorted an embattled Harry Truman, "Give 'em hell, Harry." To which he would respond, "I don't give 'em hell. I just give 'em truth, and they think it's hell."

A heckler yelled at Al Smith: "Tell them all you know, Al, it won't take long." To which Smith replied, "I'll tell them all we both know and it won't take any longer."

He wanted to run for President in the worst way—and that's what he did.

A familiar predicament for every candidate—the constituent who comes up and asks if you remember him and you don't. I once explained that of course I remembered him but his name had slipped my mind, etc. He replied, "Well, that's funny, because we have never met before."

Said a lobbyist referring to a politician, "I could buy him but I couldn't sell him."

Politicians go around shooting from the lip.

The mistake some public officials make is forgetting they've been appointed and thinking they've been anointed.

> *Alben Barkley*, Vice President (and cousin)

Sometimes in politics one must duel with skunks, but no one should be fool enough to allow the skunk to choose the weapon.

8: Democrats, Republicans and Texas

Apart from references to Lincoln and Theodore Roosevelt, the apostate Republican, the Black Book contains no comments favorable to Republicans. At the same time, it contains few derogatory comments of the crude sort common today. Humor is employed to effect, sometimes with a touch of ridicule. Many of the Black Book's comments about Republicans were less intended to influence opinion than to entertain and energize the Democratic faithful.

If the Republicans will stop telling lies about us, we will stop telling the truth about them.
Adlai II

A Republican to his chauffeur: "Drive off that cliff, James. I want to commit suicide."

It's been said that the difference between the Democratic and Republican parties is like driving a car: you put it in D for going forward and R for going backward.

And the difference between a convert and a traitor? A Republican who becomes a Democrat is a convert. A Democrat who becomes a Republican is a traitor.

The elephant has a thick skin and a head full of ivory, and as everyone who has seen a circus parade knows, it proceeds best by grasping the tail of its predecessor.

The Democratic Party is like a mule. It has neither pride of ancestry nor hope of posterity.
Ignatius Donnelly, Minnesota Legislature, 1860 (a bow to bipartisanship)

"So, you're a Democrat. Why?" asked Theodore Roosevelt. "Well, my father was a Democrat, my grandfather was a Democrat, and my great-grandfather was a Democrat." "But suppose your father had been a horse thief, your grandfather had been a horse thief, and your great-grandfather had been a horse thief," Roosevelt rejoined. "Would that make you a horse thief?" "No, that would make me a Republican."

An enthusiastic reverend at a Democratic dinner declared that God was a Democrat. Challenged to justify the assertion, the reverend said, "Well, perhaps he isn't a Democrat, but I do know the Savior did not ride into Jerusalem on an elephant."

In his book *Something of Men I Have Known*, Adlai I tells of the 1860 Illinois Democratic Convention, which approved a resolution instructing the Illinois delegates to the national convention to support Stephen A. Douglas for president. After the resolution had been enthusiastically adopted, a delegate called attention to the presence of the famed circuit-riding preacher Peter Cartwright. Immediately, "Cartwright! Cartwright!" rang from all parts of the chamber. Reverend Cartwright rose, and "with deep emotion and scarcely audible voice," began:

My friends and fellow citizens, I am happy to be with you on this occasion. My sun is low down upon the horizon, and the days of my pilgrimage are numbered. I have lived in Illinois during the entire period of its history as a state. I have watched with tender interest its marvelous growth from its feeble condition as a Territory until it has reached its present splendor as a State. I have traveled over its prairies, slept with only the canopy of heaven for a covering; I have followed the trail of the Indians, fought the desperadoes, swam the rivers, threaded the almost pathless forests, in order that I might carry tidings of the blessed Gospel to the loneliest cabin upon the border. Yes, my friends, for seventy long years, amid appalling difficulties and dangers, I have waged an incessant warfare against the world, the flesh, the devil, and all the other enemies of the Democratic Party.

(Great-great-grandfather Jesse Fell was Secretary of the Illinois Republican Party and organized its delegation for Lincoln at the 1860 Republican National Convention.)

I like Republicans, have grown up with them, worked with them and would trust them with most anything except public office.

Adlai II

It has been said of the Republican Party that their old men live in the shadow of the past—and their young men live in the shadow of their old men.

The Fish

Three hundred million years ago,
Or some such early time,
There lived a prehistoric fish
That skittered with a caudal swish
In dank Devonian slime.

Quite recently, you may recall,
Some scientific high brow
Discovered, brought to light again,
A living, breathing specimen
That hadn't changed an eyebrow.

And so we learn, my gentle friends,
(I trust I am not malicious)
Through all of evolution's range,
Two species have resisted change...
Republicans and Fishes.

Joseph S. Newman, Verses Yet!

Some fellas get credit fer bein' conservative when they're only stupid.

When Republican speakers think they are thinking, they are only rearranging their prejudices.

A Democratic committeeman paid a man $50 to carry a precinct. A Republican came along and paid him $100, but the Democrats won. Asked why, the man replied that he'd discovered the Democrats were less corrupt than the Republicans.

I remember from boyhood some rather disreputable fellows whom we never saw from one year to the next, except on election day. They had to come over the hills about twenty miles to vote, and they always did—and they always voted Republican. Somebody finally asked them if twenty miles wasn't an awful long way to come just to cast their ballots, and one of them answered, "We don't mind. The fact is, it's about the only money we make all year."

Adlai I

An independent is a guy who wants to take the politics out of politics.

In a Republican district, I was Republican, in a Democratic district, I was a Democrat, and in a doubtful district, I was doubtful. But I was always Erie.

Jay Gould, speaking of his Erie Railroad

Republicans: Men who think the American dream means falling asleep.

It takes a Republican to catch a Republican.

A Republican refused to turn the hose on his burning house because his water bill was already too high.

If you want to live like a Republican you have to vote like a Democrat.

Calvin Coolidge looked as if he had been weaned on a pickle.

Alice Roosevelt Longworth

Senator Borah rubbed his fellow Republican, Calvin Coolidge, the wrong way. Coolidge made no public comment about this until he and an aide went horseback riding. In the distance, the aide noticed another rider and asked: "Isn't that Senator Borah?" "Can't be," drawled

70

Coolidge, "The rider and the horse are going in the same direction."

Nixon is the kind of politician who would mount the stump of a redwood tree to make a speech on conservation.

Adlai II

Overheard during the Watergate scandal: The watchword at the White House is "Pardon me."

The Nixon campaign slogan has been changed from "Four more years" to "Maybe five to eight with time off for good behavior."

The Department of Interior has taken over the management of the White House staff which has been placed on the endangered species list.

(Also from the Watergate era.)

Ronald Reagan is a friend of the working men and women like Colonel Sanders is a friend of chickens.

The presidents and presidential candidates of the new era, Democrats and Republicans, have been sources of little humorous or inspirational material for the Black Book. The first President Bush, a likeable man, disparaged what he termed the "vision thing" and challenged, "Read my lips," to sensible doubters of his opposition to tax increases. He remarked after touring the Auschwitz death camp, "Boy, they were big crematoriums, weren't they." (*Chicago Sun-Times*, January 29, 1992). He makes no other contributions to the Black Book. However desultory the extemporaneity of George I, it is Olympian by comparison with his son, George II. The comments of the latter reveal a mind lacking curiosity and clearly unimproved by the study of history and prior experience on the ground in the world outside Texas, Washington, the oil industry and baseball.

The most important job is not to be governor, or first lady in my case.

George W. Bush

He is my friend, and he is not a moron.

> *Prime Minister Jean Chrétien of Canada*, denying an aide's complaint about George Bush II, 2002 (Editors of Canadian newspapers were flooded by letters expressing disagreement with the Prime Minister.)

As democracy is perfected, the office of President represents more and more closely the inner soul of the people. On some great and glorious day, the plain folks of the land will have their heart's desire at last and the White House will be adorned by a downright moron.

> *H. L. Mencken*, found framed on the wall of a tiny watch repair shop in Chicago operated by the two daughters of Japanese immigrants

Texas' first native-born governor was Democrat James S. Hogg (1891-95). Governor and Mrs. Hogg named their daughter Ima. (The Black Book records a sister named Ura, but I have been unable to verify her existence.) Her marital prospects unimproved by such parental beneficence, Miss Ima, as she was known to all, became an energetic philanthropist, a Democratic activist and enthusiastic supporter of Adlai II. Affectionate recollections of Miss Ima are the only friendly sentiments toward Texas recorded in the Black Book.

Putting the national patrimony before Texan claims to the "tidelands oil," Adlai II lost the support of Democratic governor Alan Shivers to the more expedient Dwight Eisenhower in 1952. While ambassador to the UN, Adlai II was physically assaulted by a placard bearing right-winger after a speech in Dallas. Asked if he wanted his assailant arrested, he said, "No, I want her educated." He later lamented that he had not warned the White House more forcefully against President Kennedy's fatal trip to Dallas which followed shortly.

Texas is maintaining its distinction in the Black Book. It leads the nation in executions, senior citizen poverty, and the number of citizens medically uninsured. By 2007, 60 percent of the nation's executions were carried out in Texas.

72

If I owned Hell and Texas, I'd rent out Texas and live in Hell.

P. H. Sheridan, Fort Clark, Texas, 1855

Texas is the place where there are the most cows and the least milk and the most rivers and the least water in them, and where you can look the farthest and see the least.

A Texan went to the funeral of a prominent Quaker. The Quaker conducting the service concluded his remarks and asked if anyone else cared to say anything about the distinguished deceased. After an awkward pause, the Texan stood up and drawled, "If no one wants to talk about our friend, I would like to say a few words about Texas."

Texas is also known as "outer Arkansas."

The national government will preserve and defend those basic principles on which our nation has been built up. They regard Christianity as the foundation of our national morality and the family as the basis of national life.

That quote— almost word for word from a plank in the 2006 Texas Party Republican platform—comes from the first speech by Adolph Hitler to the German people after becoming Chancellor of Germany.

Saskatchewan is like Texas; only we have friendly relations with Saskatchewan.

Governor John Peter Altgeld—the "Eagle Forgotten" of Illinois politics—possessed, it was said, the "courage to be right." The following is taken from his dedication of Illinois monuments at the battlefield of Chickamauga in 1895, a gathering addressed by nineteen other governors, two United States senators and Vice President Stevenson:

Once political parties stood for definite principles and their platforms proclaimed them boldly to the world. The tendency now is for political parties to shirk principle and follow expediency, and their platforms are often drawn to evade every live issue. The idea now is to cajole rather than convince; to ignore great wrongs and wink at abuses; to court the support of conflicting interests though it involves the deception of one or both. We are substituting office-seeking and office-holding in place of real achievement and instead of great careers in public life. We are facing a harvest of slippery, bleary-eyed and empty mediocrity.

The first Gilded Age of which Altgeld spoke was followed by reaction: progressives, populists, the muckrakers, Theodore Roosevelt and Woodrow Wilson. The new Gilded Age awaits the reaction.

Neither party has as a party any clear cut principles, any distinctive tenet.... Tenets and policies...have all but vanished. All has been lost except office or the hope of getting it.

> *Lord James Bryce, The American*
> *Commonwealth, 1889*

If politics took up the real issues, it would revolutionize the existing party system. It is not surprising, then, that our political leaders are greatly occupied in dampening down interest, in obscuring issues and in attempting to distract attention from the realities of American life.

> *Walter Lippmann*, in the 1920's

He who wrestles with us strengthens our nerves and sharpens our skill. Our antagonist is our helper.

> *Edmund Burke*

The Democratic Party is more important than any individual, and America is more important than any political party.

He serves his Party best who serves his country best.
Rutherford B. Hayes

9: Democracy and Government

I have many anxieties about this Administration and its combination of demonstrative piety and moral duplicity....This is one of those intervals in our history when the press, money, business and government have coalesced. These are imponderable forces in our national life, and as the tendency to concentration of power and influence grows, the power of coercion grows, too....We see dissent and criticism diminishing. And conformity is always the easiest way.

Adlai II, conversation reported by Collier's
Magazine,
October 29, 1955

Government includes the art of formulating a policy and using the political technique to attain to so much of that policy as will receive general support; persuading, leading, sacrificing, teaching always, because the greatest duty for the statesman is to educate.

Franklin D. Roosevelt, 1932

I believe it is easier to establish an absolute and despotic government among a people in which the conditions of society are equal than among any other.... Despotism appears to me peculiarly to be dreaded in democratic times.

Alexis de Tocqueville,
Democracy in America

Democracy remains an object of reverence in America, but in the political discourse "democracy" has become a cliché for some, a self-fulfilling, marketable system of government said to assure peace and freedom. In practice it is denigrated by its propagators. Winston Churchill was a realist. He observed that democracy was the worst form of government, except for the others. Comments on democracy and government are pervasive in the Black Book.

Democracy is morose, and runs to anarchy.
Emerson, 1841

Democracies are prone to war, and war consumes them.
W.H. Seward, 1848

Democracy gives every man the right to be his own oppressor.

J. R. Lowell, 1862

Democracy is a device that insures we are governed no better than we deserve.

George Bernard Shaw

Democracy arose from thinking that if the people are equal in any respect they are equal in all respects.

Aristotle, Politics

Definition of democracy: A charming form of government, full of variety and disorder, and dispensing a kind of equality to equals and unequals alike.

Plato

A democracy is a state in which the poor, gaining the upper hand, kill some and banish others, and divide the offices among the remaining equally, usually by lot.

Plato, The Republic

The tendency of democracies is, in all things, to mediocrity.

James Fennimore Cooper

Democracy is, by the nature of it, a self-canceling business; and gives in the long run a net result of zero.

Thomas Carlyle, 1839

A perfect democracy is the most shameless thing in the world.

Edmund Burke

In 2005, President Putin's response to the American president's sermonizing about democracy reminded the world that in 2000 George W. Bush was effectively elected by a partisan one-vote margin in the U.S. Supreme Court after having been rejected by a 5,500,000 vote majority of the American electorate. This includes the votes cast for

Ralph Nader; Vice President Al Gore won the popular vote with a plurality of 500,000. Democracy is a fragile form of government, vulnerable to abuse like all others. It is not a static system of government. It requires renewal. It demands the capacity to change and adapt. That is a function of opposition and peaceful change through dialogue and the ballot box.

President Bush preaches that it produces peace and freedom. It is a politically opportunistic message. Opponents of democracy, peace and freedom are hard to find. "Democracy" is also the latest guise for neoconservative pursuit of empire and a belated pretext for the war in Iraq. De Tocqueville warned that despotism was likely to be ushered in by the "avowed lover of liberty" who is a "hidden servant of tyranny."

Since its beginnings in Athens, democracy has been a well traveled route to autocracy and conflict. Athens was followed by Macedon of Philip and Alexander, the first French Republic by Bonaparte and Empire. The Weimar Republic led to National Socialism in Germany. Hitler came to power through the ballot box.

> Both the friends and enemies of democracy and representative government have recognized that political power based on popular rule may also be despotic. The recognition of the importance of political opposition, and the institutions and customs embodying this recognition, are perhaps the most important single restraint on what might otherwise be popular tyranny.
>
> *John Stuart Mill*, On Liberty

Alexander Hamilton warned that "the fiery and destructive passions of war reign in the human breast with much more powerful sway than the mild and beneficent sentiments of peace." It took little more than an imaginary spot of bloodied soil, an explosion in the coal bunker of an American battleship in Havana harbor, or a fictitious North Vietnamese "attack" in the Gulf of Tonkin to excite the war fevers — and the politicians. Only Senators Ernest Gruening of Alaska and Wayne Morse of Oregon, Adlai II supporters, had the wisdom and courage to oppose the Gulf of Tonkin Resolution authorizing force in Indo-China. Both were defeated in their campaigns for re-election. Rare is the Congressman Abraham Lincoln who demands evidence of the casus belli. The diplomat and historian, George Kennan, added that in war a democracy subordinates everything to the battle and "soon becomes the victim of its own propaganda."

I sense that the willingness to contrive such pretexts for war is enlarged by ideology of messianic and uncompromising purpose rooted in ignorance. The war in Iraq is a case in point.

Herman Goering, at his Nuremberg trial in 1946, explained: "Naturally, the common people don't want war....But after all it is the leaders of the country who determine the policy, and it is always a simple matter to drag the people along, whether it is democracy, or a fascist dictatorship, or a parliament, or a communist dictatorship. Voice or no voice, the people can always be brought to the bidding of leaders. That is easy. All you have to do is tell them they are being attacked (and) denounce the pacifists for lack of patriotism and exposing the country to danger."

Democracy is a breathing spell between tyrannies.

It is for this that we love democracy: for the emphasis it puts on character; for its tendency to exalt the purposes of the average man to some high level of endeavor; for its just principles of common assent in matters in which all are concerned; for its ideals of duty and its sense of brotherhood.
Woodrow Wilson

All the ills of democracy can be cured by more democracy.
Alfred E. Smith, 1933

There is one thing better than good government—which is government in which all the people have a part.
Walter Hines Page

It was government by discussion that broke the bond of ages and set free the originality of mankind.
Walter Bagehot

The only thing wiser than anyone is everyone.
Talleyrand

Democrats consider the people as the safest depository of power in the last resort: they cherish them, therefore, and wish to leave in them all the powers to the exercise of which they are competent.

Thomas Jefferson

The little people are the only important people.

We will ever strive for the ideals and sacred things of the City, both alone and with many; we will unceasingly seek to quicken the sense of public duty. We will revere and obey the City's laws: we will transmit this city not only not less, but greater, better and more beautiful than it was transmitted to us.

From the oath of the Athenian citizen

The history of direct democracy— from ancient Athens to the First French Republic to modern California—invites caution. America's founders, being conscious of the complexities of government and distrustful of public distempers, locked the doors to the Constitutional Convention, pledged the delegates to secrecy, and established a representative form of democracy with a restricted franchise, which over time was made universal.

Today, with debate dying, with politics largely reduced to money raising and marketing, with many representative institutions like the old party nominating conventions gone, with the country's social and economic inequalities of unprecedented dimensions and threats to civil liberties mounting, some question whether American government still deserves to be characterized as democratic. Communist countries characterize themselves as democratic. Some seek a degree of democracy within a one-party system. They seek some kind of social and economic equality, a democratic outcome. China seeks to narrow the gap between rich and poor, as did the old empirical American democracy. Today the U.S. consciously widens the gap.

A democracy is always temporary in nature: it simply cannot exist as a permanent form of government. *** A democracy will continue to exist up until the time that voters discover they can vote themselves generous gifts from the public treasury. *** From that moment on, the majority always votes for the candidates who promise the most benefit from the public treasury, with the result that

every democracy will finally collapse due to loose fiscal policy, which is always followed by a dictatorship.
Professor Alexander Tyler,
University of Edinburgh, 1787

One hundred and seventy three despots [are] surely as oppressive as one.... An elective despotism was not the government we fought for.
Thomas Jefferson, "Notes on Virginia"

The thing we have to fear in this county, to my way of thinking, is the influence of the organized minorities, because somehow or other the great majority does not seem to organize. They seem to feel that they are going to be effective because of their known strength, but they give no expression of it.
Alfred E. Smith, 1933

Neither democracy nor effective representation is possible until each participant in the group—and this is true equally of a household or a nation—devotes a measurable part of his life to furthering its existence.
Lewis Mumford

I believe that the community is already in the process of dissolution where each man begins to eye his neighbor as a possible enemy, where non-conformity with the accepted creed, political as well as religious, is a mark of disaffection, where denunciation, without specification or backing, takes the place of evidence, where orthodoxy chokes freedom of dissent; where faith in the eventual supremacy of reason has become so timid that we dare not enter our convictions in the open lists to win or lose.
Learned Hand

Comments in the Black Book spread from the ideals and realities of democracy to dwell on other systems and the nature of government. They range far and wide.

What is government itself but the greatest of all reflections on human nature? If men were angels, no government would be necessary. If angels were to govern men, neither external nor internal controls on government would be necessary. In framing a government which is to be administered by men over men, the great difficulty is this. You must first enable the government to control the governed, and in the second place oblige it to control itself.

James Madison, Federalist #51

Government is like a pump, and what it pumps up is just what we are, a fair sample of the intellect, the ethics and the morals of the people, no better, no worse.

Adlai II

Too many people lean upon the government, forgetting that the government must lean upon the people.

Our government is the potent, the omnipresent teacher. For good or evil, it teaches the whole people by its example.

Louis Brandeis in Olmstead v. United States

Now the excellence of rulership arises out of gentleness. . . . Now it is rare to find gentleness in men who have keen intelligence and awareness; rather is it to be found among the duller people. For an intelligent ruler is apt to impose upon the subjects more than they can bear, because he sees further than they, and can, thanks to his intelligence, foresee the consequences of any act or event; all of which spells ruin to the subjects. This is why, also the Lawgiver does not require excessive intelligence...for this may lead to oppression, misrule and the driving of the people beyond what they are accustomed to....It has thus been shown that intelligence and foresight are defects in a politician, for they represent an excess of thought, just as stupidity is an excess of stolidity. Now in all human qualities both extremes are reprehensible, the mean alone being commendable: thus generosity is the mean between extravagance and niggardliness, and courage between rashness and cowardice, and so on, for other qualities. And that is why those who are extremely intelligent are described as 'devils' or 'devilish' or something analogous

Ibn Khaldun, An Arab Philosophy
of History

While power corrupts, being out of power corrupts absolutely.

London Economist

A communist is one who has nothing and is eager to share it with others.

The communist is a socialist in a violent hurry.

G. W. Gough, 1926

Fascism gets rid of the absurdity of a senselessly obstructive Opposition, resulting in parliaments where half the members are trying to govern and the other half are trying to prevent them.

George Bernard Shaw

The great strength of a totalitarian state is that it forces those who fear it to imitate it.

Adolph Hitler

Conservatism...offers no redress for the present, and makes no preparation for the future.

Disraeli

To defend every abuse, to defend every self interest, every encrusted position of privilege in the name of country—when in fact it is only love of the status quo—that, indeed, is the lie in the soul to which any conservative society is prone.

Adlai II

There is a golden mean between being a radical and a reactionary. One can be a conservative, one who corrects

ideals with experience, or one can be a liberal, one who corrects experience with idealism. Either conservatism or liberalism will prevent one's becoming a communist out of fear of fascism or a fascist out of fear of communism.
                                                    T.V. Smith

The very essence of conservatism is awareness of the times and zeal to reduce their fevers and tensions. Conservatism recognizes that change should and must come, and demands only that change be studied and weighed before it is made. To be conservative in this true sense is to be progressive.
                              St. Louis Post Dispatch editorial
                              about Senator Ralph E. Flanders,
                              Republican of Vermont

Whatever its flaws and whatever its perils, whatever its distortions in the current political climate and whatever the crimes committed in its name, democracy is still the ideal which can animate what is best in our public life.

10: Congress and the Legislative Process

Reader, suppose you were an idiot. And suppose you were a Member of Congress, but I repeat myself.

Mark Twain

The Black Book pokes unbridled fun at Congress, legislatures and legislators of all stripes. My own experience reflects a congenial condition in the Illinois and Federal legislatures. I was sworn into the U.S. Senate in November, 1970. The majority leader was Mike Mansfield, the minority leader Hugh Scott, both gentlemen, scholars and statesmen. In those days the Senate was an aggregation of men and women (admittedly few of the latter) joined together in a near reverence for the institution. Partisan positions on issues were rare, a partisan spirit virtually nonexistent. "He's so mean he couldn't sell beer on a troopship," a moderate Republican senator once told me, speaking of a partisan colleague, a conspicuous exception who later became a Republican Presidential candidate and Viagra marketer.

Senator Paul Douglas, the Illinois Democrat, told me he once sent his friend, Senator Carl Aiken, Republican of Vermont, a $50 campaign contribution. Senator Aiken expressed his gratitude and explained that with the contribution he had raised $500 which was more than sufficient for reelection and he was, therefore, returning $25. Now senators campaign against one another and continue "dialing for dollars" after the campaign is ended, its debts paid, as they matter-of-factly acknowledge. Carl Aiken was a venerated member of the Senate when I arrived. He was not alone.

A cordial unity of purpose and reverence for the Senate prevailed, though it began to sour towards the end of my tenure. The Senate Chamber exuded a warm atmosphere conducive to congenial relationships among the Members and an informal process which facilitated the infinitely complex business of legislating. It is a different Senate today, the chamber a stark, floodlit stage for low drama, its proceedings giving a new edge to the genial mockery of the Black Book.

> Edward Everett Hale, Senate chaplain, was asked, "Do you pray for the senators, Dr. Hale?" "No, I look at the senators and pray for the country."

A new member of the House of Commons asked Prime Minister Disraeli if he should participate actively in the debates. "No, I think not; it would be better for the people to wonder why you did not speak rather than why you did."

A message once observed in the
U.S. Congress

A lank, disconsolate farmer emerged from a town hall meeting and was asked, "Who is talking in there?" "Congressman Smiffkins." "What did he say?" "Well," passing a knotted hand across his weary forehead, "he didn't say."

To a newly elected senator: "You will spend six months wondering how you got into this august body and six years wondering how the others got in."

Senator Ham Lewis of Illinois,
later attributed to Harry Truman

A senator is someone with more answers than there are questions.

A congressman is a hog. You must take a stick and hit him on the snout.

Henry Adams, quoting unnamed
member of the Grant cabinet

Horace Greeley spoke with a congressman who boasted: "I am a self-made man." To which Mr. Greeley retorted: "That relieves the Almighty of a great responsibility."

An Illinois legislator explained his switched vote to an insurance company lobbyist: "Well, I didn't know you wanted an all-day commitment!"

If we cannot get a different class of men into the Legislature, the sooner we go into the ministry the better.

John A. Dicks to Martin Van
Buren

I have long since ceased to watch the proceedings of our legislature for any other purpose than to see when they would adjourn.

Silas Wright, 1835

Returning to London from a holiday, Queen Victoria summoned her Prime Minister and asked: "Tell me sir, what has Parliament passed in my absence?" "Parliament, your majesty, has passed seven weeks, nothing more."

Bless, O Lord, the two Houses of Parliament now assembled, and overrule their deliberations for the people's good.

An old prayer in the Church of Scotland before the opening of Parliament, quoted regularly by Senator Stevenson

An ingenious doctor who seemed perfectly versed in the whole nature and system of government...directed that every senator in the great council of a nation, after he had delivered his opinion and argued in the defence of it, should be obliged to give his vote directly contrary; because if that were done, the result would infallibly terminate in the good of the public.

Jonathan Swift, Gulliver's Travels

A Russian observer of Congress, from the visitor's gallery: "Congress is so strange. A man gets up to speak and says nothing. Nobody listens—and then everybody disagrees."

Those who love sausage and the law should never be permitted to see how they are made.

Winston Churchill

A government such as ours, consisting of from seven to eight hundred Parliamentary Talkers, with their escort of able Editors and Public Opinion; and for head, certain Lords and Servants of the Treasury, and Chief

Secretaries and others who find themselves at once Chiefs and No-Chiefs, and often commanded rather than commanding, is doubtless a most complicated entity, and none of the alertest for getting on with business.
Thomas Carlyle

Nothing has ever been done so systematically as nothing is being done now.
Woodrow Wilson

A comment on a popular consul's performance in the Roman Senate: "Curse this man's virtues. They have undone the country."

One of my life's more unforgettable characters, a giant of the U.S. Senate, was Sam Ervin of North Carolina who, among other achievements, chaired the Senate Watergate Committee with rare homespun grace and wisdom. There was no hint of partisanship in the congressional Watergate proceedings, chaired on the House side by Representative Peter Rodino of New Jersey who rose to the challenge. Senator Ervin was an authority on the Constitution which he revered. As a freshman senator, I was presiding over the Senate when he sought and received my recognition. With a twinkle in his eyes, he proceeded to deliver a speech on the virtues of unlimited Senate debate—a speech by Adlai I.

The Black Book attributes the following story to Sam Ervin:

I am reminded of the two diligent party workers who were sent to a cemetery to get a list of names from the tombstones. As they went from grave to grave, one of them read the names on the stones and the other wrote them down. From one of the tombstones, the first man read: 'Beloved Husband and Father —Stuyvesant Breckenridge.' The second man started to write the name down, then paused. 'Wait a minute,' he said. 'That's a long name—we can divide it into two parts and have two votes here.' 'No, sir,' said the first fellow. 'If I'm going to have anything to do with this, it's going to have to be honest.'

Another great character and storyteller was Senator Russell Long, nephew of Huey Long, the legendary Governor of Louisiana. As chairman of the powerful Senate Finance Committee, Senator Long managed tax bills on the floor, and was fond of a ditty which always brought a chuckle from senators no matter how often they heard it: "Don't tax me, Don't tax him, Tax that fella hidin' behind the tree."

A billion here, a billion there, pretty soon you're talking about real money.

Senator Everett Dirksen, whom Adlai III succeeded in the Senate

A cartoon by J. Wesley Smith depicted a member of the Continental Congress rising to ask: "As the New Hampshire delegate, may I ask: is this Revolution going to cost very much?"

I'm agin any conspiracy I ain't part of.

Senator Robert Kerr of Oklahoma

Reforms which contributed to the metamorphosis of presidential politics also aimed to make the legislative process more accountable by making it more democratic. In his book, *On Capitol Hill,* Julian Zelizer describes with a rare perceptivity how Congress was affected. Efforts had long been underway to break down the seniority system and grip of Committee Chairmen. The efforts finally succeeded when my class entered the Senate, but without all the expected benefits. We resolved to give juniors and large states a bigger stake in the process. The juniors had gone hat in hand to the Legislative Subcommittee of the almighty Appropriations Committee to plead for larger appropriations for their offices. We were kept under control by lack of staff, especially those of us representing large states with heavy demands, like Illinois. We knew that our resources depended to a degree on good behavior and submission to the Committee Chairmen. They voted as a block, supporting one another on the Senate floor, and were rarely challenged. In 1971 we, the juniors —our numbers reinforced in the 1970 election— lined up en bloc before that subcommittee and no longer supplicated. We demanded resources commensurate with our responsibilities. Ernest "Fritz" Hollings, Chairman of the Subcommittee, faced with that phalanx of Senators, buckled. Senators from the large states acquired more staff. They deserved it. But that was the beginning of a process which had consequences which we reformers, mostly junior and admittedly eager for a larger piece of the legislative action, did not anticipate.

As one of the reform leaders, I was made Chairman of the Senate Select Committee to Study the Committee System which became known as the Stevenson Committee. It recommended measures to redistribute power among Senate committees, realign and update their jurisdictions, reduce the number of committees, and overhaul the system by which bills were referred to, and processed by, committees. The recommendations were accepted in large measure for the first major overhaul of the Senate since the Legislative Reorganization Act of 1947.

Having also proposed comprehensive ethics rules, I received for additional penance responsibility for chairing and organizing the new Senate Ethics Committee and implementing a sweeping code of ethics with power of life and death over Senators. Many hours would be spent by its Members and staff deliberating such issues as whether it was permissible for the fiancé of a staffer to accept a lobbyist's gift of frozen shrimp for her wedding reception. The attempt to proscribe misconduct by elaborate rules inevitably implied that all misconduct not proscribed was proper. Attempts to legislate (or teach) ethics have never succeeded. Ethics is propagated by example and is the product of culture which gives it definition. We took our duties seriously in the Ethics Committee, studying all complaints of misconduct and retaining special counsel as necessary. There were few credible complaints of misconduct in the 1970's, but I had the unpleasant duty of trying a Senator, a former Governor, baron of the Senate and Chairman of the Agriculture Committee, Herman Talmadge of Georgia, before the Senate after an investigation and public hearing before the Ethics Committee. He was "denounced" by the Senate for petty financial irregularities. Thus was his political career ended. Our duty as Senators was to the Senate. That duty transcended person and party. We were as one in our devotion to the upper house.

Some Senate reforms, including disclosure of financial interests of Members, the reduction in the number of committees, subcommittees and special committees and the realignment and updating of committee jurisdictions made the system more accountable and Senators more productive. But in distributing power broadly, we broke the hold of Committee Chairmen over the legislative process with results unanticipated by the reformers and the good government groups like Common Cause who urged us on. After Senator Howard Cannon, Chairman of the Rules Committee, I and others no longer remained in the Senate to enforce the reforms and some of the more promising changes, like reducing the number of committee assignments for Members, the institution succumbed to its inherent difficulty in disciplining itself.

Senators had retreated behind closed doors to draft legislation in mark up sessions and represent the public interest with impunity, as the founders did at the Constitutional Convention. We opened the doors. Senators then retreated to closed Conference Committee meetings to reconcile differences in legislation passed by both Houses and represent the public interest by removing concessions adopted in public for grateful supplicants and constituents, knowing they would disappear in secret. When their doors were opened, Senators had nowhere remaining to represent the public interest without fear of retribution from the interest groups growing more powerful and numerous with the breakdown of party organization, transcendence of money and the fresh opportunities for influence created by reforms, all adopted, of course, in the name of more democracy.

We opened up the legislative process, increased the staffing and in redistributing power, broadly left it vulnerable to pressures at many more points from think tanks, industry, financial and farm groups, environmentalists, gun control and abortion advocates, religionists, and advocacy groups of all kinds which proliferated to take advantage of reform and the mounting vulnerability of the politicians. The unintended results were due in part to the new mass media which took advantage of the reforms to be adversarial and superficial instead of availing the public of its new access to political processes and politicians, as we reformers had naively expected. Committee studies and hearings on industrial competitiveness and technology innovation, the international monetary system, and measures to prevent terrorism attracted attention from foreign media, rarely the U.S. media. Terrorism, for example, became news after the fact and too late. An Ethics Committee hearing on the pecuniary peccadilloes of a Senator packed the house. Politicians adjusted to the new environment. They competed for this media's attention with "one-liners," charges and negative attacks, accelerating the incivility and partisanship, the public's withdrawal. Some quit.

In the old days a smoke filled closed conference committee meeting of the Congressional Public Works Committees would have warmed the cockles of Boss Tweed's heart. That's where the pork was divvied up. But we were subject to more restraint and discipline. It never was an ethically pure process, as the Abscam incident implicating a Senator and several House members in an apparent bribery scheme demonstrated. But in the main we revered the Senate and earned the respect of our peers through its service. We had to satisfy economic cost-benefit ratios for Army Corps of Engineers pork projects, though they were—as the Tombigbee Canal attests—somewhat malleable, especially in Southern Illinois. Generalities are imperfect. It is all relative. But we exercised more restraint when we were less vulnerable. We fought for pork on the merits, justifying it to the Executive agencies and the Congress. We had more security in Party and were less dependent on the expectations of investors in politics and the appetites of the new media. I worked hard and successfully to bring Illinois the grants on the merits. We did not trade votes for earmarks, which were unknown. Affectations of patriotism, faith and support for social values, all taken for granted, were no part of the political culture and process.

In *The Broken Branch*, Norman Ornstein and Thomas Mann describe the demise of the House of Representatives as a deliberative body. The House is the citadel of American democracy. It is the people's house—the first House. It represents the people most directly and is the first check against excesses in the Executive Branch, they postulate. I found that the House was capable of approving irresponsible, politically convenient measures because it could count on the Senators with longer terms in office to protect the public interest from its excesses. That is no longer a prudent assumption. Ornstein, a member of the Stevenson Committee staff, and Mann are long-time, perceptive observers and participants in the Congress. They describe in grim detail the breakdown of the "regular order," the processes and procedures which had evolved over time to assure fairness for Members, the conscientious deliberation of issues in committee and on the floor, the subordinate role of professional staff, and painstaking, line by line drafting of laws by Members in the mark-up sessions to reflect faithfully and clearly Congressional intent.

Ornstein and Mann describe how the regular order was abandoned by the Republicans after they acquired control in the 1994 election. Roll calls were held open for as long as the leadership required to cajole or bribe Members. Omnibus bills of hundreds of pages were drafted at night by leadership staff and rammed through the House before Members had a chance to study them. They were loaded with hidden earmarks for the faithful, denials thereof for dissidents, and favors for the interests which had invested. By 2005, appropriations bills contained almost 13,000 earmarks at a cost of $64 billion. A 2004 tax bill aimed at eliminating an unlawful trade subsidy passed with $137 billion in new loopholes for special interests. By no coincidence, between 2000 and 2005, registered lobbyists doubled to more than 34,750, and their charges to clients increased more than 100 percent. Reported Federal lobbying expenditures for 2005 at $2.4 billion were 15 percent higher than in 2004. $2.6 billion was reported for 2006, up 11 percent. That's more than $5 million per Member. For 2007, expenditures were increased by new classes of investors, including private equity firms fearing taxes. Perhaps three to four times more is spent in "grassroots lobbying" and other unregulated efforts, according to the Committee for Economic Development. One lobby, the U.S. Chamber of Commerce and its affiliates, spent $73 million or $135,888 per Member of Congress in 2006, another record.

The lobbyists buy earmarks, loopholes and other concessions, even favors for foreign countries—especially countries like the Republic of Armenia with a local constituency. Turkey hires lobbyists to counter those of the Armenians. The Iraqi government is lobbying Congress as I write. (China and Russia have no lobbies, though China is reported to be hiring a public relations firm.) In the Black Book, Congressional leadership was zealous in defending the integrity of the legislative process from foreign influences. In the early 1960's, Senator William Fulbright and the Senate Foreign Relations committee began a lengthy investigation of foreign agents, even daring to probe Israel's espionage and unlawful organization of its lobby.

The Republican leadership after 1994 used earmarks and committee assignments to reward the faithful for raising and contributing cash to the Party coffers. In other words, committee assignments were for sale—and in both Parties. This is corruption by the standards of the Black Book, and of a scale unknown, even in the first Gilded Age when the Black Book began. The House Ethics Committee was rendered impotent by the new Republicans. Complaints of misconduct by Members are accepted only from Members!

In the new Congress, Members have little time for painstaking mark up sessions. Drafting of bills is consigned to young staffers. Bills are routinely sent to the House floor with rules that prevent amendment and debate. With little to debate and little chance to amend measures, the hours Congress is in session dwindle. The families of Members remain at home in their states. Members check into Washington for two or three days a week when the House is in session.

After the Republicans acquired control of the Presidency in 2001, the duty of the House Republican leadership was no longer to the House and the people —it was to the executive branch. Its primary purpose was to execute the President's program, and it did so ruthlessly and with contempt for democratic process. Oversight of the Executive was essentially abandoned. House districts had been gerrymandered. Few were seriously contested in general elections. In 2004 99.5 percent of incumbents won re-election, but the money pours in. Ornstein and Mann recall wistfully the days I recall and, as long-time devotees of the Congress and the legislative process, lament the Broken Branch. On January 19, 2006 they wrote in the N.Y. Times:

> We have never seen the culture so sick or the legislative process so dysfunctional....If you can play fast and loose with the rules of the game in lawmaking, it becomes easier to consider playing fast and loose with everything else, including relations with lobbyists, acceptance of favors, the use of official resources and the discharge of governmental power.

As I close the Black Book in early 2008, Democrats have taken control of both Houses. Oversight of the Executive Branch has been restored and already revealed corruption which has permeated virtually all agencies of the Executive Branch. From petty thievery to the infiltration of federal agencies with partisans, religious fundamentalists, ideologues and propagandists, the corruption is breathtaking in its sweep and audacity. Even the Justice department was corrupted, the selection and retention of U.S. attorneys politicized. Pretenses for unprovoked war were invented and implanted in Congress and complicit journalists. Ornstein and Mann report that the Congress is working longer hours under the Democrats. The earmarks have been cut back slightly. But whether "the regular order" will be restored remains to be seen. The system is basically unchanged, though the Democratic Congressional leadership is developing rules that would require lobbyists to report campaign funds they raised from others and "bundled" for Members. That would be an encouraging change.

As I write, the Congress has divided along party lines over questions of war and peace in the Middle East. The debate over Vietnam did not divide along party lines. Neither side appears capable of supporting diplomacy as an alternative to war in the Middle East. They may agree on a lowest common denominator, an ignoble exit strategy which holds Iraq responsible for its failure to meet arbitrary benchmarks of progress towards stability and self-governance, as if to blame it for having been invaded. If an end to the American occupation of Iraq was accompanied by an end to the Israeli occupation of the West Bank, Gaza

94

and the Golan Heights of Syria, as part of a comprehensive settlement and regional security arrangement, stability might be restored to the Middle East, as is near universally recognized outside Washington and Israel. The Iraq Study Group report recognized as much. But peace is beyond our political competence —and I am jumping ahead in the Black Book.

In early 2003, I called former Senator Paul Simon and inquired if Senators who voted to authorize force in Iraq were ignorant or cynical. Unbeknownst to both of us, this good man was on his death bed. He replied that a few Senators nowadays might be that ignorant, but most were cynical. Ornstein and Mann report some progress in restoring the legislative process in Congress but conclude that the jury is out. And process is not enough to assure accountability. It makes accountability achievable by Members with the "courage to be right."

> There are times when we must rise above principle.
> *Senator Eli Watson* of Indiana.

> I was sent to this body with very little opposition from the people of Indiana—and I leave it with none.
> *Senator Watson's swan song* after being overwhelmingly defeated

11: Speech and Speakers

Public speaking is very easy.
George W. Bush

Eloquent speech and speakers have always been movers in democratic systems of government, more so than all but the greatest of political writings. In the early days of the Black Book, schools in the "West" taught speech and elocution with the aid of "Readers" and "Speakers." These texts contained exercises in speech which were excerpts from literature and famous orations. *Delsarte's Speaker* illustrated poses and gestures to accompany expressions of remorse, repulsion, rejection, and patriotism. The early Speakers, like the Readers, aimed to prepare students for a life dependent on speech and one's ability to articulate, persuade and entertain. Lincoln and Adlai I parlayed their speaking skills into political careers. Adlai II followed, utilizing speech to inspire and inform—and endear the audience. Westerners began to produce more than a proportionate share of America's political leaders, or so we middle westerners believe. (The Midwest was "west" during the early years of the Black Book.)

In the early days education was an incident of religion. As time went on, the Readers and Speakers also expressed humor, Mark Twain being the much quoted, near perfect, irreverent manifestation of American humor. There followed Humorous Manuals of elocution and Humorous Recitations and minute instructions for "putting over the laugh lines." Speech was more than a means of communication in Adlai I's time. It was essential to one's vocation, most obviously in law, religion and politics. But it also animated daily life with information and entertainment. Lyceums – forums for itinerant speakers – preceded universities as a means of education. Speeches by politicians are a subject of both friendly derision and exaltation in the Black Book, with humor ever present.

First, the derision.

After an extremely long speech, the toastmaster rose and observed, "Sampson slew 1,000 in a night with the jawbone of an ass. Our guest speaker has just slain 2,000 in half the time and with the same implement."

Speeches cannot be made long enough for the speakers,
nor short enough for the hearers.
James Perry

A long-winded speaker after the first hour had few
survivors in his audience. The chairman had fallen asleep
with his head resting on the speaker's table. The speaker
in an impassioned peroration brought his fist down on the
head of the chairman, who called out wearily, "Hit me
again. I can still hear him."

Senator Tom Connelly of Texas, an impassioned orator,
was speaking "down home" and started out talking about
the beautiful piney woods of east Texas, and then he
moved on through the bluebonnets and out to the plains
and down through the Hill Country to the Gulf Coast and
then got back to the piney woods and started all over
again. When he got all around the state, he started in
again about those beautiful piney woods and the
bluebonnets. An old fellow rose up in the back of the
room and yelled out: "The next time you pass Lubbock,
how about letting me off?"

Joseph Chamberlain, prime minister of Great Britain,
told this story of himself: "I was guest of honor at a
banquet. The mayor of the city presided, and when coffee
was being served, he leaned over and asked me, 'Shall
we let them enjoy themselves a little longer or had we
better have your speech?'"

His speeches leave the impression of an army of
pompous phrases moving over the landscape in search of
an idea; sometimes these meandering words would
actually capture a staggering thought and bear it
triumphantly, a prisoner in their midst, until it died of
servitude and overwork.

Senator William McAdoo
commenting on Warren G.
Harding

Sheridan once said of a speech that "it contained a great deal both of what was new and what was true; but that what was new was not true, and what was true was not new."

The ability of various public speakers was being discussed. Someone said that Archbishop Whatley was gifted with unusual oratorical powers. Sydney Smith granted that there were some things he could indeed admire in the worthy doctor's discourses, remarking with emphasis of one particular speech: "There he had some splendid flashes of silence."

A speaker from the 1940s: My predicament reminds me of the little boy in the radio contest who was asked to tell in twenty-five words or less why he liked this particular program. After considerable effort at finding the most impressive argument he could muster, the boy uttered this testimonial: "I like the Jack Smith show because as soon as it's over the Lone Ranger comes on."

A congressman was invited to a hanging. Being a gentleman of some distinction, he was invited to have a seat with the prisoner and his spiritual advisor on the gallows. As the fatal hour approached, the sheriff advised the prisoner that he had five minutes to live and it was his privilege to address the audience. The prisoner replied meekly that he did not wish to speak. Thereupon the congressman stepped promptly to the front of the scaffold and said: "As the gentleman does not wish to speak, if he will kindly yield me his time, I will take the occasion to remark that I am a candidate for reelection, regularly endorsed by the Democratic Convention," and so it went until the prisoner, who had amidst his arrest and trial and up to this moment, with his open coffin beside him, displayed marvelous fortitude, suddenly exhibited deep emotion and piteously exclaimed, "Please hang me first, and let him speak afterward!"

One immigrant to another, "Friend, America is a grand country to settle in. They don't hang you here for murder." "What do they do?" "They kill you with elocution."

Woodrow Wilson was asked how long he would take to prepare a ten-minute speech. He said: "Two weeks." "How long for an hour speech?" "One week." "How long for a two-hour speech?" "I'm ready now."

Andrew Jackson, before he became president, made a stump speech in a small town. As he was finishing, a friend whispered, "Tip 'em a little Latin, General; they won't be satisfied without it." Old Hickory quickly recalled a few phrases, and in a "voice of thunder" concluded with, "E Pluribus Unum, sine qua non, ne plus ultra, multum in perve." The effect was tremendous; the cheers could be heard for miles.

The excitement of perpetual speech making is fatal to the exercise of the highest powers.

Pity the third or fourth speaker on a program, for whom this reverend's invocation at a banquet might be appropriate: "O Lord, help the first speaker to imbue this audience with thy spirit. O Lord, help the second speaker to inspire this audience, and O Lord have mercy on the last speaker."

A speech need not be eternal to be immortal.

If you would make a speech or write one,
Or get an artist to indite one,
Think not because 'tis understood by
Men of sense, 'tis therefore good,
Make it so clear and simply planned no
Blockhead can misunderstand.

The political speech as an eloquent expression of conscience and opinion or an instrument of inspiration and excitement has become rare, impoverishing the political discourse. Adlai I regularly spoke for two hours "journeying to and fro across the stage." His running mate in 1900, William Jennings Bryan, frequently spoke four to five hours a day, according to his widow. In 1952, the Democratic National Committee paid $1million dollars for eighteen regularly scheduled half-hour blocks of time on national television for Adlai II's eloquent addresses to cheering partisans. Today he would have difficulty financing a thirty second commercial. The discourse is increasingly reduced to sound bites and the give-and-take of news conferences, talk programs and "debates" known as cattle shows.

After winning a seat with the Free Silver delegation from Nebraska in 1896, Bryan addressed the Democratic Convention, delivering his famous speech vowing the people would not be crucified upon a "cross of gold" —the gold standard. He aimed to deflate the currency for the benefit of debtors and common people. The speech played to emotions and paid scant attention to the free silver issue. Its purpose was more to arouse than to inform.

"As he confronted the twenty thousand yelling, cursing, shouting men before him, they felt at once that indescribable, magnetic thrill which beasts and men alike experience in the presence of a master. . . . And so he had played at will upon their very heart-strings, until the full tide of their emotion was let loose in one tempestuous roar of passion," wrote Harry Thurston Peck. Following the "Cross of Gold" speech, according to Charles Warren, "There was a pause. Then occurred a wild and hysterical uprising: waves of deafening cheers and yells swept from end to end of the building and back again, unceasing in their tumult." Bryan was nominated for president then and twice thereafter largely on the strength of his oratory, the only presidential candidate in American history to be thrice defeated. He was an orator — and a highly principled reformer and progressive.

> He speaks plain cannon fire,
> and smoke and bounce ...
> Zounds! I was never so bethump'd
> With words.
>
> *Shakespeare*, King John

When Cicero finished speaking, people said, "How well he spoke." When Demosthenes finished speaking, people said, "Let us march."

Today prepared political speeches are usually the work of professional wordsmiths and spin masters who string "one-liners" together for effect according to what polls and consultants indicate is needed, and larded, as necessary, by the advice of "experts." Position papers address politically convenient or necessary subjects with input from the experts. Substantive speeches and position papers rarely proceed from the heart and mind of the wise and principled, experienced statesman. They do not shape debate, frame and define the central issues of political and economic security in a nuclear age and a resource poor, interdependent, increasingly non-polar world. Writing one's speeches is an exercise in reason for the heart and mind of the politician which is not communicable nor importable for the most part. Rare is the advisor who risks the political life of his advisee with uncomfortable truths. Lincoln was his own speech writer, as was Adlai I. Adlai II was his own best speech writer.

In this electronic era, public speaking has a visual dimension unknown to Lincoln and Adlai I. Adlai II's presidential campaigns were the first of the television era. From then on politicians would address a glass eye, the camera, with enthusiasm, empathy, indignation— whatever emotion the message required. Political oratory would adjust to an electronic, visual and episodic medium. Actors and demagogues have an advantage in this artificial environment. Demeanor and appearance acquire a new importance. "Websterian" brows retreat before the simian, air brushed brows of white male politicians who acquire a kind of sameness of appearance to mimic the discourse, though this sameness offers contrast and, therefore, opportunity to non-conformists.

The first televised presidential debate was between John F. Kennedy and Richard M. Nixon in 1960. Polls later indicated that among those who watched, Kennedy "won"; among those who listened to the radio, Nixon "won." His dark visage required a slathering of pancake makeup which melted from perspiration stimulated by the klieg lights. This fatal experience became a lesson for all politicians in the early age of television and hot lights. In 1970, moments before a joint national television appearance with my opponent, Senator Ralph Smith, I turned to him and with a note of concern whispered, "Ralph, your makeup is starting to run." The message had the desired effect. Perspiration popped from Ralph's forehead. His makeup did start to run, causing more anxiety—and more perspiration. Under seeming pressure from his opponent, poor Ralph was widely observed mopping his brow.

For the Black Book, pickings have been lean in recent years. But for those who take to the stump and the hard-roll circuit, the challenge still starts with a response to the introduction and an engaging opening.

After that ample introduction, I can hardly wait to hear what I am about to say.

Attributed by the eminent Senator
Edmund Muskie of Maine to his
Senate seatmate, Adlai III, who
attributes it to the Black Book

Apropos a warm reception: "I am reminded of the cow which, being milked one very cold morning, turned to the farmer and said, 'Thank you for those warm hands.'"

Adlai I

As speaker, my job, as I understand it, is to talk to you. Yours, as I understand it, is to listen. If you finish before I do, just hold up your hand.

Mark Twain began a lecture: "Julius Caesar is dead, Shakespeare is dead, Napoleon is dead, Abraham Lincoln is dead—and I am far from well myself."

The old Quaker Rufus Jones addressed a school commencement: "Looking at all you happy boys and happy girls recalls to me the time when I, too, was a little boy and a little girl."

Bob Hope's well tested beginning for a commencement address: "To those of you who are about to go out into the world and await my advice, here it is: Don't go!"

I feel like the eager young man who had just received his diploma at a theological seminary and exclaimed, "Now I am ready to go out and do the Lord's work wherever it may lead me, providing it is honorable!"

Newly elected Governor Al Smith of New York commenced an address to the inmates of Sing Sing penitentiary: "Fellow citizens." Then, thinking the prisoners had forfeited their citizenship, he began anew, "Fellow convicts," which, being inappropriate, prompted him to begin again with, "Well, in any case, I am glad to see so many of you here."

Senator Chauncey Depew had the unenviable task of following a speech by Mark Twain which was received with great enthusiasm. He rose to the occasion: "Mr. Chairman, Ladies and Gentlemen, before this dinner, Mark Twain and I made an agreement to trade speeches. He has just delivered mine, and I am grateful for the warm reception you have accorded it. I regret that I have lost his speech and cannot remember a thing he had to say." Depew sat down to much applause.

In a speech, jokes and anecdotes can help establish a friendly rapport with the audience. Humor can also be an effective way to denigrate the opposition without being mean spirited. It can attract media coverage without being unduly negative. "Humorous recitations" and "laugh lines" run throughout the Black Book and are often difficult to categorize except for what they are: miscellaneous and mischievous bits of wit and humor employed to engage or enlighten the audience. They reflect the differing times. What may have been amusing for one generation may not be for the next —or might be politically inappropriate. Adlai I and II found that humor was a universal language for one sensitive to cultural niceties and the temper of the moment. I found that what works in Beijing may not work in Riyadh. There have been uncomfortable moments when confronted with a mixed audience half laughing and half stony-faced following a joke or anecdote. Humor is a universal language for those who know how to speak it. Of course, much depends on translation.

After leaving the presidency, Jimmy Carter delivered a speech to a large audience in Tokyo. After translating one sequence into Japanese, the translator added, "President Carter has just cracked a joke, so please laugh." The audience roared, and President Carter was very pleased. I later met the translator who assured me the story was a total fabrication—which in this merciless business of politics detracts little from its usefulness.

The relation of the toastmaster to the speaker should be the same as that of the fan to the fan dancer: It should call attention to the subject without completely covering it.

Adlai II

Fabrications and lies are not of recent political invention, of course, though much of their color is lost, and the mendacity now transcends partisan politicking to pervade policy making and discourse at high levels.

A lie can travel half way around the world while the truth is putting on its shoes.

Mark Twain

Adlai I tells of the Honorable Frank Woolford, a member of Congress from the mountains of Kentucky who was chosen colonel of a mounted Union regiment gathered from his own and adjoining counties. "He knew how to fight, but of the science of war as taught in the schools he was ignorant as the grave. It was said that his entire tactics were embraced in two commands: 'Huddle and fight,' and 'Scatter.'"

The Colonel and General S. S. Fry of Danville were friends from boyhood and comrades in the Mexican and Civil Wars but of different party affiliations, Fry being a Republican and Woolford a Democrat. To counteract the "evil effect" of a speech to be given by the Colonel at a barbecue, the Republican State Committee engaged General Fry to attend and address the people of the county. Upon his arrival, General Fry was warmly greeted by the Colonel and invited to speak "as long as you want to. The boys have all heard me time and again. . . . When you get through, of course, if there is a little time left, I may say 'howdy' to the boys."

So General Fry did "go ahead" and discourse upon the financial question, the tariff, reconstruction, and "earnestly and at length upon the magnanimity of the Republican Party toward the men lately in rebellion against the Government." The speech concluded. Colonel Woolford arose and without a "howdy," without honoring finance or the tariff with the briefest mention, proceeded. He remarked upon the "magnanimity" of the Republican Party: "You all remember Stonewall Jackson, one of the grandest men God ever made. This same magnanimous Republican Party took him prisoner, tried him by a drum head court-martial, and shot him down like a mad dog after he had surrendered up his sword."

General Fry interposed: "Why Colonel Woolford . . . Stonewall Jackson was accidentally shot by one of his own men in battle, and his memory is honored by all the people North and South."

Colonel Woolford: "Don't try to deceive these people. We don't put on style and wear store clothes like you big folks do down in Danville . . . but if there is anything that these people do love, it is the truth. What did this same magnanimous Republican Party do with General Robert E. Lee? . . . Well, after he had surrendered at Appomattox, and his men had all laid down their arms, they tried him by drum head court martial and shot and quartered him right on the spot."

General Fry indignantly exclaimed: "It's an outrage, Colonel Woolford, to attempt to deceive these people by such statements. General Lee was never even imprisoned and is alive, the President of a college in Virginia and esteemed by everybody."

The Colonel: "Now, General Fry, you have been treated like a gentleman ever since you came to these mountains; we gave you the best we had to eat, gave you the last drop out of the bottle, and listened quietly. . . .We don't wear Sunday clothes. . .but just live our plain way in our log cabins, and eat our hoe cake and say our prayers, but if there is anything on God's earth we do love it is the truth. . . .Yes, this same magnanimous party that General Fry has been telling you about, what did they do with poor old Jeff Davis after he was captured? . . .Well, after he was in prison and as helpless as a child, what did they do with him? Why they just took him out, and without even giving him a drum head trial, tied him up and *burned him to ashes at the stake!*"

Fry sprang to his feet: "Great God! Jeff Davis is still alive, at his home in Mississippi, and has never been tried. It is damnable to make such statements to these people, Colonel Woolford!"

The Colonel with a deeply injured air: "General Fry, you and I have been friends for a life time. We hooked watermelons, hunted coons and attended all the frolics together when we were boys. We slept under the same blanket, belonged to the same mess, fought side by side at Palo Alto and Cerro Gordo. . . . I have loved you like a brother, but this is too much, it is putting friendship to a turrible test; it is little more than flesh can stand."

Pausing to recover from the deep emotion he had shown, he called out: "Bill, tell the General what you saw them do with old Jeff."

Bill, a tall, lank, one-gallused mountaineer, leaning against a sapling, deposed that he was present, saw old Jeff led out, tied to a stake and finally disappear in a puff of smoke.

At this General Fry mounted his horse and, looking neither to the right nor left, retraced his steps to Danville, where he informed the state committee that if they wanted any further debates with old Frank Woolford, they would have to send someone else.

Years later, after Adlai I had appointed "a few cross road postmasters" for Congressman Woolford, he inquired of him whether he had ever had a debate with General Fry.

"With a suppressed chuckle and a quaint gleam of his remaining eye, he significantly replied, 'It won't do, Colonel [Adlai I], to believe everything you hear!'"

> I stand by all the misstatements that I've made.
> *George W. Bush*

The Black Book differentiates between speakers and speech, and touches on the art and nature of speech and conversation, as well as abstractions about truth and falsehood and what today is called "communication."

> As empty vessels make the loudest sound, so they that have the least wit and are the greatest babblers.
> *Plato*

> Empty barrels make the most noise.
> *John Lyly*, Euphues, 1579

> Think all you speak, but speak not all you think.
> Thoughts are your own; your words are so no more.
> *Delany*

> Speech is a faculty given to man to conceal his thoughts.
> *Talleyrand*

> Speech is certainly a very effective way of concealing thought.
> *Voltaire*

> In all labor there is profit, but the talk of the lips tendeth only to penury.
> *Shakespeare*

The first duty of a wise advocate is to convince his opponents that he understands their arguments and sympathizes with their just feelings.
Coleridge

It ain't a bad plan t' keep still occasionally, even when you know what you're talkin' about.

It is sometimes better to keep still and be thought a fool than it is to speak and remove all doubt.
Calvin Coolidge

With all his tumid boasts, he's like the swordfish who only wears his weapon in his mouth.
Madden

The habit of common and continuous speech is a symptom of mental deficiency.
Walter Bagehot

He has a rage for saying something when there's nothing to be said.
Dr. Johnson

The loud voice that spoke the empty mind.
Oliver Goldsmith

The less a man thinks, the more he talks.
Montesquieu

Speech is silvern, silence is golden; speech is human, silence is divine.
German Proverb

Definition of "auditorium": Derived from audio, to hear; and taurus—the bull.

A superior man is modest in his speech, but exceeds in his actions.
Confucius

Wisdom consists of ten parts—nine of silence and one of brevity.

He draweth out the thread of his verbosity finer than the staple of his argument.

The aim of argument, or discussion, should not be victory, but progress.

Joseph Joubert, Pensées, 1842

There is always time to speak a word but never time to unspeak it.

Unknown Spanish writer in the
Golden Age of Spanish literature

But there is an art which is better than painting, poetry, music, or architecture, – better than botany, geology, or any science; namely, conversation. Wise, cultivated, genial conversation is the last flower of civilization and the best result which life has to offer us – a cup for gods, which has no repentance. Conversation is our account of ourselves. All we have, all we can, all we know, is brought into play, and as the reproduction, in finer form, of all our havings.

Ralph Waldo Emerson,
Miscellanies, 1855

A man went to the barber for a haircut, handed him a coin and climbed into the chair. The astonished barber thanked him and remarked he had never been tipped in advance, to which the customer said, "That is not a tip. It's hush money."

Never dilute the oil of anecdote with the vinegar of fact.

There is no tragedy so horrible as that of a beautiful myth being murdered by an ugly fact.

Mark Twain

The great enemy of truth is very often not the lie . . . but
the myth.
John F. Kennedy

A platitude is something that is universally agreed upon
and obviously not true.
H. L. Mencken

As scarce as truth is, the supply is always greater than the
demand.
Josh Billings

But such is the irresistible nature of truth that all it asks
and all it wants, is the liberty of appearing.
Thomas Paine

Speeches during the span of the Black Book increasingly
featured the "humorous recitations and laugh lines." Some are not
humorous or politically appropriate today but reflect their times. Many
were loosely catalogued with more sober comments under headings
which made their access in the Black Book the readier for speeches
often spurred by the moment. The potentials of some for the light-
hearted denigration of political opposition are self-evident and well
tested. More are recorded in the Afterwords.

A poor Tennessee mountain woman had ten children.
The youngest, a baby, crawled into the tar barrel and
emerged covered with tar. Asked what the poor woman
would do, she replied, 'Ah spec it'd be easier to git a new
un then clean up this un.'

Juan and Evita Peron paid a state visit to Spain which
was accompanied by much pomp and ceremony. At a
parade, Evita, on the arm of a Spanish Grandee, marched
behind Peron, the dictator of Argentina, and the King of
Spain. As the march proceeded, women in the crowd
shouted, "Puta, Puta." (Whore, Whore.) Evita was
consoled by the Grandee who turned to her, patted her on
the arm, and said, "Don't worry, dear, I've been retired
from the Army for thirty years and they still call me
General."

12: Lincoln

And so we see ourselves in Lincoln, as he saw himself in people. That greatness in him—is there not some of it in my neighbor, myself, my son? Of course there is, we tell ourselves, for Lincoln was all of us— the spokesman for all that went before him in the building of America and everything we have fought since to preserve. And so, while statesmen come and go, Lincoln in his person and in his life work remains the greatest democrat of us all, and a continuing inspiration to all mankind.

Adlai II

Lincoln was a presence in the Stevenson family. He habitually recorded stories for the telling, and may have inspired Adlai I to begin the Black Book.

> They say I tell a great many stories; I reckon I do, but I have found in the course of a long experience that common people, take them as they run, are more easily informed through the medium of a broad illustration than in any other way, and as to what the hypercritical few may say, I don't care.
>
> *Lincoln*

In an 1852 entry in the Black Book, Adlai I records seeing Lincoln alight from a stagecoach in front of the old tavern in Bloomington, "somewhat travel stained" from his sixty-mile journey from Springfield. That evening he heard Mr. Lincoln address a political meeting supporting the election of General Winfield Scott for the presidency. "The speech was one of great ability, and but little that was favorable of the military record of General Pierce remained when the speech was concluded."

My great-great-grandfather Jesse Fell was Lincoln's political sponsor and patron. At Fell's request Lincoln wrote and gave Fell his autobiographical sketch. Fell used the sketch (appended to this chapter) to promote the little-known Lincoln for president after the Lincoln-Douglas debates. This document descended in the family until it was given to the Library of Congress in 1947. It was Fell who originally proposed those debates, suggesting to Senator Stephen A. Douglas in 1854 a "joint discussion" of the critical question then pending, extension of slavery into the Territories, and Douglas' doctrine of popular sovereignty. Adlai I, then a student at Wesleyan College, was present and recorded the great Democrat's response:

"What party does Mr. Lincoln represent?" Douglas asked. "The Whig Party, of course," said Fell. Douglas declined the proposition "with much feeling," saying—according to young Adlai I— "When I came home from Washington I was assailed in the northern part of the State by an old line abolitionist, in the central part of the State by a Whig, and in southern Illinois by an anti-Nebraska Democrat. I cannot hold the Whig responsible for what the abolitionist says, nor the anti-Nebraska Democrat responsible for what either of the others say, and it looks like dogging a man all over the State."

Mr. Lincoln later called on Senator Douglas. The greeting between them was "most cordial, and their conversation, principally of incidents in their early lives, of the most agreeable and familiar character," according to Adlai I. Later Lincoln proposed the "joint discussion" to Douglas, who acceded. The seven famous debates followed. Three hours each, they were attended by thousands drawn on foot, horseback and in wagons. They brought Lincoln the national attention grandfather Fell sought. He then employed the autobiography to promote Lincoln for President in the East. Lincoln followed him. His Cooper Union speech in New York was circulated in 500,000 copies.

In 1832, the year Fell moved from Pennsylvania to settle in Illinois, Lincoln first ran for public office as a candidate for the Illinois legislature. He was defeated in that race but elected two years later. Apparently he and Fell first met in Vandalia, then the Illinois capital, when Lincoln was a legislator, and they shared a room as was common in those times. Fell was lobbying the legislature on behalf of Bloomington. Later, in 1860, Fell joined his protegé, David Davis, to organize the Illinois delegation to the Republican convention for Lincoln. That convention temporarily swelled the population of Chicago by forty percent.

> I presume you all know who I am. I am humble Abraham Lincoln. I have been solicited by my friends to become a candidate for the Legislature. My politics are short and sweet like the old woman's dance. I am in favor of a national bank. I am in favor of the internal improvements system and a high protective tariff. These are my sentiments and political principles. If elected, I shall be thankful. If not it will all be the same. (1832)

We must not promise what we ought not, lest we be called on to perform when we cannot. (1856)

No party can command respect which sustains this year what it opposed last. (1859)

Trusting in Him who can go with me, and remain with you, and be everywhere for good, let us confidently hope that all will yet be well. To His care commending you, as I hope in your prayers you will commend me, I bid you an affectionate farewell.

Lincoln's Farewell Address to the
citizens of Springfield, 1861

The dogmas of the quiet past are inadequate to the stormy present.

You cannot escape the responsibility of tomorrow by evading it today.

If there ever should be a time for mere catch arguments, that time is surely not now. In times like the present no man should utter anything for which he would not willingly be responsible through time and in eternity.

I must keep some consciousness of being somewhere near right. I must keep some standards of principle fixed within myself.

I know there is a God and that he hates injustice. I see the storm coming and I know His hand is in it. But if He has a place and a part for me, I believe that I am ready.

You may fool all the people some of the time; you can even fool some of the people all the time; but you can't fool all of the people all the time.

In a speech on July 27, 1848, Congressman Lincoln made light of General Lewis Cass' war record, saying that the general's Democratic supporters for the presidency, who were trying to tie him to "a military tail," were like "so many mischievous boys trying to tie the dog to a bladder of beans." He went on to mock himself:

> Mr. Speaker, did you know I was a military hero? Yes, sir; in the days of the Black Hawk war I fought, bled and came away. Speaking of General Cass' career reminds me of my own. I was not at Stillman's defeat, but I was about as near it as Cass was to Hull's surrender; and like him, I saw the place very soon afterward. It is quite certain I did not break my sword, for I had none to break; but I bent a musket pretty badly on one occasion.
>
> If Cass broke his sword, the idea is he broke it in desperation; I bent the musket in accident. If General Cass went in advance of me in picking huckleberries, I guess I surpassed him in charges upon wild onions. If he saw any live, fighting Indians, it was more than I did; but I had a good many bloody struggles with the mosquitoes, and although I never fainted from the loss of blood, I can truly say that I was often very hungry.
>
> Mr. Speaker, if I should ever conclude to doff whatever our Democratic friends may suppose there is of black cockade federalism about me, and therefore they shall take me up as their candidate for the presidency, I protest they shall not make fun of me, as they have of General Cass, by attempting to write me into a military hero.

Of a high official plotting against his reelection, Lincoln said, "Like the blue bottle fly, he lays eggs in every rotten spot he can find."

Lincoln told his cabinet a story of a young boy who predicted the weather for his king. Curious about the source of his unfailing predictions, the king had the boy trailed and found that he consulted a donkey. The donkey put his ears forward to indicate fair weather, backward to indicate stormy. Whereupon the king made the donkey prime minister—and from that day on every jackass has wanted to be prime minister.

Once, after a tedious courtroom wrangle in Rock Island, Illinois, Lincoln wandered to the Mississippi River bank. He found a small boy there and asked him what he knew about the river. The boy replied, "I know all about it. It was here before I was born and has been here ever since." Lincoln afterward remarked that he was glad to get where there was so much fact and so little opinion.

In Lincoln's day people could wander into the White House from the street and accost the president where they could find him. Lincoln was in this way constantly beset by job and favor seekers. Not feeling well, he consulted a physician and was told that he was suffering from a slight case of smallpox. He exclaimed, "Wonderful! Now at last I have something I can give everybody."

Responding to suggestions that he appoint a major general to a position of great responsibility, Lincoln remarked that in a recent battle the enemy had captured three major generals and four carloads of mules. He said the incident worried him; he could make three more major generals with a stroke of the pen, but he did not know where he'd get the mules. Another version has Lincoln saying, "How unfortunate—those mules cost twenty dollars apiece."

One of Lincoln's neighbors in Springfield recalled: "I was called to the door one day by the cries of children in the street, and there was Mr. Lincoln, striding by with two of his boys, both of whom were wailing aloud. 'Why, Mr. Lincoln, what's the matter with the boys?' Lincoln: 'Just what's the matter with the whole world, I've got three walnuts, and each wants two.'"

In his "spot of bloodied soil" speech, Congressman Lincoln challenged President Polk to produce with some particularity the evidence of Mexico's aggression—a challenge to which there was no response. In another context, he said that those who supposed the war was not one of aggression reminded him of the Illinois farmer who said, "I ain't greedy about land. I only want what jines mine."

Lincoln was often the despair of his generals because of his lenient treatment of soldiers absent without leave. He explained, "If the good Lord has given a man a cowardly pair of legs, it is hard to keep them from running away with him."

Lincoln replaced the hesitant General McClellan with General Hooker who attempted to create an impression of vigorous activity by reporting his movements in dispatches headed: "Headquarters in the Saddle." Lincoln remarked, "He's got his headquarters where his hindquarters ought to be."

General Grant was accused of being a drunkard. "Well, you just find out, to oblige me, what brand of whiskey Grant drinks," Lincoln said, "because I want to send a barrel of it to each of my generals."

On his way to Gettysburg to deliver his immortal address, Lincoln was urged by General Fry to hurry so as not to hold up the train.

Lincoln replied, "I feel about this as the convict in one of our Illinois towns felt when he was going to the gallows. As he passed along the road in custody of the sheriff, the people, eager to see the execution, kept crowding and pushing past him. At last he called out, 'Boys you needn't be in such a hurry to git ahead. The fun won't start till I get there.'"

Speaking of a recently deceased politician known for his vanity, Lincoln said, "If General ----- had known how big a funeral he would have, he would have died years ago."

Salmon Chase remarked that he was sorry he hadn't written a certain letter, to which Lincoln responded, "Chase, never regret what you don't write; it is what you do write that you are often called upon to regret."

Long before the Presidency, a firm inquired of Lincoln about the financial condition of a neighbor. He replied: "First of all he has a wife and baby; together they ought to be worth $500,000 to any man. Secondly, he has an office in which there is a table worth $1.50 and three chairs worth, say, $1.00. Last of all, there is in one corner a rat hole which will bear looking into."

Lincoln told of a man who was being ridden out of town on a rail. Asked how he felt, he replied, "If it weren't for the honor of the thing, I'd just as soon walk."

> How prudently we proud men compete for nameless graves, while some starveling of fate forgets himself into immortality.
>
> *Wendell Phillips* on Lincoln

Lincoln's Autobiographical Sketch, as sent to Jesse Fell:

Springfield, Dec. 20. 1859

My dear Sir:

Herewith is a little sketch, as you requested—There is not much of it, for the reason, I suppose, that there is not much of me—If anything is made out of it, I wish it to be modest, and not go beyond the materials— If it were thought necessary to incorporate any thing from any of my speeches, I suppose there would be no objection. Of course it must not appear to have been written by myself—Yours very truly…A. Lincoln

I was born Feb.12, 1809, in Hardin County. My parents were both born in Virginia, of undistinguished families —second families, perhaps I should say. My Mother, who died in my tenth year, was of a family of the name of Hanks, some of whom now reside in Adams, and others in Macon counties, Illinois- My paternal grandfather, Abraham Lincoln, emigrated from Rockingham County, Virginia, to Kentucky, about 1781 or 2, when, a year or two later, he was killed by Indians, not in battle, but by stealth, when he was laboring to open a farm in the forest- His ancestors, who were Quakers, went to Virginia from Berks County, Pennsylvania- An effort to identify them with the New England family of the same name ended in nothing more definite, than a similarity of Christian names in both families, such as Enoch, Levi, Mordecai, Solomon, Abraham, and the like-

My father, at the death of his father, was but six years of age; and he grew up, literally without education- He removed from Kentucky to what is now Spencer County, Indiana, in my eighth year. We reached our new home about the time the state came into the Union- It was a wild region, with many bears and other wild animals still in the woods- There I grew up- There were some schools, so called; but no qualification was ever required of a teacher, beyond the "readin, writn, and cipherin" to the Rule of Three. If a straggler supposed to understand Latin, happened to sojourn in the neighborhood, he was looked upon as a wizzard- There was absolutely nothing to excite ambition for education. Of course when I came of age I did not know much- Still somehow, I could read, write, and cipher to the rule of Three, but that was all- I have not been to school since- The little advance I now have upon this store of education, I have picked up from time to time under pressure of necessity-

I was raised to farm work, which I continued till I was twenty two- At twenty one I came to Illinois, and passed the first year in Macon County- Then I got to New-Salem (at that time in Sangamon, now in Menard County), where I remained a year as a sort of Clerk in a store—then came the Black-Hawk war; and I was elected a Captain of Volunteers —a success which gave me more pleasure than any I have had since. I went (through) the campaign, was elated (sic), ran for the Legislature the same year (1832) and was beaten—the only time I ever have been beaten by the people. The next, and three succeeding biennial elections, I was elected to the Legislature. I was not a candidate afterwards. During this Legislative period I had studied law, and removed to Springfield to practice it. In 1846 I was once elected to the lower House of Congress. Was not a candidate for re-election. From 1849 to 1854, both inclusive, practiced law more assiduously than ever before. Always a Whig in politics; and generally on the electoral tickets, making active canvasses. I was losing interest in politics, when the repeal of the Missouri Compromise aroused me again- What I have done since then is pretty well known.

If any personal description of me is thought desirable, it may be said, I am, in height, six feet, four inches, nearly; lean in flesh, weighing, on an average, one hundred and eighty pounds; dark complexion, with coarse black hair, and grey eyes—no other marks or brands recollected.

Yours very Truly,
A. Lincoln

J.W.Fell, Esq.

From the Library of Congress. See also Papers of Abraham Lincoln Association, Volume III, 1981, Springfield, Illinois; Recollections of Abraham Lincoln, *Ward H. Lamon;* Life of Lincoln, *Wayne Whipple for the Lincoln Centennial Association, 1908*

13: Religion and Politics

Millions of innocent men, women and children, since the introduction of Christianity, have been burnt, tortured, fined, imprisoned: yet have not advanced once inch toward conformity. What have been the effects of coercion? To make one half of the world fools, and the other half, hypocrites.

Thomas Jefferson

Politicians, including the founders, invoked God freely, but religion in the Black Book was a context for devotion, a message of charity and compassion. It was also a subject of skeptical comment and humor. Religion was connected to politics, as many tales of circuit riding preachers, lawyers and politicians attest, but without, it seems, threatening the wall between religion and government enshrined in the Constitution after centuries of religious wars and persecutions in the Old World.

This would be the best of all possible worlds, if there was no religion in it.....As I understand the Christian religion, it was, and is, a revelation. But how has it happened that millions of fables, tales, legends, have been blended with both Jewish and Christian revelation that have made them the most bloody religions that ever existed?

John Adams

During almost fifteen centuries has the legal establishment of Christianity been on trial. What has been its fruits? More less, in all places, pride and indolence in the clergy; ignorance and servility in the laity; in both, superstition, bigotry and persecution.

James Madison

The priests of the different religious sects...dread the advance of science as witches do the approach of daylight, and scowl on the fatal harbinger announcing the subdivision of the duperies on which they live.

Thomas Jefferson

The founders were creatures of the Enlightenment. The 18th century lessons of Locke, Montesquieu and Voltaire had been absorbed.

For Jefferson, the struggle for religious freedom was the "severest contest in which I have ever been engaged." When Virginia's constitution separating church and state was adopted in 1786, Madison wrote: "Thus, in Virginia was extinguished forever the ambitious hope of making laws for the human mind." God, if there was one, had given man the gift of Reason. Divine Right was dogma. The conflict between God's governance and man's self governance was resolved. Reason would govern in man's temporal universe, God in his spiritual universe.

Evangelism in the early days propagated the Gospel, preached salvation and often employed Scripture to depict a caring Jesus. Later it began to metamorphose into salvation through rebirth, the end of times and predestination, which had roots in Calvinist New England. In the Black Book this fundamentalism did not invade American politics. God, if there was one, did not demand the submission preached by Luther and Calvin or the Pope.

The Black Book recalls faith healers, creationists, camp meetings and again and again the circuit riding preachers, lawyers and politicians who sharpened their "perfervid" oratory in practice—and prospered, or not, according to their success. They were often one and the same. Preachers became lawyers, and both became politicians and judges. But the wall between church and state was not threatened.

Adlai I remembered the camp meetings as disciplined, orderly affairs with no time for merrymaking and attended by families from many miles around on horseback, in wagons and on foot with their own tents for shelter:

> The flickering lights of the camp, the dark forest around, the melodious concert of a thousand voices in sacred song, the awe-inspiring, never to be forgotten hymn, 'come, humble sinner, in whose breast, a thousand thoughts revolve'…. The orator and the occasion here met and embraced. In very truth, the joys of the redeemed, and the horrors of lost souls, were depicted in colors that only lips 'touched with a live coal from the altar' could adequately describe.

Adlai I had little sympathy for the Prophet, Joseph Smith, and the Mormons forced to flee their settlement and temple in Nauvoo, Illinois. "The history of delusions from the days of Mahomet to the present time illustrates the eagerness with which men are ever ready to seek out new inventions, and to discard the old beliefs for the new. There is no tenet so monstrous but in some breast it will find lodgment."

Religion, as practiced in the early Illinois days recorded in the Black Book, was not without antagonisms between those of different persuasions which needed to be managed by attendant politicians. Brother Peter Cartwright, the circuit riding preacher and Democrat who may be remembered from earlier references, had a horror of "immersionists" and Calvinists alike. "At the time of my appointment I had never seen a Yankee, and I had heard dismal stories about them. It was said they lived almost entirely on pumpkins, molasses, fat meat, and Bohea tea; moreover that they could not bear loud and zealous sermons, and that they had brought their learned preachers with them, and were always criticizing us poor back woods preachers." Cartwright complained of one "female" who was given over in about equal parts to "universalism" and "predestinarianism" with whom he "had a hard race to keep up with," and thus he left her "impaled for all time, a thin faced, Roman nosed, loquacious, glib tongued Yankee."

Something of these antagonisms may be gathered from the tender farewell taken by Brother Cartwright of a former associate, one Brother D, "who left the Methodists, joined the Free-will Baptists, left them and joined the New Lights, and then moved to Texas, where the Devil has him in safe keeping long before his time."

"Blessed be the tie that binds our hearts in Christian love," was too seldom heard in the rural congregations; in too many, Christian charity, even in modified form, was an unknown quality. These antagonisms between sects posed a challenge for politicians who obeyed the Apostolic injunction to be "all things to all men." Adlai I illustrates the point with a recollection:

Senator Zebulon 'Zeb' Vance of Ohio had first run for Congress in the early 1850's and told of threading his way on horseback in a wild and sparsely populated locality when he found himself suddenly in the immediate presence of a worshiping congregation "in God's first temple." It was what was known in mountain parlance as a "protracted meeting."

The flock had just been called from labor to refreshment, and he was invited to share the ham, fried chicken, salt-rising bread, corn dodgers, cucumber pickles and other wholesome edibles. The thought "uppermost in his soul" as he, the candidate, shook hands all around and enjoyed the hospitality was, "What denomination is this? Methodist? Baptist? What?" He could get no gleam of light upon this all important question when suddenly his meditations were ended by a question from one of the flock: "Mr. Vance, what persuasion are you?" The hour had struck. The dreaded inquiry had to be answered satisfactorily and at once. Laying down his chicken leg, the chunk of salt rising bread and cucumber pickle, he began:

"My sainted grandfather was, during the later years of his long and useful life, a ruling elder of the Presbyterian Church." The "gathering brow and shaking head" of a local shepherd would have been sufficient warning to a less observing man than was our candidate.

"But," he continued, "my father during long years of faithful service in the Master's cause was an equally devout member of the Methodist Episcopal Church."

The sombre aspect of the shepherd, with a no less significant shake of the head, was unmistakable intimation of danger in the air. Rallying himself for one last charge, with but one shot remaining in his locker, our candidate earnestly resumed:

"But when I came to the years of maturity and was able, after prayer and meditation, to read and understand the blessed book myself, I came to the conclusion that *the Baptist Church was right.*"

"Bless God!" exclaimed the old preacher, seizing Vance by the hand. "He is all right, brethren! Oh, you'll get all the votes in these parts, Brother Vance!"

One John Allen, an "unillustrious" Member of Congress from Mississippi, was invited by Adlai I to a seat at his table in the Senate restaurant. Asked what he would have, John replied with an abstracted air: "It makes little difference about me anyway, and, turning to the waiter, slowly drawled out, 'bring me some terrapin and champagne. . . I got used to that durin' Washington. . . By the way, did you ever hear the expression — befo' the Wah?'" Adlai I intimated that the expression had not escaped him. John continued:

"I heard it once under peculiar circumstances. Down in the outskirts of my deestrict, there is an old time religious sect known as the hardshell or ironjacket Baptists; mighty good, honest people, of course, but old fashioned in their ways and everlastingly opposed to all new fangled notions such as having Temperance societies, Missionary societies and Sunday schools. They would, however, die in their tracks before they would ever let up on the good old church doctrines, especially predestination. Oh, I tell you they were predestinarians from way back. John Calvin with his vapory views upon that question would not have been admitted even on probation.

"Sometimes the preacher during his sermon, turning to the Amen corner, would inquire: 'When were you, my brother, predestinated to eternal salvation or eternal damnation? . . .Well the answer that had come down from the ages always was, 'From the foundation of the world.'

"When I was making my first race for Congress, I spoke in that neighborhood one Saturday and stayed all night with one of the elders, and on Sunday of course went to church. During the sermon, the preacher while holding forth as usual on his favorite doctrine, suddenly turning to a stranger who had somehow got crowded into the Amen corner, said: 'My brother, when were you predestinated to eternal salvation or eternal damnation?' To which startling inquiry the stranger, terribly embarrassed, hesitatingly answered: 'I don't adzactly remember, Parson, but I think it was befo' the Wah.'"

> An evangelist was exhorting his flock to flee from the wrath to come. "I want you to know that there will be weeping and wailing and gnashing of teeth." An old woman stood up: "I ain't got no teeth." "Madam," responded the evangelist, "teeth will be provided."

The Black Book venerates Brother Cartwright, our circuit riding preacher and Democrat. He was older than Lincoln but a contemporary and Lincoln's unsuccessful opponent in the 1846 election for Congress. "My friend the Parson," Lincoln called him. Their debates are unrecorded and preceded those Lincoln held with an even more formidable opponent a dozen years later, Stephen Douglas.

> Peter Cartwright to a congregation: "Will all those who want to go to heaven please stand up?" Everybody stood up except one man. Staring at him, Cartwright demanded: "Will all those who want to go to hell, please stand up?" Still the man kept his seat. Exasperated, the preacher asked him why he kept his seat. Said the man: "I like it here."

(A variation of this story has Cartwright demanding to know where the man did want to go, to which the culprit, Lincoln, responded, "I want to go to Congress.")

> A man under sentence of death was awaiting execution. Under the ministrations of the pastor of the Baptist Church, he made "the good confession" and desired to be

baptized. The faithful pastor applied to the circuit judge for permission to have the rite observed in the Kentucky River near by. The judge—more deeply versed in Blackstone than in theological lore—declined to have the prisoner removed from jail but gave permission for him to be baptized in his cell. The physical impossibility of performing the rite in the cell being explained, the Judge, replied 'I know there is no room in there to baptize him that way. Take a bowl of water and sprinkle him where he is.' 'But,' earnestly interposed the man of the sacred office, 'our church does not recognize sprinkling as valid baptism. We hold immersion to be the only Scriptural method.' 'Well, this Court decides that sprinkling *is* valid baptism; and I tell you once for all, that infernal scoundrel will be sprinkled, or he will be hung without being baptized at all!'

(Adlai I reported that inasmuch as this decision had never been overruled by a higher court, it stands as the only judicial determination of the long controverted question.)

A Parson had to conduct the funeral service of a deceased brother whose life had been lurid: "Good bye, Mose. We hopes you's goin' whar we b'lieves you ain't."

Adlai I

Adlai I filed a Bill in chancery which sought relief in its "prayer." Opposing counsel, a fellow member of the local Presbyterian church, demurred to the Bill, denying the plaintiff was entitled to all the relief prayed for. Adlai I responded that he thought his opponent was a good enough Presbyterian to know that a man always prayed for more than he expected to receive.

Jewish story of the man who watched for the coming of the Messiah – "It doesn't pay very much, but it's steady work."

In a friendly theological dispute, Adlai I suggested that W.O. Davis, father of his daughter in law, Helen, and a Unitarian, prayed to "whom it may concern." Davis retorted that Adlai, being a Presbyterian, "believed in keeping the Ten Commandments and anything else he could lay his hands on."

Elizabeth 'Buffie' Ives, Adlai II's sister

Evangelical Christianity remains a powerful, perhaps growing, force in the lives of Americans. While mainline Protestant denominations have shrunk, evangelicals have increased and continue to derive their inspiration from a literal reading of the Bible and the resurrected Christ as their savior. Christian Zionists have become supporters of Israel's occupation of Palestine, trusting in the eventual conversion of the Jews. Preemptive war in the Middle East has toxic origins in oil and religion.

Those who can make you believe in absurdities can make you commit atrocities.
Voltaire

In the Black Book, the peccadilloes of a President and such issues as gay marriage, stem cell research and abortion rights aroused no "religious right." American politics did not exploit evangelical Christianity. It converted evangelical virtues to public policy. Politics was "applied religion." The wall between church and state was fast.

In 1780 in Hartford, Connecticut, the skies at noon turned one day from blue to gray, and by mid afternoon the city had darkened over so densely in that religious age that men fell on their knees and begged a final blessing before the end came. The Connecticut House of Representatives was in session, and many of the members clamored for immediate adjournment. The Speaker of the House, Colonel Davenport, came to his feet, and he silenced the din with these words: "The day of judgment is either approaching or it is not. If it is not, there is no cause for adjournment. If it is, I choose to be found doing my duty. I wish, therefore, that candles be brought."

Darwin's *Origin of the Species* was first published in 1859. By the turn of the century virtually all the state constitutions contained prohibitions against the teaching of religion in schools though in practice they often prohibited the teaching of sectarian religions. Adlai I's running mate in 1900, William Jennings Bryan, waged his final crusade for Christian fundamentalism, apparently expecting it to lead to economic justice and regulation of the industrial and financial interests exploiting the common people. He died all but forgotten in 1925 at the age of sixty-five, and within a few days of his devastating encounter with Clarence Darrow in the Scopes "Monkey" trial. He had defended a literal reading of the Bible and rejected Darwin. Reason reigned in America.

> The biblical record is far more concerned with events than it is with ideas. Ideas there are, but they are subordinated to events. The conviction usually unstated, is that God reveals Himself much more fully in history than in nature or in any other way....The men who wrote the words of the Bible were contented, for the most part, with telling a story.
>
> *Elton Trueblood*

As the Black Book closes, the triumph of the Enlightenment — of reason and religious tolerance — is being followed in America by a rebirth of fundamentalism, superstition and intolerance, a counter reformation. Former President Jimmy Carter, a born again Christian, complains: "The ultra-right wing, in both religion and politics, has abandoned that principle of Jesus Christ's ministry."

Some evangelicals are swayed, not by the evangelical virtues of Christian love, but by stem cell research, gay rights and abortion. Of this phenomenon—some call it class warfare—Bryan, the great commoner, would despair: common people waging war against their own class for the benefit of the rich and privileged beneficiaries and supporters of the born again President. Bush manifested the irony with an enthusiasm for preserving embryos while presiding as Governor of Texas over executions averaging one every nine days, once mocking on television a woman on death row who pleaded, "please don't kill me."

In the secular politics of the Black Book, public policy reflected a "reverence" for human life. Capital punishment was opposed by Adlais II and III. The state manifested its reverence for human life and respect for the rule of law in all its actions. The politics of old Europe with memories of religious wars and persecutions eschews this new religiosity. It still produces a firm division between church and state, and a more proactive state which leads to a more equitable distribution of income, better health care, education and an aversion to faith based war. In ways, the "old" Western Europe resembles the old America.

The new America also features the commercialization of religion on a scale never conceived by one of its pioneers, Rev. Norman Vincent Peale in the 1950's and 60's. He contrived a pseudo psychology which exploited their faith to encourage people to think of themselves, shut out reality and rely on the false promise of "positive thinking" to achieve self satisfaction and fulfillment. Psychiatrists and psychologists labeled this faith based psychology fraudulent. Some opined that it threatened the mental health of its practitioners, but it was popular and profitable for Peale, who opposed the elections of both Adlai II and John F. Kennedy. Peale became a friend and supporter of Richard Nixon.

> The apostle Paul is appealing. The apostle Peale is appalling.
> *Adlai II*

Today's non denominational megachurches are businesses. They are often planned, developed and operated by businessmen and business consultants. They pack in the crowds in shifts and by the thousands with bible classes, bands, coffee shops, rock music and feel-good preaching which typically stays away from politics, including the faith based politics of the hard right. This is entertainment and business—a commercialization of the Christian faith well described by Frances Fitzgerald in the December 3, 2007 issue of the *New Yorker* magazine. (The brilliant and perceptive Frankie Fitzgerald participated as a young woman in adventures recorded in the Black Book.) Like the law, politics and medicine, religion is commercialized in the new America. The congregations of traditional churches shrink.

Former Senator John Danforth, Kevin Phillips and others have documented and lamented the conversion of the Republican Party into America's first religious party. Perhaps Reason will return. Evangelicals have been detected taking an interest in global warming and the afflictions of the needy in the world. Republicans have been losing elections. But the commercialization of religion flourishes, unrelated, as it is, to the evangelical virtues.

From an open letter in the fall of 2004 to Senator Rick
Santorum, Republican of Pennsylvania defeated in the same year:

Dear Senator,

Thank you so much for doing so much to educate people regarding
God's law. I have learned a great deal from your speeches in support of
a constitutional amendment against "gay" marriage. I am now trying to
share that knowledge with as many people as I can.

When someone tries to defend the homosexual lifestyle, for example, I
simply remind them that Leviticus 18:22 clearly states it to be an
abomination. End of debate. I do need some advice from you, however,
regarding some other elements of God's laws and how to follow them.

1. Leviticus 25.44 states that I may possess slaves, both male and
female, provided they are purchased from neighboring nations. A friend
of mine claims that this applies to Mexicans, but not Canadians. Can
you clarify? Why can't I own Canadians?

2. I would like to sell my daughter into slavery, as sanctioned in Exodus
21:7. In this day and age, what do you think would be a fair price for
her?

3. I know that I am allowed no contact with a woman while she is in her
period of menstrual uncleanliness. Leviticus 15:19-24. The problem is,
how do I tell? I have tried asking, but most women take offense.

4. When I burn a bull on the altar as a sacrifice, I know it creates a
pleasing odor for the Lord. Lev. 1:9. The problem is my neighbors.
They claim the odor is not pleasing. Should I smite them?

5. I have a neighbor who insists on working on the Sabbath. Exodus
35:2 clearly states that he should be put to death. Am I morally
obligated to kill him myself, or should I ask the police to do it?

6. A friend of mine feels that even though eating shellfish is an
abomination—   Lev.11:10—it is a lesser abomination than
homosexuality. I don't agree. Can you settle this? Are there degrees of
abomination?

7. Lev. 21:20 states that I may not approach the altar of God if I have a defect in my sight. I have to admit that I wear reading glasses. Does my vision have to be 20/20 or is there some wiggle room here?

8. Most of my male friends get their hair trimmed, including the hair around their temples, even though this is expressly forbidden by Lev.19:27. How should they die?

9. I know from Lev.11:6-8 that touching the skin of a dead pig makes me unclean, but may I still play football if I wear gloves?

10. My uncle has a farm. He violates Lev. 19:19 by planting two different crops in the same field, as does his wife by wearing garments made of two different kinds of thread (cotton/polyester blend). He also tends to curse and blaspheme a lot. Is it really necessary that we go to all the trouble of getting the whole town together to stone them? Lev. 24:10-16. Couldn't we just burn them to death at a private family affair, like we do with people who sleep with the in-laws? Lev. 20:14

I know you have studied these things extensively and thus enjoy considerable expertise in such matters, so I am confident you can help. Thank you again for reminding us that God's word is eternal and unchanging.

> Only men who confuse themselves with God would dare
> to pretend in this anguished and bloody era that they
> know the exact road to the Promised Land.
> *Adlai II*

> Religion is regarded by the common people as true, by
> the wise as false, and by the rulers as useful.
> *Seneca The Younger*

> The Bible is not my Book and Christianity is not my
> religion. I could never give assent to the long and
> complicated statements of Christian dogma.
> *Abraham Lincoln*

14: The Press

A popular government without popular information, or the means of acquiring it, is but a prologue to a farce or a tragedy, or perhaps both. Knowledge will forever govern ignorance, and a people who mean to be their own governors must arm themselves with the power which knowledge gives.

James Madison

The press was in the family bloodstream through the *Bloomington Daily Pantagraph* acquired by Jesse Fell, and an object of passionate interest but little comment in the Black Book. The function of the press in a self-governing country was self evident. The name, Pantagraph, bespoke the obligation of the press to "print all." Named in 1848 on the prairies of central Illinois, the name also implied some recognition of democracy's origins and a familiarity with Greek classics. Now *The Pantagraph*, too, is a cog in the wheels of a media empire, a commodity which changes hands from time to time, its community roots largely severed.

From Adlai I's time, the family archives include press clippings and cartoons which depict an intensely partisan press. Cartoons from the magazine *Judge* were merciless in their colorful depictions of Adlai I, an alleged Copperhead and proudly acknowledged Democratic hatchet man. Newspapers affected little neutrality. Television was in the future. The public could not have been deceived by any pretenses to objectivity. This journalistic partisanship continued in Illinois into the 1960's. The Publisher of the *Chicago Tribune*, then the power behind the Illinois Republican Party, was Robert McCormick. He resided at Chantigny, a great estate in Wheaton, a Republican suburb of Chicago, and was an Anglophobe, isolationist and reactionary. Adlai II, asked to comment at his death, replied: "He will be missed in Wheaton."

McCormick was also an eccentric who insisted on abbreviating the English language in the *Tribune*, and reportedly gave its employees tooth brushes at Christmas. The *Tribune's* political editor, George Tagge, was also its lobbyist. In 1965, he lobbied against my bill to require registration of lobbyists and reporting of their expenditures, helping—in the name of a free press— to kill it in the Republican controlled State Senate.

Marshall Field III organized the *Chicago Sun* in the 1950's to give Chicago's newspaper readers an alternative to the illiberal, isolationist and partisan *Tribune. The Chicago Daily News*, an evening paper published by Frank Knox, a moderate Republican and later Adlai II's boss as Secretary of the Navy, fielded a formidable world wide network of foreign correspondents. Chicago had four daily newspapers in Adlai II's time, one a Hearst paper. Now it has two, a shallow, tasteless *Chicago Tribune*, part of a media empire threatened by bankruptcy, and the *Chicago Sun Times*, the latter controlled by the Hollinger interests of the neoconservative Lord Conrad Black—embroiled in litigation over corporate mismanagement and far removed philosophically and ethically from Marshall Field III, and for that matter, McCormick, neither of them known for corporate or personal improprieties. Control of the *Tribune* was acquired by billionaire entrepreneur Sam Zell at the expense of its employees. It is speculated that billionaires are targeting media for non financial, as well as financial, purposes as yet unclear but which could include ego, political influence and ideology. Also recently, Rupert Murdoch gained control of the venerable family controlled *Wall Street Journal*.

Consolidation of media in Chicagoland mirrored a nationwide phenomenon. As of 2004, of 1,500 daily newspapers, about 280 were owned independently. Five multinational corporations controlled virtually all commercial television news. News sources at large, including cable, radio and newspapers, filter the news in order to serve what the market wants. Opinionated comment on television is less expensive than world-wide news gathering for media empires focused on the bottom line. CBS (owned by Viacom) slashed its bureaus and correspondents to one correspondent in Tokyo covering all Asia, five at a "hub" office in London, three in Tel Aviv, one in Rome, and none in the Arab or Muslim world, South America or Africa. Bureaus in Washington and elsewhere are threatened. Investigatory journalism bears its share of newsroom and bureau cuts.

In 2004 CNN was spending an estimated $300 million a year to report the news. The Fox network—controlled by Rupert Murdoch — was spending about $60 million, much of it for studio based news and comment like the right-wing "O'Reilly Factor" program. Fox, an extension of the Republican Party, according to President Reagan's advisor, Michael Deaver, competes with reality shows and steals audience from other networks by catering news according to what the audience wants to hear. At a Senate hearing, I asked Rupert Murdoch about his understanding of First Amendment obligations of the press. Somewhere in the bowels of the Senate lies his unresponsive answer — but not the blank expression which implied he had never contemplated such obligations or anticipated such a preposterous question.

According to Pew Center of the People & the Press surveys, almost six in ten Americans watch local news regularly and more than three in four say that television news is their chief source of election information. While informative news programs often supported by foundations can be found on PBS, C-Span, BBC World and a few cable channels, television leaves most Americans uninformed or misinformed about public issues even as the world becomes a more complex and volatile place, the complexities of issues ever larger, requiring conscientious reporting, interpretation and honest gate keepers. Television networks increasingly rely on outside services, including newspapers, to define "news." But newspapers are dying, and cutting back reporting of news.

Spending for newspaper ads fell 9 percent in 2007. In January, 2008, the Chicago Sun Times, announced it was cutting news room staff by 19 percent, sparing photographers and sports writers. Young people in particular do not read newspapers. Of those under thirty, only one in five reads a newspaper daily. The time all Americans spend reading newspapers has fallen to 15 hours a month, a 50 percent drop since 1996. U.S. networks devote about 20 minutes a day to national and international news, going with the flow to the sensational, violent and visual, leaving Americans in some indeterminate measure with a distorted picture of a world which is not all hostile and violent.

A study of local television news coverage by the University of Wisconsin-Madison News Lab in 2007 reported that during the month following the traditional Labor Day election kickoff in 2006, thirty-six monitored Midwest stations devoted an average of 36 seconds in a typical 30-minute news program to election coverage of which by a margin of 3 to 1 the coverage was of polling, strategy, the horse race. By contrast, advertising received more than 10 minutes, sports and weather more than 7 minutes. "Government" news received about a minute, "foreign policy" 23 seconds. From January 1 to March 31, 2007, the monitored stations dedicated 1 minute and 35 seconds of a typical 30-minute news broadcast to "government." Sports and weather received 7 minutes and 41 seconds, advertising 9 minutes and 12 seconds, world affairs 24 seconds. Given the quality of U.S. television news coverage of the world, government and politics, one might reasonably query if the public would not be less misinformed with less coverage. Foreign countries, including France, plan to create or enlarge their English language programming to give Americans more objective coverage of events in the world. They too have a stake in the access of the American people to truth.

In the 1970's some 25-30 percent of Americans reported a great deal of confidence in the press, according to a Harris poll. In a 2005 poll, the press ranked only ahead of law firms, with 12 percent reporting high confidence in the media. As an ABC spokesman explained, news had become "entertainment." An American child often starts television at age three, even earlier, according to surveys, and with brain deadening implications.

Cable networks, community newspapers, satellite radio and the internet produce a myriad of information sources. Since 1990, national circulation of newspapers and the audience for evening television news has plunged. In this welter of information sources, blogs multiply with comments on personalities and issues. At the national level, political candidates are engulfed in a proliferation of messages, often from uncertain and unscrupulous sources. They are confronted by more sources than they can begin to answer or respond to. In May 2006, 37.3 million blogs were tracked. The blogosphere seems to be doubling every six months and in virtually all languages, meaning that people and organizations are everywhere acquiring new potential for organizing political power outside formal political systems —and outside the reach of traditional media. Truly democratic political systems may be the most threatened by this socialization of power, being the most permissive and tolerant.

Julian E. Zelizer in *On Capitol Hill* describes the proliferation of news sources, and the growing adversarial attitude of the media towards politicians and its focus on the sensational, scandalous and sexual. This phenomena tempts politicians to respond in kind, leaving the public with increasingly negative attitudes towards politics and the press. The Bush Administration has contributed to the demoralization by paying commentators, by deploying to the press "military analysts" with ties to the Pentagon and defense contractors, and by using government funded television stories to promote its programs.

Public relations becomes a large and challenging business in this morass of competing sources of information. It becomes an ever larger political force. According to a report prepared in early 2005 for then House Minority Leader Nancy Pelosi, the Bush Administration spent a record $88 million on public relations contracts in 2004, a 128 percent increase over 2000. According to the Council of Public Relations Firms, the country's top ten public relations firms billed clients about $2.5 billion in 2002, up from $192 million in 1968. Meanwhile, funds for public broadcasting are cut, and its programming is subjected to political pressure. The Federal Communication

Commission refuses to enforce the "public interest, convenience, or necessity" requirements of the Radio Act of 1927 and the Communications Act of 1934. The air waves are in the public domain; but the government increasingly represents the private domain. In America, news is business, and the newspaper business is no longer regarded with favor in the marketplace. The combined market value of independent, publicly traded newspaper publishers has fallen by about 42 percent from 2004-2007.

It was often difficult for politicians to communicate with the electorate through a press which Thomas Jefferson and Alexander Hamilton complained was scurrilous, but it was a press broadly recognized for what it often was: advocate and partisan. In 1980, former Congressman John Anderson—a respected, eloquent, moderate Republican of Illinois—pledged a third party, issue oriented campaign for President. The idea was newsworthy until he started to spell out his positions on issues. The public heard little of his ideas—only that he had news conferences to explain them. President Carter, in the closing days of his 1980 campaign for reelection, sought to explain his objectives for a second term in a prepared speech delivered in Texas. That is what the public at large heard—that he had objectives, not what they were. Leaving office, he was asked his greatest disappointments: "Iran and the press," he replied. After that campaign year, one defeated candidate remarked of the media, "And then they complain that we did not discuss the issues." It has been downhill since then.

In my campaign for governor of Illinois in 1982, the media ignored my program except to complain that it was too comprehensive and complex for coverage. I could feel the change. Questions were not asked about issues at news conferences. They were asked during interviews and talk programs by concerned citizens who called to ask about education, taxes and other issues. At a news conference in Springfield, Charles Wheeler of the *Chicago Sun Times* volunteered a question about education. That was the only question I could ever recall from the press about a real issue at a news conference during the entire campaign. The questions of the press were about the "game"—the money and polls, who was supporting whom, even the candidate's attire. Reporters rarely traveled with candidates, at least not with me. They stayed home and harvested and reported rumor, much of it implanted in their ready ears. I recall one out-of-state reporter traveling with me and remarking that the experience was not at all what he had been led by local reporters to anticipate. Audiences on the ground were responding as in the past, but they were largely out of the public's sight and hearing.

The media became a means of manipulating public opinion, requiring ever larger amounts of money. In the 2006 federal election cycle, about $2.5 billion was raised by candidates for federal office, about three-quarters of that from interest groups. More than $1 billion is expected to be invested in the 2008 Presidential candidates. Most of it will be spent on consultants and media, often with surreptitious, negative and false information, marketing or denigrating other candidates, simplifying "issues," undermining the democratic process even as the government's spokespeople propagate democracy to an increasingly skeptical world. The money increases with each election, pushing the public discourse to ever lower levels while indenturing the candidates. In Adlai I's time, the sporting page and comic strip had not arrived to "overbalance" the news, quoting Mark Sullivan (*Our Times*).

Frank Rich, a prominent journalist, documents in *The Greatest Story Ever Sold* the Bush Administration's exploitation of a new, impressionable mass media to deceive the public with palpable lies and utilize television for the theatrical staging of events and appearances, often at the expense of the taxpayer. Truth is not an objective of this Administration's politics, excepting where it accidentally coincides with the message and tactic. The Nixonian ethic of anything goes has been taken to an unprecedented level.

The bits of wit and wisdom which follow are neither numerous nor timely because the deliberate deception of the American people by its government through a complicit media was never experienced nor contemplated in the politics of the Black Book, nor practiced in the family's *Bloomington Daily Pantagraph*

> Were I to undertake to answer the calumnies of the newspapers, it would be more than all my time and that of twenty aides could effect. For while I should be answering one, twenty new ones would be invented....But this is an injury to which duty requires every one to submit whom the public thinks proper to call into its councils.
>
> *Thomas Jefferson*, 1798

> The first casualty of war is truth.
>
> *Hiram Johnson*, US Senator, 1917

134

An editor is one who separates the wheat from the chaff and prints the chaff. I met the scurrilities of the news writers without concern, while in pursuit of the great interests with which I was charged.

Thomas Jefferson, 1810

Mark Twain, then editor of a small Missouri newspaper, was asked by a subscriber if a spider found in his paper was an omen of good or bad luck. He responded that finding a spider in the newspaper was neither good luck nor bad. The spider was merely looking over the paper to find out which merchant was not advertising so that he could go to the store, spin his web across the door and lead a life of undisturbed peace.

Commenting on the harsh criticism from Horace Greeley in the *New York Times*, Lincoln remarked: "It reminds me of the big fellow whose little wife beat him over the head with no complaint. He explained: 'Leave her alone. It don't hurt me, and it does her a power of good.'"

The International Adlai Stevenson Center on Democracy proposed for the "farm" in Libertyville aims to bring scholars and practitioners together from throughout the world to address systemic challenges to democratic systems of government. Its first proposed major project is on media, information and democracy. Other democracies manage shorter political campaigns with less money and better informed citizens. How can the American people be empowered with truth and information in the information age?

15: Education

Education makes a people easy to lead but difficult to drive, easy to govern, but impossible to enslave.
Lord Henry Brougham

In Adlai I's time, formal education often started in a tiny one-room school that sat on a small tract carved by a farmer from a tree lot. A few are preserved in my northwest Illinois neighborhood settled in the 1830's. The students were warmed by a potbellied wood burning stove after trudging long distances on dirt roads and trails, often through the snow, from their cabins and farmsteads in the hollows and on the prairies.

Later in the 19th century it became the "central" school to which parents delivered their children for "reading, writing and 'rithmetic." The outstanding ideal of the school, as Mark Sullivan puts it, was less in the world of education than in the world of democracy. The schools were founded and maintained on the principle that all the people should be literate. So far as the schools had direct purposes, they aimed to make the students "good" men and women, good citizens, and equip them with some facility in fundamentals of reading, writing and arithmetic.

Teaching was aided by Readers, most famous of which were McGuffey's. They exposed children to vast and varied selections from literature which in turn exposed them to spelling and grammar, declamations on ethics, religion, virtues and patriotism, while imparting some knowledge of varied subject matter. The Readers attempted to serve the main educational purpose of exciting curiosity and a lifelong appetite for learning.

Discipline does not appear to have been a challenge for the schools. "Spare the rod and spoil the child" was a familiar admonition throughout my schooling. The rod, whip and switch were close at hand and applied for menial offenses such as tardiness. Standing at the bottom of the class in a dunce's hat punished a failed scholastic performance or tardiness.

At Milton Academy, the Massachusetts boarding school I attended, discipline was enforced by "old boys" armed with thick, perforated wood paddles. One subject of such discipline died of a ruptured appendix. At Harrow School outside London, which I attended in 1945-6, the preferred instrument of the "old boys" was a whip-like, less lethal switch. Youth were not "spoiled" in school even then. Methods which would now be considered child abuse and abjured by child psychologists seem to have had little adverse effect. The incidence of child delinquency, behavioral disorder and failing levels of achievement are higher in the present environment, though owing to many factors, including the intrusion of television and video games—temptations made the more so by working parents with responsibilities outside the family. Perhaps such factors explain why the highest levels of educational performance in the U.S. are achieved by East Asians, where the family survives, and education and the acquisition of knowledge remain a passion.

In the Black Book schooling was, like a responsible press, essential to responsible citizenship. It was a subject of some exhortation but little discussion. Adlai II observed in a commencement address that a college degree was like a "diaper." It was an uncharacteristically inept metaphor, but intended to suggest that with a college degree the graduate was prepared to begin his education.

Today schools are more segregated by race and economic class than before the 1954 Brown v. Board of Education decision of the Supreme Court. Disparities in per pupil spending in Illinois school districts range from $4,000 to $15,000, with the most needy districts receiving the least state aid and paying the highest rates of property taxation. Administrative costs eat up most public funds for schools because of their fractured organization at the local level and three levels of governance above. The humanities, including geography, world history and foreign languages, lose out in competition with "teaching to the tests" required by a simplistic Federal mandate. Studies reported in 2007 begin to demonstrate that the focus on math and reading to the neglect of social studies, including history, stifle curiosity, retard the mind's development, and undermine the fundamental purpose of formal education in the Black Book—exciting a lifelong learning process.

According to the National Center for Public Policy and Higher Education, only 68 percent of freshman high school students graduate, 40 percent enter college, and 18 percent graduate from college within six years of admission. According to a survey of 431 business leaders by business research organizations in 2006, three quarters of incoming high school students were viewed as deficient in basic English writing skills, including grammar and spelling. Almost 30 percent said they doubted their college graduate employees could write a simple business letter. According to another recent study, 20 percent of college bound U.S. students could not identify the ocean between California and Asia.

Surveys indicate that notwithstanding comparatively high levels of U.S. spending on education, U.S. students rank at or near the bottom of student performance as tested in all other industrial countries. In 2007, the Program for International Student Assessment reported that a test of fifteen-year-old students in the thirty industrialized country members of the Organization for Economic Cooperation and Development placed American students lower than the average in science and math for the group, and in about two dozen other countries and jurisdictions, the Americans fell in the middle of the pack in science and worse in math. The report is consistent with others which conclude that even in reading and math, test scores are falling in America. Test scores are symptomatic; they are not diagnostic. But an insatiable appetite for knowledge, quickened in the schools of the old America, may never be awakened in the new—for too many. In Western Europe, education is virtually free and near universal through the university. The quality and availability of education improves steadily in China, which increases spending on education by about 50 percent a year, albeit from a low base. At the age of six a Chinese child begins a ten-hour school day, a ten-month school year. Homework ends at 9:30 pm. Criticized for teaching by rote, the Chinese are scrambling to develop pedagogical methods for stimulating creativity, curiosity and that lifelong appetite for learning once a purpose of American schools.

In lecturing at Chinese universities over many years, I, like many others, have experienced an insatiable curiosity and appetite for information among the students, and a high level of knowledge, including about U.S. politics and contemporary events. It is a bit like the old days in America, bombarded by students with apt questions in the high schools and colleges. A twenty-year-old American college student accompanied his father to a Chinese university in 2007, and was asked," How do you manage your parents' expectations?" In China, those expectations are high.

The percentage of U.S. adults with college degrees is shrinking. Foreign graduate students pour into our universities, though the flow has been retarded by visa requirements and shifted to other countries. More and more return to their origins, especially in East Asia, where larger opportunity awaits them after graduation.

Some speculate that an unspoken political conspiracy in the U.S. seeks to keep Americans undereducated in order to make them more susceptible to deception and political control. What is clear is that the old test of teaching for the sake of democracy is being failed. In a post industrial economy, the test of education for national economic competitiveness is also failed. Other developed and many developing countries, especially in East Asia, have demonstrated the political competence to effectively organize and fund public education for eager publics.

Our only hope of making the atom servant rather than master lies in education, in a broad education where each student within his capacity can free himself from trammels of dogmatic prejudice and apply his educational accoutrement to besetting social and human problems.

Henry Woodburn Chase

In the conditions of modern life the rule is absolute, the race which does not value trained intelligence is doomed. Not all your heroism, not all your victories on land or at sea, can move back the finger of fate. Today we maintain ourselves. Tomorrow science will have moved forward yet one more step, and there will be no appeal from the judgment which will then be pronounced on the uneducated.

Alfred North Whitehead, 1916

Your days are short here. This is the last of your springs. And now, in the serenity and quiet of this lovely place, touch the depths of truth, feel the hem of heaven. You will go away with old, good friends. Don't forget when you leave why it is you came.

Adlai II, Commencement Address, Princeton University, 1963

Whom, then, do I call educated? First, those who manage well the circumstances which they encounter day by day and who possess a judgment which is accurate in meeting occasions as they arise and rarely miss the expedient course of action; next, those who are decent and honorable in their intercourse with all men, bearing easily and good naturedly what is unpleasant or offensive in others, and being themselves as agreeable and reasonable to their associates as it is humanly possible to be; furthermore, those who hold their pleasure always under control and are not unduly overcome by their misfortunes, bearing up under them bravely and in a manner worthy of our common nature; finally, and most important, those who are not spoiled by their successes and who do not desert their true selves, but hold their ground steadfastly as wise and sober-minded men, rejoicing no more in the good things which have come to them through chance than in those which through their own nature and intelligence are theirs since birth. Those who have a character which is in accord, not with one of these things, but with all of them—these I maintain are educated and whole men, possessed of all the virtues of a man.

Isocrates in "Panathenaicus, 398 B.C .

A kind of liberal education must underlie every wholesome political and social process, the kind of liberal education which connects a man's feeling and his comprehension with the general run of mankind, which disconnects him from the special interests and marries his thought to the common interests of great communities and of great cities and of great states and of great nations, and, if possible, with that brotherhood of man that transcends the boundaries of nations themselves.

Woodrow Wilson

We're going to have the best educated American people in the world.

George W. Bush

My education message will resignate amongst all parents.

George W. Bush

Quite frankly, teachers are the only profession that teach our children.

George W. Bush

If a nation expects to be ignorant and free in a state of civilization, it expects what never was and never will be.

Thomas Jefferson

16: Crime and Justice

Injustice will be ended when those who are not wronged are as indignant as those who are.

An Athenian

In the Black Book, life, in the words of Albert Schweitzer, is "revered." The state in all its actions seeks to enhance respect for human life and the rule of law. It does neither when it takes life in criminal proceedings, usually the lives of the poor without adequate means of defense, sometimes the lives of the innocent. Prosecutors have lower rates of conviction in proceedings against business executives represented by lawyers frequently compensated by the corporations they have robbed than in proceedings against common criminals.

Over the span of the Black Book, the U.S. became the only western, industrialized nation to practice capital punishment. By 2006, more than one hundred and thirty countries had abolished capital punishment legally or in practice. The U.S. was one of six countries accounting for 90 percent of executions known to have been carried out that year, according to Amnesty International. The others were China, Iraq, Pakistan, Iran and Sudan. As of 2008, the U.S. also had 2.3 million people convicted of crimes behind bars, far more than any other nation in both relative and absolute terms. The U.S. had 751 persons incarcerated for every 100,000 in population. The median for all nations was 125. In the America of the Black Book, the U.S. incarceration rate was low and stable. From 1925 to 1970, it was about 110 per 100,000. Alexis de Tocqueville observed: "In no country is criminal justice administered with more mildness than in the United States." In the new America, however, it became popular to "get tough" on crime with long sentences. Uniquely in America, state judges, as well as legislators, are elected.

The U.S. also acquired the highest rates of violent crime of all developed countries, driven in part by drugs and guns. Other nations have effective gun control, including sweeping measures to outlaw automatic weapons, and outlaw or restrict access to hand guns, the crime guns. Australia's enactment of strict gun controls was immediately followed by a drop in violent crime rates. I was regularly targeted by the gun lobby for authoring state and federal measures to license hand gun owners and register the weapons. You don't need a snub nose .38 or AK 47 to hunt ducks, I explained. Ready accessibility to hand guns facilitated crimes often committed in moments of passion.

Possession of an unlawful weapon in suspicious circumstances gave law enforcement officers a charge. Registered weapons used to commit crimes can sometimes be traced to the perpetrator through the registration system.

The American gun lobby doesn't represent most responsible hunters, myself included. Its opposition was a badge of political honor. Most citizens understood. Nowadays this lobby is more capable of intimidating politicians. Unrestricted gun ownership and possession is promoted as a means of self defense and a constitutional right. Random killings by deranged people with automatic weapons are becoming common. Australians, like Canadians, are fond of guns, but their politicians appear to have more integrity or less vulnerability.

If present incarceration trends continue, by the end of the decade, one out of ten male Americans will have been in jail at one time or another, some of them for crimes they did not commit. One out of nine black males can already expect time in jail. (A 2005 Report of the American Bar Association identified 150 people convicted in 31 states and the District of Columbia who served a combined total of 1,800 years in prison for crimes of which they were later exonerated by DNA evidence.)

Though there have been recent exceptions to the rule, despoilers of American politics, like those of finance and industry, have been known to receive preferential treatment in the criminal justice system. The Incas of Peru had a different practice. The penalties inflicted upon civil servants were always greater than those involving ordinary citizens, and their severity increased with rank because, it was argued, the first obligation of men who have been chosen to punish others is to commit no offense themselves. The Confucian ethic is similar. Korean Presidents go to jail. An American President was pardoned. President George W. Bush ignores his Administration's insistence on enforcing harsh sentencing guidelines to commute the jail sentence of his assistant, Lewis "Scooter" Libby, convicted of obstruction of justice and other offenses.

Poverty is the parent of revolution and crime.
Aristotle

The greatest of evils and the worst of crimes is poverty.
George Bernard Shaw,
Major Barbara

Justice is the great interest of man on earth. It is the ligament which holds civilized beings and civilized nations together.

Daniel Webster

Vice is a monster of so frightful mien,
As to be hated, needs but to be seen;
Yet seen too oft, familiar with her face,
We first endure, then pity, then embrace.

Alexander Pope

The real significance of crime is in its being a breach of faith with the community of mankind.

Joseph Conrad

Make me know the measure of their crimes, that I may minister to them accordingly.

Shakespeare, Measure for
Measure

Manners are of more importance than laws. Upon them in a great measure, the laws depend. The law touches us but here and there, and now and then. Manners are what vex or soothe, corrupt or purify, exalt or debase, barbarize or refine us, by a constant steady, uniform insensible operation like that of the air we breathe in.

Edmund Burke

Society prepares the crime; the criminal commits it.

Henry Buckle, English Historian
(1812 -1862)

17: Law and Lawyers

Lincoln, while practicing law in Springfield with Herndon, was approached by a man who wished to press a claim for several hundred dollars against a poor widow and her six children. Lincoln wrote: "We shall not take your case, though we can doubtless gain it for you. Some things that are right legally are not right morally. But we will give you some advice for which we will charge nothing. We advise a sprightly, energetic man like you to try your hand at making six hundred dollars in some other way."

Adlais I, II and III were lawyers, albeit with other pursuits for which the study of law was preparation. The practice of law was also a profession to fall back on in the lean years between public duties. A reverence for the law is undiminished throughout the Black Book. A reverence for the practice of law—the most honorable of human callings, the "safeguard of society," the "palladium of liberty"—is diminished over time, not by the worthiness of the calling but by the metamorphosis of its practice. It too became commercialized.

Recollections of the practice in Illinois begin in the 1840's. The term of court in most counties was rarely more than a week because of the time it took judges and lawyers to travel on horseback. Thus, it was said by Governor Ford of a judge whose district extended from Quincy on the Mississippi River in central Illinois to Chicago: "He possesses in rare degree one of the highest requisites for a good circuit judge—he is an excellent horseback rider."

Adlai I observes that the "monster libraries" of later days had not arrived. To an Illinois lawyer upon the circuit, a pair of saddle bags contained his library and "a change or two of linen." The lack of volumes of adjudicated cases was not, however, an unmixed evil. Causes were necessarily argued upon principle. Adlai I quotes a Professor Phelps as saying, "it is easy to find single opinions in which more authorities are cited than were mentioned by Marshall in the whole thirty years of his exemplary judicial life; and briefs that contain more cases than Webster referred to in all the arguments he delivered." The lawyers of these times were with few exceptions—like circuit riding preachers and politicians—in close touch with the people, easy of approach and obliging. A lawyer's office was as open to the public as the Courthouse. The lawyer's surroundings were "favorable to the cultivation of a high degree of sociability." Story telling at country taverns helped to while away the long evenings. At times,

'The night drave on wi's sangs and clatter.'
Robert Burns

When an important case was being tried all other pursuits were
suspended. People for miles around were in attendance. The litigation
was different from what would come soon enough. The "restraints and
amenities of modern society were in large measure unknown, and
altogether there was much to be, and was, 'pardoned in the spirit of
liberty.' There were no great corporations to be chosen defendants."
Much of the time of the courts was taken up by suits of ejectment,
actions for assault and battery, breach of promise and slander. "One, not
infrequent, was replevin, involving the ownership of hogs, when by
unquestioned usage all stock was permitted to run at large." Criminal
trials, especially for murder, aroused the greatest interest. To these
people came from all directions, "as if summoned to a general muster."
Such occasions furnished exceptional opportunity to the gifted
advocate: ". . . the general acquaintance thus formed, and the popularity
achieved, have marked the beginning of more than one successful and
brilliant political career."

Adlai I observes that the thorough knowledge of the people thus
acquired —their condition, necessities and wishes—resulted often in
legislation of enduring benefit to the new country. Politics in the
modern sense, "for what there is in it," was unknown, he claimed. The
caucuses and primary elections were yet to come. It was possible for
aspirants to public office to present their claims directly to the people.
Bribery at elections was rarely heard of, Adlai I claims. As late as 1858
when Lincoln and Douglas vied for the Senate, "every voter was a
partisan of one or other; there was never, from either side, an intimation
of the corrupt use of a farthing to influence the result."

Of the early Western bar, Adlai I's recollections are also
sanguine. He quotes a "distinguished writer":

Not only was it a body distinguished for dignity and
tolerance, but chivalrous courage was a marked
characteristic...insulting language and the use of
billingsgate were too hazardous to be indulged where a
personal accounting was a strong possibility. Not only
did common prudence dictate courtesy among the
members of the bar, but an exalted spirit of honor and
well bred politeness prevailed. The word of counsel to

his adversary was his inviolable bond. The suggestion of a lawyer as to the existence of a fact was accepted as verity by the court. To insinuate unprofessional conduct was to impute infamy.

From the Western bar Adlai I goes on to enthuse about the indispensability of the law to the "progress of society":

With the coming of the lawyer came a new power in the world. The steel clad baron and his retainers were awed by terms they had never before heard and did not understand, such as precedent, principle, and the like. The great and real pacifier in the world was the lawyer. His parchment took the place of the battlefield. The flow of his ink checked the flow of blood. His quill usurped the sword. His legalism dethroned barbarism. His victories were victories of peace. He impressed on all individuals and on communities that which he is now endeavoring to impress on nations, that there are many controversies that it were better to lose by arbitration than to win by war and bloodshed.

Adlai I's paeans to the rule of law are not unlike Lincoln's of near the same time and place: "The sure rock of defence in the outstretched years as in the long past, will be the intelligence, the patriotism, the virtue of law abiding, liberty loving people. To a degree that cannot be measured by words, the temple of justice will prove the city of refuge. The judiciary has no guards, no palaces, or treasuries; no arms but truth and wisdom; and no splendor but justice."

In Adlai II's time lawyers flocked to the Roosevelt, Truman and Kennedy Administrations, as they had to his Administration in Illinois, and, their work done, returned to their firms, rarely abusing any privilege or confidence gained. The "revolving door" was a source of vitality for private and public sectors. Now it is regulated in a futile attempt to prevent persons from leaving government to take unfair, even corrupt, advantage of their information and connections. Law firms have become "monstrous" far beyond Adlai I's imaginings. Like businesses, some advertise their services, which was unimaginable in the Black Book. Calling cards were inappropriate in my time at the law firm of Mayer, Brown and Platt. In March, 2007 that firm "eliminated," to quote press reports, forty-five of its partners. Its managing partner

146

explained the firm needed to keep up its "stock price." The press matter-of-factly referred to the "business of law." Law firms keep up their "profits per partner" ratio as a means of competing for the rainmakers, those who pull in the business. When I entered that venerable law firm in 1958, it had sixty-seven partners and was part of a proud profession. Partners were tenured for life. In 2008, it was sued for alleged complicity in a large financial fraud, and concurrently, to "strengthen the brand," its name was shortened to Mayer, Brown. This is not atypical.

Demeaned and burdened by the commercialism of a profession revered in the Black Book, lawyers are dropping out. Recruits to the profession are judged by their billable hours. They experience the entrepreneurial pressures and ethics of a business—not the honorable profession they entered.

In legislatures, lawyers made a special contribution, versed as they were in common law traditions, procedure and the Constitution. They shared a commitment to process for its own sake. Lincoln studied law and prepared for its practice as an elected state legislator. Unto my time, party organizations commonly endorsed lawyers to serve in the law making branch of government. As Adlai I pointed out, lawyers also had a knowledge of the human condition born of their general practice. Justice Felix Frankfurter told me as a law student that the best advocates before the Supreme Court came from small towns; they were unspecialized and dealt with all manner of human situation. In legislatures where lawyers were traditionally predominant, they have been largely supplanted by doctors, businessmen of all stripes, persons of any notoriety or the ability to raise money or appeal to "single interest" voters in primary elections. Until he was indicted, a born again pest exterminator from Texas, appropriately known as the Hammer, served as the Republican Majority leader in the U.S. House of Representatives.

The Stevensons combined their reverence for the law with humor as usual, but as with comments on politics and politicians, the Black Book's light hearted jokes about lawyers acquire an edge in the new America.

I used to be a lawyer, but now I am a reformed character.
Woodrow Wilson

A farmer engaged a city lawyer. When his bill was presented after winning the suit, the sum seemed exorbitant and the farmer complained that the case had only taken two days. The lawyer explained what had gone into preparing him to be a lawyer. Whereupon the farmer handed the lawyer a check and remarked, "Here's your money this time, next time I'll hire a lawyer that nature has done something for."

Speaking of a lawyer, Lincoln said: "He can compress the most words into the smallest ideas better than any man I ever met."

Counsel opposing Lincoln in a trial objected to a juror on grounds that he knew Lincoln. As the objection reflected on the honor of counsel, Justice Davis overruled it. Lincoln, examining the jurors, found that three knew his opposing counsel. Exasperated, Justice Davis charged Lincoln with wasting the court's time since a juror's knowledge of counsel did not disqualify the juror. Lincoln responded, "but I'm afraid some of the jurors may not know him, which would put me to a disadvantage."

The law protects everybody who can hire a good lawyer.

A woman client of Clarence Darrow gushed after he had won her case: "How can I ever show my appreciation?" "My dear woman, ever since the Phoenicians invented money there has been only one way to answer that question."

Commenting about a wordy and long paper written by a lawyer, Lincoln observed: "It's like the lazy preacher that used to write long sermons. The explanation was, he got to writin' and was too lazy to stop."

A lawyer asked to campaign for a candidate replied, "I can't. I've retired from criminal practice."

Law, reverence for the laws—let every American, every lover of liberty, every well wisher to his posterity, swear by the blood of the Revolution never to violate in the least particular the laws of the country, and never to tolerate their violence by others. – Let reverence for the laws be breathed by every American mother to the lisping babe that prattles on her lap; let it be taught in schools, seminaries, and in colleges; let it be written in primers, spelling books, and in almanacs; let it be preached from the pulpit, proclaimed in legislative halls, and enforced in courts of justice. – As the patriots of '76 did to the support of the Declaration of Independence, so to the support of the Constitution and laws let every American pledge his life, his property and his sacred honor. Let every man remember that to violate the law is to trample on the blood of his fathers, and to tear the charter of his own and his children's liberty.

Abraham Lincoln, Springfield,
Illinois, January 27, 1838

18: Money and Economics

During the summer of 1905, Nicholas Murray Butler, President of Columbia University, was granted an audience by the German Kaiser. They discussed   various subjects relating to their countries, including finance. Who, asked Wilhelm II, managed governmental financial matters in the U.S.? Answered Dr. Butler, "God."

Making money for the sake of making money was of no interest to Stevensons. They were addicted to farming, practicing law, newspapering and government service. They earned it thusly and saved it patiently. They also made money by marrying it. Adlai II, the downstate boy, married into the socially prominent Borden family of Chicago which had made a fortune mining in Colorado. Maternal grandfather John Borden speculated and lost his fortune during the Great Depression. The Stevensons' modest wealth descended from great-great-grand father Jesse Fell of Bloomington. He was heralded in Harold Sinclair's novel about America, *The Years of Growth*. Fell speculated in land.

> ....in Central Illinois Jesse Fell had dabbled his fingers in more of the rivulets than almost any other man. And almost everything he had touched had been for the public good. Of course, he profited himself; he was wealthy now. But he had given away as much as he had kept — more, if the value was computed as of now.... He had promoted schools and roads and railroads and agriculture and temperance movements; founded towns; participated in dozens of business enterprises whose probable financial success was dubious but which he thought would serve a need in the community. From some he had profited handsomely. From others he had nothing but trouble and loss.

Sinclair goes on to describe how Fell founded the first public college beyond the Appalachians, now Illinois State University, and homes for orphans. He planted trees, established parks and acquired the *Bloomington Daily Pantagraph* which his son-in-law managed. Sinclair describes how Fell, a lawyer, gave rise to a young law partner, David Davis, and how they "nursed the gawky country youth named Lincoln and saw him go beyond them into immortality."

He describes how later Fell and Davis would retire behind locked doors to deliberate the details of Lincoln's estate and the "financial aberrations" of Mrs. Lincoln. Fell was a community booster, political activist and humanitarian, asking nothing, so far as the record discloses, for his benefactions, and in them gave, as much as any man, Lincoln to America—of whom he asked nothing. Lincoln made Fell, the Quaker, an Army paymaster during the Civil War. Davis, he appointed U.S. Supreme Court Justice.

Stevensons were not handicapped by more than a passing formal education in the "dismal science" of economics. They adapted to the changing circumstances and its exigencies in their private and public lives, with finance and economics gradually requiring a larger share of attention. From bank lawyer, starting in 1958, to State Treasurer, Member of the Senate Banking Committee and Chairman of the Subcommittee on International Finance, Co-Chairman of the East Asian Financial Markets Development project and efforts to develop financial markets and a regional monetary regime in East Asia, to trans-pacific investment banking, founder and Co-Chairman of the first Sino U.S. investment bank, much of my life has been in finance. Finance occupied an ever larger place in the dynamics of the American economy and world—and politics. An education in economics and finance, as it were, was acquired on the ground, including East Asia, and utilized on the ground.

Adlai I faced different times. He observed of Governor Oglesby that he stood in the front rank of campaign orators when slavery, rebellion, war and reconstruction were the stirring questions of the hour. But when the once vital issues were relegated to history and succeeded by tariff, budgetary and other "every day" questions, he was greatly hampered. "Othello's occupation was gone. Cold facts, statistics, figures running up into the millions, gave little opportunity for the play of his wonderful imagination." In a speech during his second race for Governor, Oglesby said in a deprecatory tone: "These Democrats undertake to discuss the financial question. They oughtn't to do that. They can't possibly understand it. The Lord's truth is, fellow citizens, it is about all we Republicans can do to understand that question."

Harvard did not grant a doctorate in economics before 1876. Economics in America had roots in the Social Darwinism of Herbert Spencer and the *laissez faire* of Adam Smith. The fittest would survive; the others did not matter. Entrepreneurs would spur production and employment if sufficiently incented to invest. The benefits of an unregulated market economy would trickle down. Robber barons of the first Gilded Age seized on this economics to justify their predatory practices, great wealth and the incidental poverty and oppression of the laboring classes, many of them immigrants piling into America's slums where their refuge was the settlement house, the church or perhaps the political machine of the Democratic Party. Tammany Hall was also a philanthropic organization. The machine offered them sustenance, for some a job and route to the middle class.

In this economics, also seized by the rich slave owning class in the South, there was little social ethic or role for the government as a dispenser of justice and opportunity for the masses. The government was to be minimized, the market left to allocate resources. Growth would be spurred by owners of the engines of industrial production. For Karl Marx, the vision was of endless, deepening poverty and ignorance for the masses. In the Black Book muckrakers exposed its abuses and appealed to the American conscience. Progressives and Democrats responded. Whigs led the way. They followed in the foot steps of Alexander Hamilton whose vision of a strong central government included a national bank and tariff to protect infant industries from foreign competition.

Lincoln entered politics as a candidate for the Illinois General Assembly in 1832, the year Alexis de Tocqueville concluded his trip to America and Jesse Fell arrived in Illinois from Pennsylvania. De Tocqueville was struck by the equality of the human condition in the new world and its contrast with the inequalities in the old world. The vast multitude of Americans were neither very poor nor impoverished, and "possessed of sufficient property to desire the maintenance of order, yet not enough to excite envy. Such men are the natural enemies of violent commotions; their lack of agitation keeps all beneath them and above them still, and secures the balance of the fabric of society."

Lincoln was heir to Henry Clay, the Whig, whose American System included a national bank to provide a sound currency, high tariffs to nurture infant industries, and federal support for development of infrastructure —the system of "internal improvements." Lincoln succeeded where Clay failed. He was elected President.

> "This middle-class country had got a middle class president, at last."
> *Ralph Waldo Emerson*

For Lincoln, the American government was "for" as well as "of" and "by" the American people. His struggle to preserve the Union is associated with a moral abhorrence for slavery, but Lincoln was a practical man, his wisdom acquired from experience, much of it harsh. His was also a struggle for opportunity for all, including the black man. He understood that an American people with the opportunity to get ahead by saving and hard work would have a stake in the stability of the American republic. He said his politics was "short and sweet like the widow's dance." But as President he signed into law the National Banking Act which revived the national bank and gave the country a sound, single currency. He signed into law acts of Congress which gave land to settlers in the West and to the states for colleges which created higher educational opportunity for ordinary people. Another act chartered the first transcontinental railroad system.

In the Black Book, the American Dream spelled opportunity—the opportunity to enjoy the fruits of one's labor and, by work and saving, to get ahead. The human spirit triumphed over adversity and the meaner instincts. The first Gilded Age followed Lincoln. Business was organized in ever larger units. Scandals multiplied. Social Darwinism and *laissez faire* were the order of the day as Adlai I began his political career. As Vice President he was never close to the conservative but principled Grover Cleveland. The tariff had become a costly tax upon the poor for the benefit of industry. Cleveland fought it. Bryan and Adlai I were defeated in 1900, but the Progressive movement followed. Authors and journalists exposed the conditions of laborers and immigrants, corruption in politics. Reform resumed with the Interstate Commerce Act of 1887 and Sherman Antitrust Act of 1890.

Theodore Roosevelt, Adlai I's victorious opponent, understood the power of the bully pulpit. He tackled the railroads and trusts, supported food and drug safety legislation. He took on the robber barons. William H. Taft followed and a return to Republican normalcy. Roosevelt broke with his party, effectively electing Woodrow Wilson. Wilson is a hero in the Black Book, a personal acquaintance of Adlai I's son, Lewis, who unrealistically sought the Vice Presidential nomination in 1914. Wilson's reformism was born of intellect, not the harsh experience of Lincoln, but the American Dream of opportunity and fairness for all became a political and moral imperative for Wilson. He was also a practical politician who knew how to beat the New Jersey machine politicians and make them like it. He was a model for Adlai II. Wilson is commonly associated with the League of Nations and his uncompromising commitment to self determination. But he reduced tariffs, shifting revenues from consumption to a progressive tax on incomes. He helped craft the Federal Reserve Act of 1914 to modernize the banking system, and the Federal Trade Commission and Clayton Antitrust Acts to put teeth in antitrust policy. Child and worker protection laws were enacted under Wilson. War and the 1920's would follow. Social Darwinism and *laissez faire* economic orthodoxy, in the persons of Warren G. Harding, Calvin Coolidge and Herbert Hoover returned —and another Gilded Age. Harding was sworn into the Ku Klux Klan in the White House, on his knees, his hand upon a White House Bible. Intolerance and prejudice greeted waves of immigrants— for a time.

Franklin Delano Roosevelt was slow to reject the orthodoxy of minimal government and balanced budgets. But he became the great innovator. He was willing to experiment, and he relished his enemies in the moneyed classes who viewed him as a traitor. In his 1944 State of the Union address, Roosevelt enunciated a Lincolnian Bill of Rights for Americans, a reaffirmation of the American Dream:

The right to a useful and remunerative job in the industries or shops or farms or mines of the nation.

The right to earn enough to provide adequate food and clothing and recreation.

The right of every family to a decent home.

The right to adequate protection from the economic fears of old age, sickness, accident and unemployment.

Social Darwinism returns in different guises. In the Black Book, government was not the problem. It was part of the solution. Hubert Humphrey looked down from our airplane one night in 1969 as we returned to Chicago from a meeting of the Democratic Study Group in Springfield. (As state treasurer, I had organized this group in the Illinois legislature along lines of a similar group in the U.S. House of Representatives to discuss and formulate policy for the Democratic Party.) He looked down at a rural Illinois sprinkled with lights as far as the eye could see and remarked that forty years earlier we would have looked down at blackness. Government engineered the electrification of rural America.

The purpose of studying economics is not to acquire a set of ready made answers to economic questions, but to avoid being deceived by economists.
Joan Robinson,
Cambridge University, 2007

Leave it to the "magic of the marketplace," went Ronald Reagan's mantra. A veneer of academism labeled supply-side economics postulated that decreasing marginal income tax rates for the wealthy and cutting Federal spending would increase investment, producing economic growth and employment. In *The Moral Consequences of Economic Growth,* Benjamin M. Friedman documents the absence of any empirical evidence to support the ideology of decreased taxes, primarily taxes on unearned wealth such as dividends and estate taxes, to produce savings and growth. George H. W. Bush called it "voodoo economics" before he, a practical man, converted. Supply-side economics became a political statement, a disguise for the old social Darwinian trickle-down economics, and a rationale for cutting taxes for the wealthy as a means of spurring investment.

It does not work in the real world, as Friedman demonstrates. Under Chairman Paul Volcker, the Federal Reserve squeezed inflation out of the economy with double digit interest rates, causing unemployment to soar to nearly 10 percent in 1982 and 1983. The low inflation caused by the Federal Reserve Bank's draconian interest rates laid the foundation for economic revival and demonstrated the harsh effectiveness of monetary policy. It disproved, again, the value of tax cuts for the wealthy as a means of stimulating investment and growth. The 1950's and 60's were associated with high levels of taxation, savings and growth. Under President Eisenhower, Republican, the highest income tax rate was 91 percent.

Trickle-down economics continued with George W. Bush, a living reproach to Social Darwinism. Taxes were cut for the wealthy; child welfare, Medicaid and education were cut for the poor. Expenditures were increased, mainly for the military and "homeland security." The budget plunged from surplus to deficit at the fastest rate in history, leaving the U.S. with the first consecutive annual negative savings rates since the Great Depression when people had to dip into savings to survive, as they do today, faced with declining real incomes and rising costs for debt service, education, healthcare and energy. Fiscal profligacy, an accommodative monetary policy, unsustainable household and mortgage debt, a leaking bubble in the property market, foreign credit and investment kept the American economy afloat. But the dollar begins its slide. As I write in March, 2008, the credit rating of the U.S. government is endangered. The commoditization of debt by intermediaries with esoteric and deceptive means of packaging, valuing and marketing it begins to reveal the consequences of monetary, regulatory and fiscal promiscuity. The U.S. Federal Reserve postpones the reckoning with low interest rates and an ever weaker dollar. The executive and legislative branches will, it seems, stimulate the failing economy by borrowing to finance tax rebates and consumption of goods produced in part abroad, while neglecting the long term investment needed for structural reform of the failing U.S. economy. The consequences of continuing monetary and fiscal promiscuity and structural weakness are experienced within a global economy lacking a sound monetary system, all countries put at varying degrees of risk by the weakness of the world's reserve currency and the political immoderation of its source.

As Friedman demonstrates from the historical record, higher marginal tax rates are associated with savings, investment and high economic growth rates. Under Presidents Bush I and Clinton, marginal tax rates for the wealthy increased—and revenues. Economic growth followed, owing much to increases in productivity which owed little to the bond market and interest rates and more to the information technology revolution—a product of American ingenuity fueled in part by public policies, including government support for civil research and our measures in the 1970's to stimulate technological innovation.

The Stevenson Wydler Technology Innovation Act and its companion, which I also authored (later misnamed the Bayh Dole Act), facilitated cooperative research, opened the government national laboratories to "technology utilization," and made it possible for the private sector, including universities, to acquire proprietary interests in government funded research. But President Clinton sacrificed investment in America to accommodate the bond market—his former Secretary of Labor, Robert Reich, a realist, laments. Education, the aging infrastructure, and research were neglected. The magic of the marketplace reigned under the Democrat. Debt soared, but it was private debt, the debt of households and financial service companies. Under Clinton, U.S. credit market debt increased by 72 percent. The financial sector's share of total debt rose to more than 30 percent by the time he left office. Far from challenging oligopolistic concentrations of economic power, Clinton signed legislation in 1999 which brought down the last barriers separating commercial banking, insurance, mortgage lending and securities. A consolidated, oligopolistic financial service sector became America's largest. It financed an explosion of mortgage and consumer credit, leveraged buyouts, recapitalizations, stock buy backs, hundreds of billions of dollars annually of investment in global bond and equity markets, and with the growth of derivatives, a

massive range of often opaque credit instruments for a global
community of highly leveraged speculators. This debt does not finance
education, the infrastructure and civil research. It finances consumption,
speculation and bubbles—not the production of real goods for a global
marketplace.

Starting with President Reagan, Federal support for civil
research was slashed. Our efforts in the 1970's to promote energy
conservation and develop alternative energy sources were abandoned to
the marketplace. The Enron debacle followed and rolling black outs in
California. Spending for the military was steadily increased. In the
Black Book, the military stood down when the conflict ended. From
1870 to 1913, years of rapid industrialization and economic
development, military expenditures amounted to about 1 percent of net
national income or GNP.

The 2007 Report on "Technology-based Competitiveness of 33
Nations" by Georgia Tech University, financed by the National Science
Foundation, concluded that China's technological standing was higher
than that of the U.S. Judged by numerous "high tech indicators," China
demonstrated steady progress toward world technological leadership
over a fifteen-year span. U.S. technological primacy peaked in 1999 and
since then has experienced rapid decline. Japan also declined in relative
technological standing. Europe, though not treated as an entity, was
gaining. One of the report's authors observed that China's technological
pre-eminence combined with its manufacturing strengths "won't leave
much room for other countries." Recent statistics on the value of
"technology products" exported —a "key component of technological
standing" already put China on a par with the U.S.—even as the U.S.'
self inflicted wounds are aggravated by barriers to the immigration of
the scientists and engineers it fails to produce at home. A broader focus
on relative Chinese economic dynamism would include its financial
resources and high savings, its rapidly developing modern physical
infrastructure, human resources, financial service sector and its good
will in the developing world, including resource rich Russia. China does
not rely on the magic of the marketplace. As the ideologues were
arriving in Washington in the early 1980's, they were leaving China.

Adlai II was advised by John Kenneth Galbraith and other
Keynesian realists. Some had served with him in the strategic bombing
survey after World War II which concluded that the economic cost of
bombing Europe was higher for the bomber than for the bombed. The
Great Depression had ignited an explosion of intellectual activity, much
of it rooted in the macroeconomics of Maynard Keynes. Like him, most

of these intellectuals were practical men with experience in the real world. They moved in and out of business, academe and government. They began to critically examine corporate governance and oligopolistic characteristics of the economy. They moved beyond Keynes to make qualitative judgments about government spending and taxing, its efficiency, and its stimulative and distributive effects. Their history is well told in *The Life of John Kenneth Galbraith* by Francis Parker. They fueled the New Deal— and the Deals to follow, including Adlai II's New America. During the Eisenhower interregnum, they manned the Democratic advisory bodies set up by Adlai II, and later piled into the New Frontier and Great Society to implement policies they had designed.

> Every gun that is made, every warship launched, every rocket fired, signifies, in the final sense, a theft from those who hunger and are not fed, those who are cold and are not clothed. This world in arms is not spending money alone. It is spending the sweat of its laborers, the genius of it scientists, and the hopes of its children.
>
> *Dwight D. Eisenhower,*
> Farewell Address, 1960

The international order created with U.S. leadership after World War II included an international system of fixed exchange rates. Currencies were linked to the dollar which was linked to gold. The transition from sterling to dollar went smoothly and symbolized the passing of the British Empire and the rise of the new. The International Monetary Fund was established to police the fixed rate foreign exchange and monetary system, and provide balance of payments financing. This system, engineered by Keynes (who preferred a world currency) and the U.S. Treasury, served the world well until 1973 when President Nixon was forced to suspend dollar convertibility and surrender to the marketplace. U.S. gold reserves were dwindling.

I conducted the Senate hearings on Nixon's action. It was "our currency," the Secretary of the Treasury said, "other peoples' problem." Little did former Governor John Connelley of Texas know how right he was. Other peoples would take measures to protect themselves from their problem even as the U.S. became steadily more vulnerable to flight from its problem, an unsound dollar. "Sound as a dollar" disappeared from the American discourse. After Nixon's decision, the U.S. Treasury's "interventions" to support the dollar with resources of the

Exchange Stabilization Fund were reported to me in confidence weekly. Nowadays in Washington, China's interventions to support its foreign exchange regime are labeled "manipulations" by members of Congress.

Members first discovered the Exchange Stabilization Fund after it was used to bail out Mexico in the 1980's and, then, it too became politicized. Thailand was not bailed out in 1997— a contradistinction well noted in East Asia, which quietly develops a regional free trade area and behind the closed doors of finance ministries and central banks, also at the Asian Development Bank, a regional monetary regime and currency unit to relieve it and eventually the world of dependence on the undependable dollar.

On September 11, 2001, the day of the infamous attack against the World Trade Center in New York City, I was in Hong Kong, keynoting a conference on East Asian financial regionalism co-hosted by the World Bank and Hong Kong Monetary Authority. All the speakers supported an East Asian regional monetary regime and currency unit in principle, and they all expressed skepticism about the political will and competence in the vast region to achieve it. But that was before the dollar lost its role as a store of value for the world, and before Congressional attempts to politicize the World Trade Organization and the International Monetary Fund by making them exchange rate policemen. Efforts to achieve East Asian financial regionalism began with the Chiang Mai initiative (a modest system of swap agreements for support of currencies) and has spread to other regions, including the Arabian Gulf. They may be followed by efforts to create a global unit of value and, in the meantime, more de-linking of currencies from the failing dollar. Kuwait has already done so. America is forfeiting the considerable economic advantages associated with maintaining the world's reserve currency.

Fernand Braudel, the French historical economist, described one economy—the world's—long before globalization became a clichê, a phenomenon treated by some as a doctrine of free markets and floating exchange rates, in reality a fact and condition to be managed by business and government. It was always a global economy, but no longer divided by Cold War fault lines and restricted by limits of technology which now speeds the reach of traders and producers in all parts of the world to all others. Trade barriers, transportation costs and capital controls have come down. By some estimates globalization, including trade and investment liberalization, adds between $500 billion and $1 trillion in annual income to the U.S. economy. But within this global economy with infinite possibilities, America is retreating. Its current account and fiscal deficits are not sustainable without foreign credit which is becoming wary of U.S. financial assets. The benefits of globalization are not spread equitably in America. The tides of protectionism are rising. Neoconservatives place their faith in God and the marketplace. Democrats threaten retaliation against China and trade protection. They terminate the President's trade negotiating authority. Democrats and Republicans preach fiscal orthodoxy; neither practices it, or neo-Keynesian realism.

The American Empire is losing comparative advantages not to an irremediable fate but to nations and regions more pragmatic and rational in a highly competitive post-industrial era and global economy. In the real world, a weak dollar does not reduce the trade deficit as economic orthodoxy postulates and insignificant monthly statistics might indicate. It did not do so after the dollar devaluation in 1971, after the Plaza accords appreciated the yen against the dollar in the 1980's, or after the Euro began its appreciation against the dollar. The U.S. ran trade surpluses when the dollar was strong, and made the imports of its industrial companies relatively cheap and facilitated their far flung investment in the world. In the real world there are no quick fixes like a devalued dollar. OPEC oil producers increase the price of dollar denominated oil to offset the dollar's decline. That increases the U.S. trade deficit and benefits European competitors of the U.S. by reducing their relative cost of oil. Europe's exports increased as its currency appreciated against the dollar.

China's foreign investments, like its imports, are made cheaper as its currency appreciates. Its foreign direct investment is increasing annually by more than 40 percent as I write. It was about $3 billion between 1986 and 1991. By 2006 it had reached $70 billion. America's leaders, Republicans and Democrats, are turning their country into a bargain basement for China and other foreign investors while blaming foreign competition for the U.S. current account deficit. As the world's reserve currency loses its value, central banks are forced to diversify investments and develop alternatives, perhaps in time a world currency, as Maynard Keynes dreamed. Sovereign wealth funds are created to diversify the investment of their reserves and serve national interests.

The new America is at risk of following Spain and the Hapsburgs, Holland and Great Britain. They too produced wealth and became its managers. Accounting, law, consulting, tax preparation, gambling and financial services are growth industries in America. Salaries in the investment banking sector are the nation's highest even as its bundling and marketing of dubious debt rattles markets, undermines the balance sheets of creditors, and threatens innocent debtors with loss of their homes.

In the life cycle of nations and empires, economies progress from agricultural to mercantile and industrial stages and through what Kevin Phillips in *American Theocracy* calls "financialization"—which is often accompanied by costly militarism, decadence (self-indulgence) and decline. Managers outsource production of industrial goods, commodities and services to nations at an earlier stage in the life cycle. Even American farmers threatened by restraints on immigration propose to outsource production. The management of wealth gets separated from its ownership and invites the development of ever more unregulated liquid financial markets, increasingly complex financial instruments and fund management companies, many of them highly but obscurely leveraged. Financial institutions expand through consolidation and manage investments in companies for which they also provide financial services.

In 1997, American observers smugly attributed the financial crisis which swept out of East Asia to "crony capitalism." Since then one example after another of crony capitalism has swept the U.S. financial sector: Enron and Arthur Andersen, WorldCom, Hollinger, Tyco, Revco, the mutual fund and insurance industries. The largest U.S. investment banks followed. Incented by compensation based on short-term corporate performance, their executives rewarded themselves at the expense of their banks' long term profitability and solvency. The U.S. government went along. It offered moral hazard in the U.S. as it denounced it in foreign countries. American regulators seem to have studied economics without discovering Gresham's law: Bad money drives out the good. The good investment is hoarded, the bad is circulated— until the crash. Large U.S. investments banks are reporting losses in the tens of billions of dollars for 2007—and bonuses of $40 billion for the culpable executives of the five largest, up 10 percent over the preceding year.

In the late 1990's the traditional "basket" of costs used to calculate the U.S. Consumer Product Index (CPI) was modified to underweight food and energy, home ownership and energy costs while attributing cost decreases to subjective measures ("hedonics") stemming from improvements in television, computers and other such products. This methodology seems to have reduced the CPI by about 2 percent annually, automatically cutting social security and other benefits pegged to the CPI, while causing a comparable increase in gross domestic product (GDP). It is not clear that other countries have modified traditional methods similarly nor that all central banks, sovereign wealth funds and other investors appreciate the degree to which inflation is understated and growth overstated in the U.S. and in relation to other countries.

Manipulating economic statistics, concentrating economic activity in the financial service sector while bailing out banking conglomerates, embracing moral hazard and using tax policy to widen the wealth and income gaps does not address structural weaknesses in the once productive and competitive U.S. economy. Interest rate cuts for the banking sector will further weaken the savings rate and the dollar. A world alert to such realities, including East Asians and oil producers with control of most of the world financial reserves, is being incented to delink currencies and the pricing of oil from the dollar and hasten development of substitutes for the dollar as a reserve currency. The American house of cards is trembling. Robber barons of the first Gilded Age built industries and railroads. Now they mostly manage money—and mismanage it.

> A money changer's desire is not of glory, but of gain; not of public wealth, but of private emolument; he is, therefore, rarely to be consulted on questions of war and peace, or any designs of wide extent and distant Consequence.
>
> *Dr. Johnson*, a Tory

The human costs of Social Darwinism are expressed in comparatively low levels of educational achievement and motivation, a widening gap between the haves and have-nots, and a divided people. The wealth and income disparities in America rival those of the Gilded Age and exceed those of all other industrial countries, with the possible exception of Switzerland. Nobel Laureate economist Robert Solow said what is happening is "nothing less than elite plunder," the redistribution of wealth to the wealthy and power to the powerful. Nearly all the wealth created in the last twenty-five years has been captured by the top 20 percent of households. Since 1970 the median income of American families has stagnated even as husband and wife both work, and for longer hours. Thanks to the Bush Administration's tax cuts, taxpayers earning more than $10 million a year pay a lesser share of their income in taxes than those making $100 thousand. Executives justify compensation packages and perquisites by claiming they are determined by the market—as if they were commodities auctioned to the highest bidder. Their failures are routinely rewarded with multi-million dollar "golden parachutes."

> ...men very powerful in certain lines and gifted with the money touch, but with ideals which in their essence are merely those of so many glorified pawn brokers.
> *Theodore Roosevelt*

From within China I have seen a meritocracy rising as the Party loosens its grip for purposes of policy and patronage while maintaining control at a doctrinal level. It liberalizes the foreign exchange regime and capital account gradually and in tandem as it develops its financial services sector. The Chinese have learned from the tragic results of Washington's economic orthodoxy in Russia during the early 1990's and elsewhere in the world, including East Asia after the 1997 financial crisis where it joined with the International Monetary Fund to accelerate capital flight and a collapse of currencies for the benefit of foreign creditors and predators. They cannot fail to be unimpressed by what neo-liberal economic orthodoxy and politics have done to the American economy. Oblivious to the irony, western disciples of this "free market" orthodoxy compete fiercely for stakes in China's "socialist market" economy, even as China's banks and securities companies quietly begin to internationalize their operations and in time compete with America's financial institutions. In China, Reason reigns, or as Lee Kuan Yew— father of modern Singapore—puts it, pragmatism is China's ideology.

In the new America, reaction waits—or in Arnold Toynbee's phrase—the "response" waits. In the 1970's we addressed structural weaknesses in the U.S. economy, studying the industrial policies of other countries, notably Japan. In 1980, Senate Democrats developed a comprehensive economic strategy, including structural measures to enhance U.S. competitiveness. Japan implemented some of its provisions to foster technological innovation. In America the effort died with the election of Ronald Regan. It should be resumed with a government operated universal health care system; job training for a post industrial era; investment in the aging infrastructure, including public transportation financed by increased gas taxes; reform and support of early childhood, elementary and secondary education; universal education through the university for those qualified; a restoration of the draft to improve military manpower while lowering its cost and diminishing enthusiasm for war; alternative energy projects and a national oil company to produce from the public domain for the public and bring America's bargaining power to bear with the national companies of the producing countries; and measures to redistribute wealth and the benefits of globalization, break up or regulate the financial oligopolies, and strengthen the social safety net. Many such measures and policies have long been on the drawing boards. Funding for redundant and irrelevant weapons systems, earmarks, self perpetuating war, farm subsidies, ethanol and pork could be slashed. But the old political will and competence have been lacking.

> I don't like doles. I don't like subsidies. I don't like any interference with free markets, free men and free enterprise. But I know that there can be no real freedom without economic justice, social justice, equality of opportunity and a fair chance for every individual to make the most of himself.
> *Adlai II*

> These businessmen and lawyers were very adroit in using a word with fine and noble associations to cloak their opposition to vitally necessary movements for industrial fair play and decency. They made it evident that they valued the Constitution, not as a help to righteousness, but as a means of thwarting movements against unrighteousness.
> *Theodore Roosevelt*

> The businessman dealing with a large political question is really a painful sight. It does seem to me that businessmen, with a few exceptions, are worse when they come to deal with politics than men of any other class.
> *Sen. Henry Cabot Lodge, Sr.*
> (an imperialist)

Alvin (Shipwreck) Kelly was a popular hero who devised a new form of popular entertainment: He sat on flagpoles. For the most part, he remained motionless during his performance, but he would occasionally pull a bucket aloft that contained food, newspapers and the four packs of cigarettes he smoked each day. When Kelly descended from a flagpole on the morning after the great stock market crash, reporters asked him what he thought of the Wall Street disaster. Kelly considered the matter and replied: "If people took up flagpole-sitting it never would have happened. Flagpole-sitting learns you discipline. The thing that everybody hasn't got nowadays is discipline."

David Alexander, Panic
(on the 1929 crash)

A feast is for laughter and wine maketh merry, but money answereth all things.
Ecclesiastes 10:19

Gold has a certain very pronounced affinity for a certain type of men. Did you ever notice that?

Anybody can lose his shirt on Wall Street provided he has enough capital and inside information.
Joseph P. Kennedy

They are not prosperous; they are only rich.
George Bernard Shaw

I hope we shall crush in its birth the aristocracy of our money corporations, which already challenge our government to a trial of strength, and bid defiance to the laws of our country.
Thomas Jefferson

Gasoline was never much higher. But there you have a business that is in the hands of a few men, and they see that the price is kept up. It's not regulated by supply and demand, it's regulated by manipulation.
Will Rogers, 1931

If capital and labor ever do git together, it's good night fer the rest of us.
Mr. Dooley

There was a time when a fool and his money were soon parted. Now it happens to everybody.

I believe emphatically in what is called for want of a better word 'free enterprise.' But free enterprise…must be a source of well being for the many, or it won't be free very long.

Adlai II

19: Diplomacy and Foreign Policy

We must thread our way between imperialism and isolationism, between the disavowal of the responsibilities of our power and the assertion of our power beyond our resources.

Adlai II

The Black Book reflects foreign policy formulated and implemented by officials with extensive experience on the ground, in the world, and some understanding of the crosscurrents of cultures and history, the intertwined dynamics of economics and politics, and their management by statecraft. It records vignettes from on the ground and in a real world which often bear little resemblance to the stereotypes which inform debate and the images projected by the mass media. Its perspectives are far from those ivory towers of arm chair strategists and polemicists.

These officials who formulated and implemented policy were predominantly in the State Department. Foreign service officers were embedded with the peoples to whom they were accredited throughout the world. They learned on the ground and rose in the ranks. The State Department was the repository of responsibility for the nation's foreign policy. It reported to the President and was not subjected to "coordination" by a National Security Council led by ambitious and transient scholasticists. (Zbigniew Bryzinski, President Carter's National Security Advisor, an academic, would become a wise and courageous commentator on contemporary events, including the Middle East). The Pentagon did not exist for most of this history, nor myriad intelligence services. America's ambassadors did not bid for embassies with campaign contributions in the diplomacy of the Black Book. They rose in the foreign service or from distinguished careers in other branches of government and the private sector. According to the Center for Responsive Politics, the George W. Bush Administration has awarded forty-three ambassadorships to its campaign donors. Each curtails the career of a foreign service officer, contributing to the demoralization of America's once vaunted foreign service.

Lobbying by foreign ambassadors on Capitol Hill was an improper intrusion into State Department authority as late as the early 1970's. By the end of that decade even foreign ambassadors were lobbying, and foreign governments were hiring public relations firms and lobbyists. Politics never truly stopped at the water's edge, as claimed by Daniel Webster, according to the Black Book, but diplomacy was not formulated by ideologues in the executive branch or Members of Congress unchastened by experience in the real world.

Foreign service officers were martyred for reporting the truth about China in the 1940's. But McCarthysism was an aberration. The Senator was disciplined by his peers. Demagogues, "realists" and idealists are part of a recurring pattern. Realists, so called, in recent times often lacked experience in the real world. They may have been students of Count Metternich and 19th century balance of power politics, but they were unrealistic. War in Indochina, the Nixon Doctrine, the "tilt" to Pakistan in its civil war, the assassination of Allende in Chile, NATO's U.S.-led war in Kosovo— such exercises in selective "realism" were unrealistic—and predictably so from on the ground where the archetypal realists seldom tread. Atrocities in Sierra Leone, the Congo, Algeria, Rwanda, and Sri Lanka they selectively ignored.

A poster from the 1900 campaign portrays William Jennings Bryan and his running mate, Adlai I, and beneath: "The Republic, not the Empire." Empire—always in the ostensible cause of liberation, freedom, civilization or democracy, and inflamed by the likes of William Randolph Hearst then and Rupert Murdoch later—won. McKinley agonized over what to do with the "liberated" Philippines until his prayers were answered by God. America was called upon to Christianize the Filipinos, most of whom were Roman Catholics. In His name the Philippines was colonized brutally—for a time. Cuba was liberated by the U.S. from Spain—and in time, liberated by Fidel Castro from corrupt and dictatorial minions of the U.S.

In the Black Book the Republic wins. Diplomacy is an alternative to war. America's diplomacy embraced the world's pluralism and propagated democracy and human rights by example and with development assistance. It reflected a recognition that the power of a great country requires the exercise of its restraint. Carlos Romulo, foreign minister of the Philippines, explained that the more powerful the nation, the more amenable it should be to reason and negotiation with the proverb: "The taller the bamboo grows, the lower it bends."

War can be a politically convenient alternative to diplomacy. Fears and fevers are easily inflamed and then exploited by politicians. Medals, monuments and campaign contributions are not for the peacemakers. In the spring of 1960, when Adlai II was being urged to seek the Democratic Presidential nomination for a third time, he was invited to meet with Ambassador Menshikov of the Soviet Union at its Embassy in Washington. Two chairs were placed in the room—away from the walls to signify the conversation was confidential. The

Ambassador explained that he had received instructions from General Secretary Khruschev to inform Governor Stevenson that the Soviet Union was prepared to assist his presidential candidacy. To draw out the Ambassador, the Guv inquired as to the kind of assistance Mr. Khruschev had in mind. His inquiry had been anticipated. The Ambassador replied that he was instructed to invite suggestions from the Governor, who then rejected the proposal.

A year and a half after this incident, the Soviet Union was detected placing missiles in Cuba. Within the Administration, Ambassador Stevenson proposed a compromise. To stand down from nuclear confrontation, he proposed the exchange of obsolete U.S. bases in Turkey for withdrawal of the missiles. This proposal was leaked to the press and used to pillory the Guv for being "soft." In public, the Kennedy Administration took a hard line.

In May, 1962, Adlai II presented proof of the missile emplacements to the UN Security Council in a dramatic confrontation with Soviet Ambassador Zorin which swung world opinion behind the United States. The Soviet Union backed down; the missiles were removed. But the diplomacy was flawed. The Kennedy Administration had agreed with the Soviet Union to take its obsolete bases out of Turkey, as the Guv had proposed, but insisted on keeping that part of the deal secret. Years later Secretary of State Dean Rusk acknowledged the arrangement. Thus, Kennedy won applause for his toughness, but Khruschev was humiliated by his capitulation. His deal on the bases was secret. The balance of terror and peace were preserved. But Khruschev's humiliation contributed to his downfall. He was succeeded by a reactionary collective leadership from which Leonid Brezhnev emerged the leader. The hard liners in Moscow succeeded Khruschev. The strategic arms race escalated, costing the U.S. far more than the Soviets.

The Guv, a friend of the world and Khruschev's erstwhile presidential candidate in 1960, indicted and convicted Khruschev's government in the "court of world opinion." Later, the American Secretary of State, Colin Powell, unintentionally convicted the U.S. government in the same court by presenting false evidence of Iraqi weapons of mass destruction in Iraq. The Bush Administration ignored the Security Council's interest in stabilizing the Middle East while containing Saddam Hussein. An oblivious Condoleeza Rice dubbed Secretary Powell's presentation to the Security Council an "Adlai Stevenson moment." The strategic arms limitation process begun by the Guv has long been abandoned.

Khruschev was plain spoken, a de-Stalinizing reformer and a dove by Soviet standards. He also had a sense of humor—rare for the Soviet leaders I came to know later, including Brezhnev. Sir Brian Urqhart, former Deputy Secretary General of the UN, marvels to this day at the diplomatic skills of Adlai II, remarking that his counter parties in negotiations sometimes did not realize they were in negotiations. According to Urqhart, Adlai II could even make the dour Soviet Foreign Minister, Andrei Gromyko, laugh. Secretary Khruschev once invited my brothers to remain in Moscow and marry two "nice Russian girls."

Korean description of a diplomatic contretemps: "If it had not been for your fence, my cow would not have broken its horns."

Ceylonese (Sri Lanka) proverb: "Hatred is dispelled not by hatred, but by kindness. This is the eternal law."

Finnish proverb: "Better a meager agreement, than a satisfactory disagreement."

In diplomacy: "A gentleman's agreement is an agreement no gentleman would put in writing."

Three rules of diplomacy:
Never lose the initiative;
Never triumph over a victory;
Never get between a dog and the lamp post.
Harold Nicholson

I live in a sea of words
Where the nouns and the adjectives flow
Where the verbs speak of actions that never take place
And the sentences come and go.
Adlai II, composed at a UN
meeting in London

The Cabinet Ministers go to their dinner
Their Secretary sits getting thinner and thinner
Rocking his brains to get into his head

What he thinks that they think that they ought to have said.

Diplomacy is the business of handling porcupines — without disturbing their quills.

When will people learn that it is the spirit we are of, not the machinery we employ, that binds us to others.
Macauley

Diplomacy consists of protocol, alcohol and geritol.
A weary Adlai II

We can afford to exercise the restraint of a great power which knows its power and refrains from misusing it.
Woodrow Wilson

The acts of governments are transitory while relations between peoples are lasting.
Sumner Welles

Take away the sword; states can be saved without it.
Richelieu

Another lesson that we shall have to learn is that we cannot deal with questions of foreign policy in terms of moral absolutes. Compromise is not immoral or treasonable. It is the objective of negotiation and negotiation is the means of resolving conflict peacefully. But when we negotiate we have to have something to negotiate with as well as for. If rigidity and absolutist attitudes deprive our representatives of anything to negotiate with, then there is nothing they can negotiate for.
Adlai II, Harvard University, 1954

I will have a foreign handed foreign policy.
George W. Bush, Redwood,
California, September 27, 2000

The fundamental question is, will I be a successful president when it comes to foreign policy? I will be, but until I'm the President it's going to be hard to verify that I think I'll be the more effective.

George W. Bush, New York
Times, June 28, 2000

We'll let our friends be the peacekeepers and the great country called America will be the pacemakers.

George W. Bush, Houston, Texas,
September 6, 2000

In recent years, efforts to embrace the world's pluralism and break down barriers behind which ignorance and fear can fester have been scarce. While representing the U.S. in the Pacific Economic Cooperation Council (PECC) in the mid 1990's, I ignored policies of U.S. and South East Asian governments isolating communist Vietnam, and after advising then Secretary of State Warren Christopher of my intentions, traveled to Hanoi, its capital, where I received a warm welcome. I opened its way into PECC, the route to APEC (Asia Pacific Economic Cooperation), ASEAN (Association of Southeast Asian Nations) and the world. Normalization of Vietnam's relations with the U.S. and the East Asians followed. The U.S. has a trade agreement with a friendly, economically dynamic Vietnam which recently hosted an annual APEC meeting attended by President Bush. Little warrant exists in history for U.S. efforts to isolate and castigate its pariahs. It isolates itself.

In the 1970's I tried, as a Senator, to wean Eastern Europeans of dependence on the Soviet Union by developing trade and investment instead of forcing them into the ruble bloc, effectively enforcing for the Soviets post war arrangements for the division of Europe agreed at Potsdam. The Jackson-Vanik Amendment, adopted in 1974, conditioned U.S. trade and credits for "non market" i.e. communist, countries, on findings of "free" emigration policies, subject to annual review and approval by the Congress until these countries were "graduated" by Congress to normal trade status. The only emigrants of interest and concern were Jews seeking emigration from the Soviet Union and subject to an emigration tax, a singularity of purpose underscored when President Carter explained the amendment to Deng Tsiao Peng in 1979. Deng, leader of non market China, was reported to have inquired "how many millions do you want?" The normalization of relations with countries of Eastern Europe was politicized and retarded. The amendment's first beneficiary was the infamous Ceausescu regime of Romania which promptly made Bucharest an entrepôt for any Jews escaping the Soviet Union. Its first victims were Jews, their emigration curtailed by the Soviet Union after the amendment was approved by Congress.

With responsibility for "east-west" trade, I explored Eastern Europe. I met Ceausescu—after traveling by car to his retreat in the Carpathian mountains of Transylvania—and other Communist bosses, including Janos Kadar, the leader of Hungary whom I met in Budapest, and Todor Zhivkof of Bulgaria, whom I tracked down to his retreat on the Danube near the Black Sea. Kadar was intelligent, but for the most part, the communist leaders in Eastern Europe were plain men of simple origins, leaders of the resistance against Germany. They were nationalists and, like their peoples, yearning for freedom—with a mild qualification for Bulgaria which was liberated by Russian arms from the Ottomans. Throughout Eastern Europe, the leaders and ordinary people I met were nationalists first, collectivists as much from necessity as conviction, though East Germany was murky and hard to penetrate. Except in that walled-off slice of Germany, I was warmly received throughout Eastern Europe and encouraged to persist, a lonely American seeking to break down their isolation. Even Bulgaria encouraged the effort with a decoration.

I supported the Jackson-Vanik Amendment, a bizarre product of the Israeli lobby and Richard Perle, then an aide to Senator Henry "Scoop" Jackson, who reciprocated my support with his support for what became known as the Stevenson Amendment. As Congress unwittingly helped contain East Europeans in the Soviet orbit, Secretary of State Kissinger, the "realist," pursued "detente" with the Soviet Union by granting it more than a billion dollars worth of cash and credits in one year. Thus, the Soviet Union was being subsidized by the U.S. while the East Europeans were being punished by the U.S. The Stevenson Amendment put an end to Kissinger's pursuit of détente with money. It conditioned cash and credits for the Soviet Union on periodic Congressional review, thus effectively ending his unwitting efforts to prolong the life of the Soviet Union. Unaided, it would collapse of its inner contradictions and weight, and thus would the Eastern Europeans and the Republics of the Soviet Union be finally freed—under President Michael Gorbachev.

I visited China in 1975 as a member of the first congressional delegation to visit that country, then enduring the last years of the cultural revolution. We were "running dogs of capitalism." People in the streets, all dressed in their shapeless Mao jackets, feared being detected communicating with us. We met Deng Tsiao Peng on that trip, and I served briefly as an escort during his trip to Washington in 1979. China's reforms followed that trip to Washington, the overtures of the Nixon Administration and its opening to the world. Formal normalization of relations followed under the Carter Administration. The process and the dissimulations and deceits which made it possible to open China to the world are well described in Patrick Tyler's *The Great Wall.* The right wing had to be bought off by playing China off against the Soviet Union, the China Lobby assuaged with military assistance for Taiwan. China opened to ideas and information— to the sunshine. Its "peaceful rise" and development followed.

A prudent diplomacy recognizes that fear and hostility flourish in beleaguered isolation and darkness. North Korea is a case in point. U.S. pressures are often counterproductive. Countries are unlikely to do under pressure, that which they might without it. The Castro regime in Cuba has survived eight U.S. presidents already. It had America's embargo to blame for the plight of the Cuban people. Other countries invest and pick up the business in Cuba. Americans are denied a market. Such attempts at pressure and isolation were once known as examples of the "if you don't behave, I'll shoot myself in the foot again" syndrome.

Iranians are joined in a reluctant defense of their autocratic regime by the noisy hostility and sanctions of the U.S. Its hostility undermined the reformist President Khatami and strengthens hard liners as I write. Dissent in Iran implies complicity with a U.S. which intervened to overthrow the popularly elected President Mossadegh in the 1950's, threatens pre emptive war against an "axis of evil," and seeks sanctions. In January, 2008, President Bush belatedly visited friendly countries in the Arabian gulf for the first time. He furtively dropped in on Baghdad's Green Zone by plane and quickly exited. President Ahmadinejad of Iran followed with a parade in the streets of Baghdad and was hailed by large crowds, including the Iraqi President and Prime Minister. Throughout the Gulf, customarily polite and deferential Arabs took to the streets and protested President Bush's visits. The normally deferential Arab press protested, too:

> President Bush chose Abu Dhabi and the midway point
> of his Middle Eastern sojourn to attack Iran. It was, as
> usual, a display of the fairly muddled thinking behind the

current   foreign policy of the United States. Bush said Iran funds terrorist extremists, undermines peace in Lebanon, sends arms to the Taliban, seeks to intimidate its neighbors with alarming rhetoric, defies the United Nations and destabilizes the entire region by refusing to be open about its nuclear program. If the part about sending arms to the Taliban were removed, it would be easy to mistake this description of Iran for a description of Israel. The difference is that Iran has just agreed to respond to the unanswered questions about its nuclear program.

The Saudi Gazette, January 14, 2008.

We do not need more threats of war. Warmongering has already created the greatest level of regional instability in 60 years. Bush's inflammatory threats against Iran ride roughshod over the counsels of peace that he has heard from every Arab government on his Middle East visit. Whatever threat Iran may constitute, now or in the future, must be addressed peaceably and through negotiations. The consequences of further war in the region are hideous, not least because they are incalculable. Even Bush, with the ruin of Iraq before him, must surely see that. Yet in his confrontational remarks about Iran, he offers no carrot, no inducement, no compromise —only the big U.S. stick. This is not diplomacy in search of peace. It is madness in search of war.

Arab News, January 15, 2008

Destabilization of the middle east spreads to Afghanistan and Pakistan. General Carl von Clausewitz (1780 -1831) in his classic *On War* explained that ". . . war is not a mere act of policy but a true political instrument, a continuation of political activity by other means. . .Subordinating the political point of view to the military would be absurd, for it is policy that creates war. . . .War is an act of force to compel the enemy to do our will." Optimally war is defensive. Clausewitz was a creature of the Enlightenment, and he knew something of war.

As I wrap up the Black Book, the U.S. is building an embassy on one hundred four acres in Baghdad's Green Zone with more than twenty buildings, including six apartment complexes, two office complexes for one thousand employees, a beauty salon, shopping market, food court, movie theatre, gymnasium, tennis court, a school and American club for social gatherings, residences for senior diplomats —all behind a nine foot wall. America's embassy in Iraq has its own military and mercenaries recruited at home and in the world for $10,000 per month. The maintenance of this scandal plagued fortress, some call it a "crusader castle," is expected to cost more than $1 billion per year. Congress has already appropriated $592 million for its construction. Diplomats of the new America are sealed off from the peoples to whom they are accredited. They travel in armed convoys guarded by contractors to whom military duties are outsourced by the State Department at a cost to tax payers of billions of dollars, much of it stolen or otherwise misappropriated. Across the world, the stately residences of American Ambassadors are being sold by the State Department and replaced with new, "secure" buildings walled off from the people.

> The time for diplomacy is now.
> *Condoleeza Rice*, Secretary of
> State designate, January 17, 2005

The 2007 annual survey of the International Institute for Strategic Studies noted the continued decline of American authority in the world and that the deterioration of American power had led to a "non polar" world in which other actors, citing Russia, were able to assert themselves. American power was "diminished and demystified," with adversaries believing they will prevail if they manage to draw the U.S. into prolonged engagement. The loss of U.S. influence in the Middle East encouraged countries —notably Iran —to flex their muscles. The U.S. provides ammunition to radical groups seeking to discredit the leaders of countries maintaining solid links with the U.S. and encourages other countries to hedge their diplomatic relations with the U.S. The survey concluded that the "restoration of American strategic authority seems bound to take much longer than the mere installation of a new president."

On September 13, 2007, President Bush pleaded with Americans to support the recommendations of generals led by David Petraeous, including a "surge" of U.S. forces. He evidently aims to prolong the Iraq war into the next Administration. In the Black Book, the military was subordinate to civil authorities which formulated policy and managed

diplomacy. Harry Truman discharged General Douglas D. MacArthur
for insubordination. It was a highly unpopular act, but it may have
spared the country war with China on the Asian mainland after
MacArthur had defied the civil authorities by invading North Korea.
(Lincoln observed that he could make generals with the stroke of a pen.
Finding enough mules at $20 dollars a head was more difficult.)

> War is too important to be left to the generals.
> *Premier Georges Clemenceau,*
> 1918

The reassertion of American diplomacy grows more difficult as
the U.S. blind support for Israel's colonization of Palestine, the
invasions of Iraq and Afghanistan, attacks against the Northwest frontier
areas of Pakistan, the collateral killing and wounding of the innocents,
the torture, secret prisons and renditions spread jihad and the threat from
Al Qaeda to Central and South Asia and new regions in Africa, Asia and
Europe. More than four million Iraqis have been displaced. Afghanistan
is being engulfed by Taliban, emboldened and encouraged by the
corrupt Karzai government. All Pakistan is endangered. Iran rises – and
Hamas and Hezbollah. India may in time be threatened by its ties to the
U.S. and the rising Islamic insurgency. The most radical Islamism,
including Whahhabi Islam supported by Saudi Arabia, spreads in
Central Asia. Poverty, ignorance, hunger, and anger combine to isolate
the U.S. and its perceived accomplices. This phenomena is no secret –
except to the American people. Innumerable proposals have been made
for international diplomatic efforts to bring about a regional security
arrangement. It might be led by the UN and involve all the affected
countries. All have a common interest in political stability and heading
off world threatening instability. India and Pakistan are nuclear states.
    Failures of U.S. militarism may revive diplomacy's search for
peace by the UN and other nations –and a new American President. But
the hour is late. As told in the following chapters, peace is hard, war is
easy, and for American politicians, peacemaking in the Middle East can
be fatal.

> I dread our own power and our own ambition; I dread our
> being too much dreaded.... We may say that we shall not
> abuse this astonishing and hitherto unheard of power. But
> every other nation will think we shall abuse it. It is
> impossible but that, sooner or later, this state of things

must produce a combination against us which may end in our ruin.

Edmund Burke

20: War Is Easy

Seen through spectacles, war is easy.
Arab proverb

After the armistice which ended World War I, world leaders, led
by President Woodrow Wilson, resolved to end war for all time and
make good the promise of the future. Margaret MacMillan in her epic
Paris, 1919 about the peace conference which followed the war, tells of
Wilson's trip by train at night from the French port of Brest to the
conference in Paris. Families lined the tracks the entire distance, their
heads bared in respectful silence, as they sought a glimpse of the train
which brought the American President and the promise of a better
world. President Wilson received a tumultuous welcome in Paris. He
was a didactic and difficult man but of high principle, intelligence and
purpose. Like Theodore Roosevelt, no friend, he had been something of
an imperialist during the country's brief flirtation with imperialism at
the turn of the century, but became an internationalist and peacemaker.
His Fourteen Points, including the worthy but naive principle of self
determination for all peoples, guided the Paris Conference, though
European imperialists betrayed the Arabs and carved up the Ottoman
Empire, planting seeds of discord and instability in the Middle East.
      Wilson's proposal for a League of Nations was, with varying
degrees of enthusiasm, supported by all the leaders at the Conference.
The League would give the world a chance to prevent war and achieve
peace for all time.

The tents of humanity have been struck. And mankind is
once more on the march.
Gen. Jan Christian Smuts, 1919,
speaking of his plan for the
League of Nations

Here musters not the forces of party, but the forces of
humanity. Men's hearts wait upon us—men's lives hang
in the balance—men's hopes call upon us to say what we
will do....There must be not a balance of power, but a
community of power; not organized rivalries, but an
organized, common peace.
Woodrow Wilson, Second
Inaugural Address

The League, and in particular Article X, which bound Members of the League to defend one another against external aggression, was opposed by the Republican Old Guard in the U.S. Senate led by Henry Cabot Lodge. Wilson rallied the country but was uncompromising and dying. The Treaty of Versailles and the League were rejected by the Senate. Mankind's march was arrested.

Failed in the high enterprise, yet greatly failed.

The fruits reaped by the sinews of the victors have been destroyed by the pens of the statesmen.
Duke of Wellington

As Wilson predicted, another World War followed.

"Lieutenant," asked my gunny (platoon sergeant), "what's the worst: the sights, sounds or smells of war?" Sergeant Harry Harbor had fought with the Marines in the warm battlefields of the South Pacific Island campaigns of World War II. I turned the question around and asked him the same. He responded with conviction and no hesitation: "The smells."

It was not until early 1971 that I began to understand his answer. Nancy and I were in Dhaka, capital of what was then East Pakistan, now Bangladesh. The Pakistani civil war was winding down. At night we could hear the crackle of gun fire as old scores were settled. The Indian army had come to the rescue of the Bengalis in the East after the Nixon Administration "tilted" to the Pakistani government of President Yahya Khan. In cables to the State Department, the American Consul General in Dhaka, Chicago native Archer Blood, protested Pakistan's "genocide." He urged his Government to act. For his efforts he was cashiered by President Nixon and his National Security Advisor, Henry Kissinger. By some estimates, three million Bengalis were slaughtered.

To communicate their outrage at the atrocities of the West Pakistanis and the complicity of the U.S. government, our Bengali friends insisted on taking us to an excavated mass grave. That's when I understood Gunny Harbor's answer; the smell is not a sensation washed away by time. Like many, that slaughter was little noted in its time nor remembered. More ordinance was dropped on little Laos by the Nixon Administration than on Europe during World War II. Children by the hundred are still being killed by the bomblets. The sights, sounds and smells of war are not recorded in the Black Book, and they are the least of it—mere symptoms of the suffering and dehumanizing consequences, the economic, political and cultural upheavals wreaked by war.

At the American military cemetery outside Manila in the Philippines, Asian tourists once pondered white crosses marching silently over the surrounding hills, remembering thankfully America's defense of their countries. They contemplated the names of thousands of Americans missing in action etched upon the stone face of the mausoleum. I found MIA's once on a mountain top in Korea after stumbling through the unmarked northern perimeter of a minefield. It never occurred to Marines in those days to do anything except leave their pitiful remains in the undisturbed peace they had finally found. In Vietnam and North Korea, MIA's would later be commercialized and politicized, grieving families given false hope, millions of tax payer dollars spent to dig up and sift through such sad remains. That mausoleum contains a brilliant depiction in mosaics of the epic struggle to first defend Southeast Asia and then wage war, island by island, across the Pacific to Japan, where General Curtis LeMay's low flying bombers dropped napalm, fuel oil and phosphorous on the tinderbox residential areas of the cities. It was reported the flight crews could smell the death and destruction they were wreaking below. As many as eighty thousand women, children and old men were incinerated in one night of fire bombing Tokyo. The young men were away at war.

A lonely stone temple in the Nihonbashi district of Tokyo survived, and contains a row of oil paintings beneath its eaves depicting the great earthquake's aftermath in 1923, and beneath it a row of photographs depicting Tokyo's other great disaster, the American fire bombing. In the photographs, rubble stretches to the horizon, interrupted only by the remains of occasional stone buildings and a few stark tree trunks. In the forefront are piles of what one can barely discern to be the charred and shapeless forms of the victims. There was no escaping the holocaust ignited by LeMay's bombers on the wooden homes of the Japanese in their cities. A few years later, villages and civilian populations of North Korea would be destroyed by American bombers, industries and populations driven underground. In Europe, memories long dormant of American bombings of civilian targets in the last days of World War II have been revived by American atrocities in Iraq.

In Vienna, I heard recorded communications of American bomber pilots targeting civilians and the palaces and cathedrals of the Hapsburgs—broadcast in 2005 on the 60th anniversary of the end of World War II. (The British, led by Winston Churchill, were more indifferent to the suffering of civilian populations.)

Adlai II's generation, led by Presidents Franklin Roosevelt, Truman and Eisenhower, resolved to try again where Wilson had been defeated. President Eisenhower knew something of war. So did Harry Truman, an artillery officer in World War I. They faced the opposition of Republican isolationists and disciples of the old power politics of nations. Henry Cabot Lodge had been succeeded by Robert Taft as leader of the Old Guard in the Senate. But Democrats and moderate Republicans prevailed, and in doing so made America the leader of an evolutionary process with tribal and feudal origins which had led to the nation state, a 17th century doctrine of non interference in the affairs of others, the Congress of Vienna in the early 19th century, and finally, to a world order which required a sacrifice of some sovereignty and relied on economic assistance, the rule of law, arms control, law enforcement, and in all things, international cooperation to foster peace and human progress in an interdependent world. From the ashes of the League of Nations and World War II, America aided the fallen enemy, albeit later in the name of resisting communism, and led the creation of a United Nations and its host of international organizations. America was a superpower then. Freedom was not a pretext for war. President Franklin Roosevelt's Four Freedoms included freedom from war.

In the Black Book America was great, Americans secure when America was waging peace, respecting the opinions of mankind and building coalitions of nations which could guarantee collective security. The Republican Old Guard which rejected the League of Nations and resisted the post World War II order reflected a strain of exceptionalism and insularity going back to Washington's Farewell Address. The Black Book articulates an internationalism born of war. The new Old Guard sees the world in Manichean terms; theirs is a war for empire and against evil, as they see it. Its apostles, one is tempted to say its Ayatollahs, include religious Zionists, Jewish and Christian, with Biblical visions of a greater Land of Israel and its "realm."

There is little new in wars and persecutions driven by religiosity or waged in the name of God and destiny. Ecclesiastical discords, notably Christian intolerance, were critical factors in the downfall of the Roman Empire, according to Edward Gibbon. For centuries Europe suffered dynastic and religious wars and persecutions. The European heads of state all waged World War I in the name of God. "On me, the German Emperor, the spirit of God has descended. I am His sword, His weapon and His Vice Regent. Woe to the disobedient and death to cowards and unbelievers." To his generals, Kaiser Wilhelm was "Your Chief War Captain."

America's self described "War President," George W. Bush, propounds a doctrine of preemptive war, including the use of weapons of mass destruction against, selectively, nations which might possess or develop them, while withdrawing from the Anti-ballistic Missile Treaty, undermining the Nuclear Non Proliferation Treaty by disseminating nuclear technology to India, deploying a national missile defense system, and supporting the militarization of outer space and a new generation of useable nuclear weapons for a nation which already has six thousand—two thousand of them armed for launch within fifteen minutes. He evidently sees nothing anomalous in this proposition and seeks some kind of global hegemony, a unipolar world, the New American Century of the neo conservatives, in a multi or non polar reality—an un-American and unrealistic proposition.

Great empires were creditors and producers; they invested in their domains, reaped rewards and bestowed benefits before they failed. They manifested in different ways the "tolerance" cited by Amy Chua in her book, *Day of Empire: How Hyperpowers Rise to Global Dominance—And How They Fall.* Japan contributed to the industrialization and agricultural development of Formosa after the war of 1895, later but harshly, also of Manchuria and Korea when the military controlled in Japan. European imperialists were more exploitive. They all failed. The U.S. follows. It was the world's great producer and creditor; now it is the world's great debtor and consumer. It relies on America's first standing, professional military for empire. Britain's colonies supplied troops—roughly half its troops in World Wars I and II. The U.S. does not have colonies. Its coalitions are increasingly unwilling. The high tech weaponry of empires could with efficiency and near impunity kill the natives.

In 1957, in the torrid summer heat of Omdurman near Khartoum in the Sudan, Nancy and I pondered the site where in 1898 Anglo Egyptian forces used artillery and maxim guns to slaughter thirteen thousand lightly armed Sudanese, losing forty-eight British troops. They were restoring their authority and avenging the death of Governor General Gordon in Khartoum. The Sudanese had been inspired by the Mahdi, a pious, charismatic predecessor of Osama Bin Laden, to rise up for their faith, their brethren and their lands. They had defeated the Anglo Egyptian forces, taken Khartoum and killed Gordon.

Vietnam, Laos, Cambodia, Korea, Haiti, Kosovo, Bosnia, Somalia, Cuba, Nicaragua, Afghanistan, Iraq—one has to go back through all the wars, strikes and incursions to World War II, to find a U.S. military operation with a successful political outcome, unless one counts the invasion of Grenada. Most were counterproductive. More are under way, as in the Horn of Africa. More are on the neo conservative drawing boards, as in Iran and Syria. As for Grenada, Prime Minister Thatcher was puzzled, to put it diplomatically, by her "Ronnie" Reagan's unforewarned invasion of a tiny member of the British Commonwealth.

World War II was an heroic war of national defense. Before it, America's attacks, wars and incursions were often counterproductive, as in the Philippines, though then, as always, cloaked in lofty purpose. This sad story of America's popular, self righteous military adventures for ulterior purposes and the cumulative counterproductive consequences is well documented by former *New York Times* foreign correspondent Stephen Kinzer in *Overthrow: America's Century of Regime Change from Hawaii to Iraq*. It is not ended.

Economic sanctions are a form of warfare; export and investment controls were for many years my direct responsibility in the Senate, and a subject of much study by my Subcommittee on International Finance. As mentioned in the preceding chapter on Foreign Policy and Diplomacy, we sought to break down the calculated U.S. isolation of countries and open them to the sunshine. Sanctions typically impoverish and demoralize innocent people, especially the most vulnerable. The elderly and children are often consigned to slow death from malnutrition and insufficient medical care. (Upwards of forty thousand children may have lost their lives to the U.S. led sanctions in Iraq.) Leaders like Saddam Hussein remained unscathed. Like Fidel Castro, they have Americans to blame for the suffering of their demoralized peoples. Foreign economic competitors pick up the business in Cuba, Iran, Myanmar and elsewhere. Embargoed countries develop their own technologies with military applications, most obviously in Russia and China. Its sanctions exhausted, the U.S. has shot itself in the foot again and shot its wad—short of military force. But the U.S. military is already stretched thin by small wars. So, the U.S. becomes dependent on other nations. China quietly comes to the diplomatic rescue in North Korea and Sudan. Arab states of the Gulf Cooperation Council quietly negotiate trade and security arrangements with Iran as the U.S. and some Europeans try to tighten sanctions. They invest in Iran—and hedge their relations with the U.S., seeking stability in a region destabilized by the U.S. The U.S. is sanctioning itself.

Von Clausewitz continues to be vindicated. America's economic warfare is costly and ineffectual, at best. The inefficiencies of conventional war mount as the military industrial complex develops ever more expensive technological fixes for the failures of the last war and the antiseptic, politically correct requirements of the next. According to the General Accounting Office, the Pentagon doubled the amount committed to new weapons systems from $790 billion in 2000 to $1.6 trillion for 2007. Ninety-five major systems exceeded their original budgets by $295 billion and are being delivered almost two years late on average. In most cases the systems also fail to deliver promised capabilities. High tech "megasystems" include $5.2 billion for one Littoral combat ship, and escalating billions for advanced submarines, destroyers, fighters (planned for Cold War with the Soviet Union) and high tech tanks and other energy inefficient vehicles unusable in terrain such as I faced in Korea as a tank platoon commander. My jeep took me on reconnaissance missions where no Humvee could go. Our tanks served mundane purposes in the real world, like providing close cover and transport for weary infantrymen. The fuel guzzling new tanks throw off too much heat. Such realities on the ground are far from the realities in Washington today. Air strikes against insurgents embedded in civilian populations carry ever larger political, moral and financial costs. The war is on the ground, the terrain of the "insurgents." The Pentagon's response in 2007—popular in Congress—includes fifteen thousand new "bomb resistant" vehicles for $2.4 billion, plus. These fuel guzzling vehicles must be transported by air and weigh in at around thirty thousand pounds. One of them has already been destroyed by a bomb which probably cost about three hundred pounds of fertilizer.

The new American soldier is catered and laundered by the likes of Halliburton and Kellogg, Brown and Root. A grievously wounded veteran, Tammy Duckworth, reports that troops in Iraq are catered dinners of lobster and filet mignon by Halliburton, per its cost plus contract with the Pentagon. A Ghurka did not require a kevlar vest at $10,000, let alone lobster and gambling and beauty parlors for America's new "professional" military. Sergeants did not require pedicures in my time. Corporals did not become pregnant. Military duties were not outsourced to Blackwater and other costly, politically connected contractors. Their immunity from prosecution for violent crimes in Iraq is costly, too. In Japan, American forces, including dependents, were confined in February, 2008 to their bases in an attempt to assuage public opinion outraged by another alleged rape. Prime Minister Fukuda publicly complained of a U.S. failure to "control" its military.

The cost of four of years of war in Iraq and Afghanistan adjusted for inflation runs several times the cost of Vietnam, not counting costs of reconstruction. No end is in sight. The Bush Administration 2009 budget will increase defense spending 70 percent since it came to power even without funding for more than a small part of its wars in Afghanistan and Iraq for 2009. According to Secretary of Defense Gates, total defense spending for the year could exceed $685 billion. Costs of war estimates vary; no one can foresee the costs of an endless war against shadows and the jihad it spreads. The cost of operations in Iraq, Afghanistan and "elsewhere" could amount to $1,700 billion between 2001 and 2017, according to the Congressional Budget Office. It is already more than the inflation adjusted cost of World War II—a war with the armed forces of Japan, German and Italy.

According to a study by Linda Bilmes of Harvard and Nobel Laureate Joseph Stiglitz of Columbia, a "moderate" cost scenario of the Iraq war as of January, 2007 had already produced a cost of $1,184 billion, including medical and rehabilitation treatment, increased debt service and higher recruitment costs, but not including costs to other countries and such subjective consequences as more power to the jihadists and loss of authority and security for the U.S. The cost of cultural atrocities in Mesopotamia, the "cradle of civilization," is inestimable. After occupying Baghdad, U.S. authorities allowed the fabled National Museum to be plundered. Archeological sites across Iraq are still being looted. To this day, U.S. bases are located and heavy equipment moved with little concern for the archeological costs of war. The ruins of Babylon, stretching back three thousand years, are host to a U.S./Polish transport depot.

Even with misleading assumptions about defense spending and budget cuts for law enforcement, environmental protection and health and human services, the Bush Administration has proposed a $3.1 trillion Federal budget for fiscal 2009, an increase of 50 percent in seven years. American soldiers pay the costs of war with broken lives and bodies.

Samuel Adams warned that standing armies were "always dangerous to the liberties of the people." The tradition of the citizen soldier sustained civic engagement, protected liberties and guaranteed political accountability.

Overgrown military establishments are under any form of
government inauspicious to liberty, and are to be
regarded as particularly hostile to Republican liberty.

President George Washington,
Farewell Address, 1796

Letter to his unborn son found on a British soldier killed
in World War I:

The spirit of wonder and adventure, the token of
immortality will be given you as a child. May you keep it
forever, with that in your heart which always seeks the
gold beyond the rainbow, the pastures beyond the desert,
the dawn beyond the sea, the light beyond the dark. May
you seek always in good faith and high courage in this
world where men grow so tired. Keep your love of life
but throw away your fear of death. Life must be loved or
it is lost, but it should never be loved too well. Keep your
wonder at great and noble things like the sunlight and
thunder, the rain and the stars, the wind and the sea, the
growth of trees and the return of harvests and the
greatness of heroes. Keep your heart hungry for new
knowledge; keep your hatred of a lie; and keep your
power of indignation.

Since the government no longer has the competence to adopt a
draft which could address inefficiencies of war while practicing the
democracy for which it is ostensibly fought, enlistment bonuses run to
$40,000 for the Army and Marines, with re-enlistment bonuses as high
as $150,000. Raising bonuses, offering lifetime benefits, lowering
standards with "moral waivers" for recruits who have committed
multiple misdemeanors and/or felonies, luring foreigners with promises
of citizenship, the Army and its growing army of recruiters still cannot
lure enough young men and women to meet its quotas. Half its recruits
without a high school education do not complete basic training.
Increasingly, young, highly trained commissioned officers opt out of the
Army after five years of service. By outsourcing military duties to
politically connected contractors, it stimulates competition for
manpower and higher costs in other countries as well. The funded
lifetime cost of a U.S. soldier already exceeds $4 million. Military

manpower objectives may be achieved by the economic misery and unemployment to which American militarism contributes.

As a percentage of GDP, the costs of the military-industrial-intelligence complex might have been afforded by the old America with a dynamic, globally dominant economy. But these costs for the new accelerate its decline in a highly competitive global economy. Expenditures for health and human services, law enforcement, the environment, education, research, foreign economic assistance, Medicare, and the infrastructure are cut or neglected. In Illinois a corporation with a promising Internet-based system for managing energy efficiently shifts resources to homeland security because "that is where the money is." A $3 trillion plus deficit budget must be financed by more debt. The White House acknowledges that national debt will nearly double from $5.7 trillion at the end of President Bush's first year to an estimated $10.38 trillion in 2009. The military is stretched thin, and the new America depends on China and other countries to finance its wars with credit—or to buy its assets.

Military planners cannot be expected to weigh the implications of their planning and spending for the economy. They do not balance the nation's liabilities against their assets, let alone weigh the effect of their expenditures on the country's precarious economic condition and its implications for national security. In the name of national security, the government buys national insecurity. Congressmen go along; indeed, they often accelerate the decline. They defend redundant bases in their districts and the weapons systems of defense contractors. They equate defense with money and cannot afford to be "soft" on defense. This is a generalization unfair to some, but Congressmen, like elected judges, tend to go along with their investors, including defense contractors—and the military—and local constituents at defense installations. There are no peace contractors. They must support a nation at "war," as Alexander Hamilton warned and Herman Goering explained. It's easy.

As the inefficiencies of conventional warfare increase, the efficiencies of asymmetrical warfare increase. Its practitioners learned at Omdurman and from Ho Chi Minh to disperse. They have access to modern weapons and technology. They utilize television for propaganda and blackmail, the Internet for command and control and to disinform their enemies. Many have little to lose except their tortured lives and paradise to gain. The American military did little to plan or train for asymmetrical warfare until too late. That warfare requires language training and cultural sensitivity, more quick witted boots on the ground than the new military can afford. Locals it hires in Iraq for $10 per day are being killed; besides money is not a substitute for loyalty. And it will run out. "Insurgents" from many nations receive invaluable training and experience in Iraq and Afghanistan. As has been mentioned, they infiltrate countries far distant and destabilize a nuclear Pakistan. The most imminent nuclear threat, acknowledged by Mohammed El Baradei, Chief of the International Atomic Energy Agency, is not from a nation which would be "pulverized" (Iran) but from extremists, nurtured on "anger, humiliation and desperation." Nuclear materials are disappearing, he reports. For terrorists, deterrence is not a relevant concept. Terrorism becomes the international "terrorist scene" which I predicted in 1979 (see the following Chapter) spreading like a contagion through inspired but disconnected cells and individuals to countries perceived to be aligned with the new America and Israel, the occupiers of Islam, and America's "apostate" allies in the Islamic world.

The Black Book comprehends all manner of politician but not a "War President" who, lacking experience in foreign affairs, international finance and the military or even a detectable prior interest in the world, takes his certitude from God and advisors with messianic motives, limited real world experience and cunning partisan purpose to wage undeclared and unprovoked "war." For them and many politicians war is easy.

> We cannot have peace if we are concerned only with war. War is not an accident. It is the logical outcome of a certain way of life. If we want to attack war, we have to attack that way of life.
> *A. J. Muste, 1967*

> Why must you defend the country when your country seems to lie in peace around you?....It is not to make good the errors of the past that you are here but to make good the promise of the future.
> *Governor Adlai E. Stevenson,*
> Democratic candidate for
> President, September 20, 1952,
> addressing the commissioning
> ceremony for Adlai III and his
> fellow Marines, Quantico,
> Maryland

If we win men's hearts throughout the world, it will not be because we are a big country, but because we are a great country. Bigness is imposing, but greatness is enduring.

According to President Bush's Chief of Staff, Andrew Card, announcement of the war against Iraq was put off to September, 2002 because: "From a marketing point of view, you don't introduce new products in August."

21: Peace Is Hard

It is much easier to make war than peace.
Premier Georges Clemenceau, 1919

In the course of our global explorations, Nancy and I trailed the Israeli troops into the West Bank of Jordan and the Golan Heights of Syria after the 1967 Six Day War. We were on a junket to Israel sponsored by its Weizmann Institute. Expense paid junkets to Israel are routine for American politicians. I was a newly elected Illinois State Treasurer. But Nancy and I took an unexpected detour through the Golan Heights, Jordan and West Bank. We saw evidence of what in another time and place would be called ethnic cleansing—a city in the West Bank with no sign of inhabitants except one old man sitting on a doorstep, too frightened or shocked to speak.

Israel had spurned a cease fire with Egypt to occupy the West Bank of what was then Jordan and also attack Syria. We managed to clear an Israeli Army checkpoint, enter the Golan Heights of Syria and circumnavigate the Sea of Galilee by car. Most of the reported Syrian resistance to the Israeli attack had been to the north. In the area we traversed, homes had been abandoned, family possessions left behind, a child's book left open on the parlor table of a home we entered. Our photographs record a deserted city street, all the buildings severely and identically damaged with their characteristic metal shutters blown out from inside, contents spilled on the street. We saw no sign of human life in the Golan Heights beyond the checkpoint and little of shelling or combat, as if the inhabitants had been surprised and killed, expelled or without resistance had fled the sudden approach of Israeli troops. This impression is reinforced by reports of the destruction of Quneitra to the North. Israelis attribute its destruction to war damage, combat and resistance. Visitors report no signs of war damage or resistance, only the same signs of systematic destruction of a city fled by its inhabitants, which we recorded. (In 2005, U.S. and French officials complained about the Syrian presence lingering in Lebanon after its forces were invited in to establish and maintain stability in the 80's. Israel's uninvited presence in the Golan Heights of Syria was ignored.)

Our impressions are consistent with the theory of Admiral Thomas Moorer, former Chairman of the U.S. Joint Chiefs of Staff, that the carefully reconnoitered Israeli attack first by Mirage and Mystere jets and afterwards by torpedo boats against the USS Liberty, an American spy ship a few miles off the Sinai coast, was intended to prevent the Americans from monitoring Israeli communications and discovering Israel's plans for a surprise attack against Syria in the Golan Heights. That attack followed within twenty-four hours Israel's attack against the Liberty. Thirty-four Americans were killed; one hundred and seventy-one more were wounded, with more to die later from the trauma and neglect they suffered. The incident was hushed up and ascribed to a mistake—which Secretary of State Dean Rusk later acknowledged it was not. More recently, Ward Boston, Counsel to the U.S. Navy Court of Inquiry convened to investigate the incident, broke thirty years of enforced silence to confirm that the Court had been ordered to cover up the attack. He was angered by continuing attempts to whitewash the incident.

We visited a Palestinian refugee camp in Jordan, heard angry claims of Israeli atrocities in the West Bank and witnessed the horrible conditions in which another generation of displaced Palestinians was growing up. We crossed the Allenby bridge over the River Jordan (called the Hussein bridge by the Jordanians) to the West Bank where we were met by Bill Mauldin, famous cartoonist and dear friend, and Seymour Simon, a Chicago Democratic Ward Committeeman, later to become Cook County Commissioner and Illinois Supreme Court Justice.

In 1976, I visited the major Arab capitals of the Middle East and Tehran as Chairman of the Senate Subcommittee on International Finance, occasionally donning a black hat as Chairman of the Senate Subcommittee on the Collection and Production of Intelligence, to drop out of sight and meet with CIA station chiefs, a practice I followed in other regions, including the Soviet Union. They told me more of intelligence "sources and methods" than I was intended, or wanted, to know, and always seemed grateful for the unaccustomed attention.

The Operating Directives of these brave civil servants reflected the preconceptions of Washington and focused everywhere in those days on activities of the Soviet Union, to the neglect of turmoil beneath their feet. Recent critics of the CIA fail to recognize that foreign intelligence, an inherently flawed and fragile process, usually supports foreign policy—its collection priorities and estimates determined by the consumers, not the producers, of intelligence. The U.S. relies on foreign intelligence services which then included the Shah's service, Savak, for intelligence on Iran. It still relies on Israeli intelligence services for intelligence in the region. Foreign services support their own governments' policies. Israeli intelligence, which reportedly corroborated evidence of weapons of mass destruction in Iraq in 2002, may not have been flawed, as was later claimed. It may have been supporting Israeli government policy, luring the Bush Administration into an inexplicable war in Iraq, just as Savak lured the Nixon Administration into complacency about Iran.

After meetings with Syrian officials in Damascus, including a three hour meeting with President Haffez Assad, I drove to Beirut with Bill Buell, an accomplished and cheerful senior foreign service officer on loan to my staff. We were met at the Syria-Lebanon border by Al Fatah guerillas and—with submachine guns on the floor boards beneath our feet—careened down mountain passes to Beirut to meet with Yassir Arafat in his grubby headquarters. An explosion detonated outside the headquarters, perhaps for effect. Arafat and his aides—isolated from contact with American officials, then and thereafter, by politically opportunistic edicts reflecting and protecting U.S. preconceptions and ignorance—presented us a detailed proposal for systematic withdrawal of Israeli forces from the occupied territories accompanied by a UN peace keeping force and buffer zone. It was another proposal for a demilitarized West Bank and a peace agreement that respected the Jewish character of the State of Israel. In that conversation and in all but two of the conversations at the highest and at lesser levels throughout the region, we found an explicit willingness to accept the UN resolutions supported by the U.S. for a lasting settlement: a negotiated two state solution along the boundaries which pre-existed the1967 war. Though it was difficult to get a reading in Lebanon, which seemed hopelessly at war with itself, all Arab governments, also Iran and the PLO, were willing to accept Israel's existence as a state with minor border revisions and some provision for Palestinian refugees denied their right of return, as a basis for peace. This was confirmed many times over many years in conversations with American experts, as well as Arab officials in the region. It was confirmed publicly by the Palestinians in 1988, at Oslo in 1993, and at Taba in 2000.

The only Middle East governments which rejected this basis for settlement in my conversations in 1976 were those of Iraq and Israel. After delivering the Arafat proposal to the Shah of Iran (Ambassador Richard Helms in attendance), thinking he might have influence with the Israelis to whom Iran supplied oil (he assured me he would refer it to his foreign minister), we returned to the United States and delivered the proposal to the State Department where it was promptly leaked, forcing Arafat to repudiate it. No Arab leader could publicly agree at that time to sacrifice the Palestinian refugees' "right of return" except as part of a comprehensive settlement on UN lines which they were all willing to support, except in Baghdad. There, my Kurd driver— who worked for the U.S. Representative (the U.S. had no embassy)—limped because his toenails had been torn out by minions of Iraq's Baath regime for having been insufficiently forthcoming during one of his periodic interrogations. This was Saddam Hussein's regime, soon to be supported with cash and intelligence by the Reagan Administration when it was using weapons of mass destruction against Iranians and Iraqis. (According to reports out of Jordan, the Iraqi Baathists were also supported by the U.S. in the 1960's when they were contesting with the communists for power.)

My Report to the Senate in April 1976 predicted an "explosion" in Iran which was soon to follow with the demise of the Shah's government, a product of American regime change in the 1950's and object of American assistance, including transfers of nuclear technology by the Nixon-Kissinger Administration. The Shah's government was a jewel in the crown of the Nixon Doctrine, which also postulated the incompetent and corrupt Lon Nol regime in Cambodia as a regional center for defense against the spread of Soviet communism. (Lon Nol's regime led to the cruel "ruralization" of Cambodia by the demonic Khmer Rouge regime and invasions by Vietnam and China.) The Report also predicted the downfall of President Sadat of Egypt who, like Prime Minister Rabin of Israel, his fellow peace maker, would soon fall victim to assassins doing "God's work."

In 2001, Prince Abdullah of Saudi Arabia (now King Abdullah) with whom I had met in 1976 at Riyadh, together with the infirm Prince Fahd, later to become the infirm King, publicly proposed a settlement along the lines of the UN resolutions. By then, all the Arab states, even Iraq, publicly accepted this formula for peace in the Middle East—but not the Likud government of Israel. It was still creating the "facts on the ground" that would make peace impossible. My official Report to the Senate observed of Israeli officials: "It is ironic but not unusual; a democratic government is hemmed in by the immoderate and passionate sentiments of a minority. Israel's settlements in the West Bank and Golan Heights are defended angrily in public—not at all in private. . . As Israeli analysts said, the military balance is shifting the wrong way. But war in the Middle East is easier than peace."

More recently all the Arab States have officially affirmed their willingness to accept the Abdullah proposals, including recognition of the State of Israel, on this basis once supported by the U.S. The Report of the Iraq Study Group acknowledged the centrality of the Israeli-

Palestinian issue to peace throughout the Mideast. It, too, recognized the only formula for peace. But war is easier.

In 1976, there were only about forty-five hundred Israeli settlers in the West Bank. But Palestinian bitterness and frustration was mounting. (Since 1948, more than eight million Palestinians have been uprooted and torn from their homeland to make way for Jews seeking a homeland.) In Jordan I visited a Palestinian school for the children of "martyrs," the combatants, including terrorists, who had lost their lives in the Palestinian resistance. It was not difficult to divine horrors to come unless the U.S. represented its interests— and Israel's —in peace. Anyone who made the effort could see reality. It required no foreign intelligence: only a willingness to confront uncomfortable truths and intelligence of a cerebral sort. Ignorance is often convenient and, to repeat, easily acquired, even required in the U.S. American officials were blind to Arab perceptions by choice and governmental edict, forbidden contact with the Palestinian Liberation Organization. Arabs once contributed to this reciprocal exercise in enforced ignorance, foolishly trying to isolate Israel with an economic boycott.

Offended by that assault on American sovereignty, I authored the Arab Anti-Boycott Law which made it unlawful for American companies to comply with the boycott of Israel. It was possible to represent Israeli and American interests. But by design and ignorance, American politics was largely cut off from Middle East reality and prey to stereotypes. The U.S. was isolating itself. Peace was made impossible, war easy. As is described from on the ground by British journalist Robert Fisk in *The Great War for Civilization,* the "peace process," including the Oslo Accords, destroyed all hope for peace. It became a process for temporization, requiring the Palestinians to guarantee the "security" of their occupiers, an impossible contradiction which enabled Israel to continue cementing its presence in Palestine while consigning the stateless Palestinians to impoverished, disconnected ghettos. President Bush's 2007 "peace" conference in Annapolis is but the latest example of this temporization called "peace process."

In *The Accidental Empire: Israel and the Birth of the Settlements 1967-1977,* Gershom Gorenberg details how between the 1967 war and 1977, Israel's indecisive government slid down the path of least resistance to seek biblical redemption and security in land with settlements in the West Bank, Gaza, Golan and East Jerusalem which it annexed. For a time the Israeli government attempted to conceal the illegality of its settlements by calling them military encampments. A senior Israeli official wept at the sight of Israeli bulldozers crushing Palestinian homes and orchards—and his dreams of a democratic Israel at peace with its neighbors. He was symbolic of many, but the religionists and militarists carried the day. Empire prevailed. The U.S. did little to resist Israel's defiance. Henry Kissinger quietly assured the Israeli leadership that the U.S. would never require a return to the 1967 boundaries, and with characteristic guile, the "realist" advised Israeli officials not to advertise the settlements.

The Likud came to power in Israel in 1977. Its leaders, notably Menachem Begin—the first Likud Prime Minister and former leader of the terrorist Irgun gang—proclaimed that ancient Judea and Samaria, the West Bank, were part of the Land of Israel; or as Defense and Foreign Minister Dayan had put it earlier, the "Empire of Israel." Israel's objectives had become overtly those of its religious, nationalist right, defying the ideals for which it was created with American leadership and the liberal, humane traditions for which Jews are still noted.

The morning after signing the Camp David accords in 1978 which promised "autonomy" for the Palestinians after a five year interim, or so Presidents Carter and Sadat thought, Begin came to a closed meeting with Senators where I heard him repudiate autonomy. In retrospect, autonomy may have meant for him autonomy for Palestinians, not for Palestine—a distinction missed by Presidents Carter and Sadat of Egypt, but not their associates, according to my friend, then Vice President Mondale. Egypt's Foreign Minister resigned in protest. With Egypt neutralized by a "peace agreement" with Israel, the Likud government aggressively promoted settlement of East Jerusalem, the West Bank, Golan Heights and Gaza. It was creating "facts on the ground" which would make autonomy for Palestine—and peace—impossible on the "land for peace" formula of the UN Resolutions supported by the U.S. The religious claims of Zionists and the secular claims of Palestinians were irreconcilable. The U.S. was subsidizing Israel's defiance of U.S. policy which deemed the settlements "obstacles to peace." Isolated incidents of terrorism, an ancient tactic, were occurring in other parts of the world, notably in Northern Ireland. I decided it was time to begin the first in-depth Congressional study of terrorism. By subsidizing the Likud's illegal expanding occupation of Palestine, the U.S. would become vulnerable to attack. The Palestinians had no tanks and Apache gunships for their resistance. They would perforce resort to asymmetrical methods. Bill

Buell and I had sensed something of such preparations in the Palestinian school for the children of martyrs.

A year long study by the Senate Subcommittee on the Collection and Production of Intelligence led to the Comprehensive Counter Terrorism Act of 1979 which I introduced in the Senate, with the warning that it would be "irresponsible" to assume "it can't happen here." The statement went on to explain that:

> terrorist groups, finding their more common tactics such as airplane hijacking, no longer have their former shock value, will turn to more spectacular acts of mass disruption or destruction....Terrorism is increasingly becoming an international phenomenon as terrorist groups have formed various connections across national borders...what has emerged is not a terrorist international, in which a terrorist group in one country typically acts on behalf of a foreign group or power; rather it is an international terrorist scene...in which groups from different countries offer each other training, financial and operational support, and safe havens.

The Act conferred on the President statutory authority to organize government at all levels for management of disasters, and amended the Foreign Intelligence Surveillance Act to liberalize standards for judicial approval of electronic surveillance to help penetrate terrorist cells and prevent disasters. As mentioned earlier, we feared an overreaction to an act of terrorism, and sought to balance the claims of privacy and security with a standard that would better enable the authorities to anticipate and prevent terrorism.

Civil libertarians opposed it. The effort was ignored by the American media. In 1980, I offered an amendment on the Senate floor reducing U.S. assistance to Israel by $200 million per annum until such time as the President could certify that its settlement policies were consistent with U.S. policy. (By 2006, U.S. annual assistance for Israel amounted to about $4 billion.) The $200 million was an estimate of what the U.S. government contributed to Israel's illegal settlements in the West Bank and Gaza. I did not expect the amendment to be approved, but wanted to demonstrate that—given a choice between supporting the U.S. or Israel's defiance of the U.S.—the Congress supported Israel's lobby—and defiance.

No Senator defended the settlements. Some raced to the floor to record their opposition to the amendment, arguing that the timing of the amendment was wrong, we had to give the Israelis confidence, they couldn't be pressured and so on. Senator Jacob Javits of New York suggested I be "even handed." I pointed out that the bill authorized no money for Palestinians, implying that to be even handed, the Senate would eliminate all funding for Israel. He offered no response. The amendment received seven votes, one of them cast by the redoubtable Majority Leader, Robert Byrd, who then and many times since has demonstrated the "courage to be right." After the vote, the late Senator Quentin Burdick, a craggy faced friend with a big heart, representing North Dakota which was not exactly a citadel of Zionism, said ruefully, "Sorry, Adlai, but I am up for re-election." Campaign contributions go a long way in North Dakota, and it doesn't matter any more if they come from out of state. The amendment would have received more votes in the Knesset. War, like ignorance, is easy, not peace. The President and Congress failed to act until after 9/11, and then—as we feared— overreacted, playing into the hands of terrorists. The mere claim of a "war" on terrorism confirms for many Osama Bin Laden's complaint of a "war" against Islam. The American media ignored the vote on my amendment, but not the Israeli lobby.

Terrorists have many motives and methods. Generalizations are difficult. The sophisticated, politically animated terrorist seeks a reaction. Gavril Princip, the Serb nationalist who in 1914 assassinated the Austro-Hungarian Archduke in Sarajevo, did not expect to bring down the empire. He expected a reaction. The Austro-Hungarian empire obliged with an ultimatum which triggered World War I and the empire's demise. The Bush Administration has obliged with reactions that far exceeded the expectations of Osama Bin Laden. According to a recent statement attributed to Bin Laden, he expected an "economic" reaction. As mentioned in the preceding Chapter, the federal budget has plunged from surplus to deficit at the fastest rate in history, the federal debt increased to $1.9 trillion in fiscal 2008. The U.S. is rendered dependent on foreign creditors and investors, not to mention its dependence on a destabilized Middle East and Russia for oil. (Only 10 percent of the world's oil reserves are controlled by Western companies.) The costs to the economic and political security of the U.S. are not quantifiable. Osama Bin Laden received an "economic" reaction far beyond any conceivable expectations – and more. The U.S. was far more secure before 9/11.

After letting Osama Bin Laden escape in Afghanistan by pursuing him with bombers, the Bush Administration attacked his enemy, the secular Baathist regime of Saddam Hussein in Iraq, where jihaadists are now propagated and trained. That regime was also the enemy of Iran. Now, as I have already mentioned, Hezbollah and Iran are ascendant. The Taliban are recovering in Afghanistan and may come to terms with Iran, their former enemy. The U.S. has virtually isolated itself in the "court of world opinion." Suffice it to say, the Bush Administration took the bait. Nineteen men armed with box cutters could not bring all America down. Only its government can do that.

The many proposals for engaging Iran and all the countries of the region in a regional security arrangement require a resolution of the Israeli Palestinian conflict, as the Iraq Study Group and all Arab governments recognize. Since 1976, the U.S. subsidized Israeli occupation of Palestine has produced a Jewish population of about four hundred fifty thousand in about 40 percent of the West Bank and East Jerusalem. Israel spent over $14 billion on settlements, including infrastructure, but not on social services. Road blocks and curfews combined to cause a hopelessly disconnected, ungoverned, desperate Palestinian community. Of that, little needs to be said here. Even the American media gives some coverage to Israeli actions to oppress and intimidate Palestinians and cripple their Authority, kidnapping their elected leaders, while complaining of its inability to provide "security." Hamas, Hezbollah, Islamic Jihad, the Muslim Brotherhood and other militants, some of whom accepted the 1967 borders as a basis for settlement, gained support with the attack in 2006 against Lebanon and with the killing of each Palestinian child. A million bomblets were scattered over the southern Lebanese population of six hundred fifty thousand, many of them made in America. Lebanese children will die and be maimed for a long time to come. Israel loses control. The Palestinians have little control to lose. Terror spreads as Israel is reduced to building a wall. As I write, a majority of Israelis and the government of Prime Minister Olmert acknowledge that the settlements were a mistake—too late.

Indignation towards Israel and its U.S. patron spreads throughout the world, leaving Americans and Israelis everywhere more vulnerable and alone. As is often the political dynamic, militants in Israel and Islam gain the upper political hand and produce relentless cycles of mutual violence, ignorance and hatred. Palestinians, like Iraqis, lacking Apache gunships, use their bodies for delivery of weapons against civilian and military targets. They, and their brethren throughout the Islamic world, Shiites and Sunnis, acquire more sophisticated weapons. Chemical, radioactive and biological weapons, the poor man's weapons of mass destruction, are not far beyond their reach, nor the nuclear materials for bomb production. Collective martyrdom is not inconceivable in Israel. Moderate Sunni governments are threatened. The contagion spreads. There is not now and never was a "peace process" —only that process for temporization as the levels of violence and intolerance mount and "facts on the ground" are created to make the two state solution and peace more remote.

In early 2008, the annual Global Peace Index drawn up by the Institute for Economics and Peace, together with the UK-based Economist Intelligence Unit, ranked 140 states according to their peacefulness as assessed by their international policies and domestic conditions, including crime and incarceration rates. Iraq ranked last, thanks to the U.S. led invasion. Iceland ranked first owing to its political stability and good relations with other countries; it has no standing army. Israel ranked 136 after Chad and before Afghanistan. Of the most peaceful states, 16 of the 20 were European. China ranked 67th. The U.S. ranked 97th. War is easier than peace.

All that is necessary for the triumph of evil is that good men do nothing.
Edmund Burke

Practical men, like owls, see clearly in the dim twilight of their preconceptions and are blinded by the bright light of truth.
Sir Francis Bacon

I know of no country in which there is so little independence of mind and real freedom of discussion as in America. The majority raises formidable barriers around the liberty of opinion; within these barriers an author may write what he pleases, but woe to him if he goes beyond them.
Alexis de Tocqueville, Democracy in America

In no part of the Constitution is more wisdom to be found than in the clause which confides the question of war or peace to the legislature, and not to the executive department....War is in fact the true nurse of executive aggrandizement. In war, a physical force is to be created; and it is the executive will which is to direct it. In war, the public treasures are to be unlocked; and it is the executive hand which is to dispense them....It is in war, finally, that laurels are to be gathered, and it is the executive brow they are to encircle. The strongest passions and most dangerous weaknesses of the human breast; ambition, avarice, vanity, the honorable or venial love of fame are all in conspiracy against the desire and duty of peace.

James Madison

22: Epitaph for Adlai III

I quarrel not with far-off foes, but with those who, near at home,
cooperate with, and do the bidding of those far away, and without
whom the latter would be harmless.
Henry David Thoreau

I did not seek reelection to the Senate and left it in January, 1981
when my second term expired. A year later I ran for Governor of
Illinois, seeking to get my hands on the "levers," reform the government
of a state which had been good to my family for many generations, and
perhaps influence national policy from the Governor's office as my
father had.

I won the Democratic nomination with little opposition and
pledged to make the election a test of American politics, demonstrating
that it was still possible to "trust the people with the truth, all the truth."
The results were ambiguous. I detailed a program for state economic
development and reform. I campaigned the county courthouses, the
streets and byways of Illinois, as in the past, debated "early and often"
and took no polls, explaining I did not need them to tell me what was
right. I knew the people of Illinois in my bones and needed the money
saved. Support from organized labor was lukewarm, largely because of
my opposition to trade protection and support of pro-competition
policies. The Israeli lobby was the problem. Word spread from its nerve
center, the American Israeli Political Action Committee (AIPAC) in
Washington, through its network of organizations and political action
committees across the country. Campaign contributions dried up and
shifted to the opposition. Nancy and I were reviled as anti-Semitic.
Some in the press turned hostile. Jewish Democratic Committeemen
wilted under pressure. Jewish friends and supporters were also reviled.
They included Philip Klutznick, former U.S. Ambassador at the U.S.
Mission to the UN, Secretary of Commerce and Chairman of the World
Council of Jewry, who was a family friend and advisor. Klutznick was a
veteran of the real world and an embodiment of the liberal, humane
Jewish tradition. Like many, he supported my opposition to the
settlements policy of the Likud. Unlike some, he was steadfast in my
support.

Nancy and I shared a country home with Milton Fisher and his
family. He was a former law partner, treasurer of my campaigns, and
Jewish. He called AIPAC headquarters in Washington to inquire why it
was waging an aggressive campaign against Stevenson who was

running for governor and would have no say over foreign policy. Fisher, the anonymous caller, was told Stevenson was anti-Semitic and that if he was not stopped in Illinois he would run for President—a thought which had in fact crossed my mind.

The Lobby, known as THE Lobby, attacked most every candidate for any public office who opposed Israeli policies or its radical formulations of Israeli policy. It aims to intimidate American Jews and politicians —and succeeds. Since Israeli atrocities are well documented by Israeli organizations such as B'Tselem, the Public Committee against Torture in Israel, Physicians for Human Rights Israel, and independent organizations such as Human Rights Watch and Amnesty International, and the facts of its occupation are beyond any rational dispute, the reflexive charge of anti-Semitism has been institutionalized as a response to criticisms of Israel.

In *Beyond Chutzpah,* Professor Norman Finkelstein explains that since Israel is the "Jew among nations," any criticism of it is seen as anti-Semitic. Thus, Jews as well as non Jews are anti-Semitic. He was strongly supported by the faculty and students of DePaul University, but first denied tenure by its administration for no apparent reason, except his courage; later he was denied a classroom and forced to resign from the faculty. In early 2006, Professors John Mearsheimer of the University of Chicago and Stephen Walt of Princeton published an article in London after its rejection in New York, explaining at length why U.S. policy toward Israel should be a subject of debate in the U.S. Their intellectually unassailable suggestion attracted the familiar, automatic complaints of anti-Semitism, thereby underscoring their point. In 2007, they published *The Israeli Lobby* which documents in three hundred fifty heavily footnoted pages the atrocities of Israel, the tactics of The Lobby, and the price paid by Israel and the U.S. for its intimidation of American policy makers. The authors were routinely invited by the Chicago Council on Global Affairs to discuss their book at a Council program. The President of the Council later withdrew the invitation, explaining that it was unable to secure representatives for the "other side." There is no "other side" to the documented, observable facts of Israel's occupation of the West Bank, Gaza, East Jerusalem and the Golan Heights, which is why The Lobby resorts to character defamation, charges of anti-Semitism, and such heavy-handed tactics as suppressing speech. A book by Jimmy Carter which likened Israel's policies in occupied territories to apartheid provoked the same familiar response.

The consequences of U.S. support for Israeli policies in the Middle East cause these tactics to backfire. They draw public attention to its power to intimidate American politicians. All 2008 Presidential candidates swear unqualified support for Israel, the Middle East's "democracy" and America's ally, though Barack Obama had the temerity to express sympathy for Palestinians for which he was chastised. One candidate, a Republican, proposed extending the U.S. nuclear umbrella to Israel by giving it NATO membership.

The Lobby's control of U.S. policy in the Middle East, its espionage and illicit origins as a foreign agent, are documented in *Foreign Agents* by Grant F. Smith. Finkelstein, Mearsheimer, Walt and others explain that The Lobby represents neither Israel nor the liberal, progressive opinions of most American Jews. It is The Lobby by default with a well-developed network of individuals and organizations trained to react against critics of Israeli policies and reward its political minions with money. It preempts and intimidates mainstream Jews. Organizations like Israel Policy Forum, Americans for Peace Now and Brit Tzedek v'Shalom are simply outgunned. Members of Congress follow The Lobby no matter the policies and interests of Israel or the U.S. Israeli Prime Minister Rabin complained of The Lobby's hard line. The 1995 Act of Congress supporting movement of the U.S. embassy in Israel from Tel Aviv to Jerusalem was embarrassing to the governments of the U.S. and Israel. "New Jews," including organizations like the Jewish Institute for National Security Affairs and Washington Institute for Near East Policy, have taken over and coalesced with neoconservatives and Christian fundamentalists to undermine the U.S. and Israel. Indeed, neoconservative and Jewish authors of the project for the New American Century— the program for Greater Israel and regime change in Iraq, Iran and Syria—are largely one and the same, and no part of U.S. and Israeli mainstream opinion. As Israeli commentator Tom Segev wrote in Haaretz: "Had the U.S. saved Israel from itself life today would be better. . .the Israel lobby in the U.S. harms Israel's true interests." (Daniel Levy, a former advisor in the Israeli Prime Minister's office, elaborates at length in *The American Prospect*, July/August, 2006.)

Polls in Europe demonstrate that anti-Semitism is now largely a function of Israel's policies in Palestine. Anti-Semitism becomes a tragic creation of Israel and its lobby. Critics of Israeli policies, Jews and Christians, dreamed of a democratic Israel at peace with its neighbors. Now Israel lies behind a wall which disconnects Palestinians from one another and Israel. The history of walls is not reassuring. To preserve a Jewish majority in Israel, the government could be reduced to more ethnic cleansing.

> A Jewish Professor at the University of Illinois: "I may be required to wear the yellow star of David before I die." "Why?" from an incredulous Adlai III. "The American people may discover what their support of Israel has done to their country."

A week before the 1982 gubernatorial election in Illinois, I was losing by about 18 percent, according to self-fulfilling media polls which can dry up money and human energy. With little money for television, I spent the last days of the campaign barnstorming inner city communities, flailing away at the "flesh, the devil and all the other enemies of the Democratic Party," including Illinois' incumbent Republican Administration. I picked up some television news coverage, an unfamiliar experience. Harold Washington, my old friend and seat mate from the Illinois House of Representatives, the dynamic African American Congressman (later Mayor of Chicago), pitched in on the streets and at the subway stations. Come election night with almost all the counties reported, I was 200,000 votes ahead. But DuPage County, a large, suburban Republican county, held back reporting its returns. Late in the night it reported enough Republican votes to put my opponent ahead by 5,013 votes, 14/100 of 1 percent of the votes tallied for governor.

The campaign was re-energized and immediately exercised its right under Illinois law to examine ballots, fielding an army of volunteer lawyers in Illinois' 102 counties. They found widespread irregularities in many counties, including evidence of fraud. In Kankakee County, a public housing project came in 90 percent for me, as was to be expected. Absentee ballots from residents of the project came in 100 percent straight Republican. In little Washington County in southern Illinois, straight Democratic ballots were not counted. That was not part of "God's work" for its lone election judge. In other counties tens of thousands of ballots had not been initialed by an election judge, as required by law, though probably innocently. Cook County, the Democratic bastion, was using the now infamous punch card system for the first time. It was raining in northern Illinois on election day. Hands were wet; long lines formed as voters fumbled with damp cards and unfamiliar machines. The turnout in Chicago was far larger than expected. The polls were not kept open, and thousands of voters were turned away.

Our lawyers discovered the hanging and dimpled chads, the spoiled and uncounted ballots, the disenfranchised voters later to become famous. Experts then and since have also explained the ease with which the Diebold company's electronic voting machines can be programmed or hacked to produce the desired electoral result. (The CEO of Diebold, Walden O'Dell, wrote on August 14, 2003 that he was "committed to helping Ohio deliver its electoral votes to the President next year.") Our observers at DuPage County's central "remake center" on election night witnessed officials systematically punching the card ballots to "reflect the intention" of voters. Any such attempt in Democratic Cook County would have been met with nationwide howls of indignation and derision. Ukraine's central counting and remake center excited universal condemnation in its 2004 Presidential election for the same offense. Its Supreme Court ordered a new election which reversed the outcome. The evidence of massive voting irregularities was promptly presented to the Illinois Supreme Court by John Schmidt, former Associate Attorney General of the United States. Unlike the U.S. Supreme Court which heard the evidence one day and ruled the next in the Presidential election of 2000, the elected members of the Illinois Supreme Court tolled the clock. The justices waited until three days before inauguration of the Governor to rule by one vote that the evidence of irregularities was insufficient and that the Illinois recount statute was unconstitutional. There were no recounts under Illinois law.

Two Democratic Party leaders had warned me that one of the four Democratic Justices of the Illinois Supreme Court would vote with the three Republican Justices to deny a recount. He was a Zionist they explained, and what is more, his family received business from my opponent, Governor James Thompson. That Justice was Seymour Simon, the same Seymour Simon who, with Bill Mauldin, had met Nancy and me when we crossed over the Allenby Bridge into the occupied West Bank from Jordan in 1967 and demanded a detour to Nablus to see if what we had heard about ethnic cleansing was true.

To paraphrase the Black Book's story about the Coroner's Jury, the cause of my political death was "an act of God under suspicious circumstances." But for my efforts to disassociate the U.S. from the Israeli government's self destructive and defiant settlements policy in 1977 and prevent terrorism, the election outcome would never have been in doubt.

Unable to secure a recount, the Stevenson campaign could not quantify the under count later demonstrated in low income Democratic jurisdictions using the punch card system. The only study of the 1982 election concluded that the people of Illinois had been deprived of their choice for governor. In the election of 2000 after the punch card system finally attracted media attention, the Cook County Clerk found that one hundred twenty thousand ballots were not recorded for President in that County. Not until the Florida election of 2000 could anyone appreciate the extent of the 1982 debacle in Illinois when the voters of northern Illinois were contending on a rainy day with the punch card system for the first time. By then it was forgotten.

In his Farewell Address to "Friends and Citizens" in 1776, George Washington warned:

> So likewise, a passionate attachment of one nation for another produces a variety of evils. Sympathy for the favorite nation, facilitating the illusion of an imaginary common interest exists, and infusing into one the enmities of the other, betrays the former into a participation in the quarrels and wars of the latter, without adequate inducement or justification. It leads also to concessions to the favorite nation of privileges denied to others, which is apt doubly to injure the nation making the concessions, by unnecessarily parting with what ought to have been retained, and by exciting jealousy, ill-will, and a disposition to retaliate, in the parties from whom equal privileges are withheld. And it gives to ambitious, corrupted, or deluged citizens (who devote themselves to the favorite nation), facility to betray or sacrifice the interests of their own country, without odium, sometimes even with popularity; gilding with the appearances of a virtuous sense of obligation, a commendable deference for public opinion, or a laudable zeal for public good the base or foolish compliances of ambition, corruption, or infatuation.

I was re-nominated for Governor in 1986 with the largest plurality of all candidates of both parties. The outcome of the general election was not in doubt. However, a funny thing happened to me on my way to Springfield (paraphrasing Adlai II on his way to the White House thirty years earlier). Mayor Harold Washington and Edward

"Fast Eddy" Vrydolyak, Cook County Democratic Chairman, were contesting control of the Chicago City Council. They both supported me, but the Democratic Cook County organization paid little attention to the primary contests for State offices since the endorsed Democratic candidates had no serious opposition. The Organization was more concerned with local contests, especially in Chicago. Supporters of the Lyndon LaRouche cult filed candidates for Lt. Governor and Secretary of State. They had smooth Anglo Saxon names, Fairchild and Hart. The Democratic Party's endorsed candidates for Lt. Governor were George Sangmeister, a respected senior State Senator from suburban Will County, and Aurelia Pucinski, a bright and respected Cook County Clerk whose father, a Congressman, had lost the Senate contest to Charles Percy in 1966. Their central European names implied association with the Cook County Democratic organization, the Machine, which never sat well downstate and in suburbs. Voters went to the polls unaware of contests for these offices, and, unfamiliar with the candidates, abstained or voted in ignorance. I should have organized challenges to their nominating petitions, a fatal mistake. LaRouche candidates were nominated for Lt. Governor and Secretary of State. Party organization and responsibility were breaking down, and I was slow to appreciate the changes in American politics which I, the reformer, had helped set in motion.

The governor and lieutenant governor candidates were connected like Siamese twins—one vote for both. I could not shake the LaRouchie nominated for Lt. Governor or in good conscience ask voters to cast a vote for him, an anti-Semitic cultist who, if elected, would be within the proverbial heart beat of the governor's office. What is more, I feared their presence on the Democratic ticket would cost other candidates straight Democratic ticket votes. So, I resigned the Democratic nomination and organized a third Party, the Solidarity Party, which endorsed me for Governor, Mike Howlett Jr. for Lt. Governor, and Jane Spirgel for Secretary of State. We were then endorsed by the Democratic Party State Central Committee.

It was a forlorn and hopeless effort. But the Democratic Party, including Washington and Vrydolyak, pulled together and waged an energetic and imaginative campaign to educate voters to vote the straight Democratic ticket, and then cross over and also vote the Solidarity ticket. Howlett and Spirgel were dynamic, talented campaigners. Richard Dennis, a public spirited securities trader, believing the people of Illinois were entitled to a contest for governor, contributed $500,000. The Stevenson family put up some money (at about $100,000, it was a lot by our standards). But the Solidarity candidates were impoverished and running as candidates of an unfamiliar Solidarity party urging voters to vote Democratic. When the votes were counted, the regular Democratic state-wide candidates had won. As the Solidarity Party candidates, Mike Howlett and I received 40 percent of the votes cast for Governor and Lt. Governor.

The Illinois Democratic Party's most senior leaders urged me to run for Governor in 2002, assuring me no primary opposition. I missed the opportunity in 1976 when Mayor Daley urged me to run for President—and again in 2002, for Governor, the office I had always sought. It was too late in life. I declined the opportunity. Rod Blagojevich raked in the most money, won the nomination for Governor and was elected. He was the popular choice—not the Party's choice.

> A strong political tide washed a Congressman out of office, much to his surprise. At a victory dinner for his opponent, the old lawmaker was called upon for a few remarks. He rose and said dryly: "I am reminded of an epitaph on an old tombstone in the town cemetery. It reads: "I expected this, but not so soon."

23: China and Eight Immortals Crossing the Sea

To see the future, you must see the past.
Winston Churchill and *Confucius*

At times it is difficult to understand why or how a piece found its way into the Black Book, seeming to bear remotely, at most, on underlying themes of government, politics and peace. The Black Book acquires dimensions in time and space, becoming more ecumenical as it proceeds. There is no singularity to the Black Book, except its humor, faith in the human spirit and Reason, and aversion to the profane. Each leaf covers a surprise. The last is in China, where my adventures in the world will end.

The Black Book records no introduction to this Chapter. The Immortals originate with Tao in the Han dynasty. They were spiritual creatures who bridged the earthly world of yin and yang with Tao, a spiritual universe which animated all beings and things.

According to a Chinese legend, the Eight Immortals were celestial beings who performed miraculous feats. They could travel vast distances in a few seconds, produce any thing desired out of thin air, move mountains and seas at will and overcome evil enemies with magic weapons. One day the Eight Immortals were on their way to attend the birthday party of the Queen of Heaven when they were challenged to a battle by the King of the Dragons, ruler of the East Sea, who had many followers including the Clam Fairy, the Turtle Fairy and the Carp Fairy, as well as innumerable crabs, lobsters and other inhabitants of the sea.

After a fierce contest of magic, the Eight Immortals defeated the forces of the King of the Dragons and arrived safely for the birthday party of the Queen of Heaven. Each of the Eight Immortals had his own magic weapon and had achieved his immortality in a different way.

Chang Ko Lao - He was an elderly immortal. During the battle, he is said to ride his magic donkey and point his magic cane in the direction of the King of the Dragons.

Whenever he did not need the donkey for traveling, he would fold it up like a piece of paper and put it in his pocket, thus solving his parking problems. When he was about to travel, he would unfold the donkey and revive it with a sprinkling of water.

Han Shong Tse - He was a romantic immortal. He played his magic flute to benumb and paralyze the followers of the King of the Dragons. He could make himself invisible or change into any kind of person or animal merely by blowing on his own hair. After years of self-cultivation, he ascended to Heaven on the back of a flamingo.

The Kuai Lee - He was a crippled immortal. He used magic rays from his gourd to blast the King of the Dragons. An explanation of his being a cripple is that on one occasion when his spirit left his body to commune with the infinite, he left word that his body should be cremated if his spirit did not return after seven days. However, his disciple miscounted and cremated his body on the sixth day. Upon returning to earth, his spirit had to enter the only available body, the corpse of a crippled beggar.

Yu Tong Ping - He was a bearded immortal. He wielded a magic sword in his right hand and directed magic rays from his left hand against the King of the Dragons and his followers. One day he was invited to dine by a celestial emissary disguised as an old peasant. Before dinner, he drank some wine and became drowsy. In a dream, he saw himself achieving wealth, fame and position, finally becoming the most powerful person in the land. But after many years, when he was aged and feeble, he was deprived of all his possessions and reduced to utter poverty. Sighing, he woke up. Conscious of the futility of worldly effort, he decided to become a discipline of the celestial emissary and was subsequently taught the secret of immortality.

Ho Shan Koo - She was a girl immortal. She was the only female in the group and fought the King of the Dragons with her magic water lily. She was the fiancé of the Bearded Immortal. After he became immortal, he visited her in another guise to test her fidelity. Turning himself into a handsome young man of wealth, he courted her with all that money could buy. She resisted all his temptations. When he was convinced that she was true to him, he reverted to his own appearance and gave her a magic peach. Upon eating the peach, she became immortal and ascended to Heaven with him.

Chao Kuo Chiu - He was a Prince Immortal. He used his magic castanets against the pearl cannon balls emitted by the Carp Fairy, one of the Dragon King's followers. A brother of an Empress, he searched for the secret of immortality for many years. Finally, the Queen of Heaven appeared before him and asked: "What is the secret of life?" He did not reply a word but merely pointed first to Heaven and then to his own heart. Thus he was admitted to the ranks of Immortals and ascended to Heaven on a cloud. Later he returned to earth to test the honesty of human beings by peddling flower vases stuffed with money. Those who called him back to return the money were rewarded a thousand fold.

Han Tsung Li - He was the uncouth immortal. He used his magic fan against the Dragon King's lobster supporters. His fan had a magic mirror which reflected the whereabouts of evil spirits and annihilated them. A recluse who achieved immortality through the contemplation of nature, he needed no nourishment and subsisted on pure air. At night he would hang a bottle on the wall, jump into it and emerge the next morning.

Lang Tsai Ho - He was a young immortal. He is said to have been a boy genius. One day he followed a wood-cutter into a cave which led to a beautiful garden adjoining a magnificent palace. He spent several days in the cave and was given a basket of flowers on leaving. When he emerged, he discovered that several hundred

212

years had elapsed. The flower basket proved to be a
perpetual source of elixir and   secret weapons. He
dropped flower bombs on the Dragon King's Navy.

After I left the Senate in 1981, I returned to East Asia, albeit
with interruptions for the two campaigns for governor. The world's
economic and political centers of gravity were continuing to shift. On
numerous policy related and business assignments I began to cross and
re-cross the sea. (See footnote).

Of East Asia, there are few skeptics among those who can
remember it as I do. When I served in Japan and Korea with the Marines
in 1953-4, this vast kaleidoscopic region of some two billion people—
stretching from the Russian far east to Indonesia and Papua New
Guinea— commanded about 4 percent of global GDP. Korea was
devastated. The suffering was terrible: Korea had no economy to speak
of and was exporting human hair. Japan's economy was in ruins. The
insurgencies were under way in South East Asia and would continue
well into the 1970's. The Guv was downed in a helicopter over guerrilla
infested jungles of Malaya that year of 1953. China had been savaged
by world war and civil war. It was being isolated, contained by the
West. It awaited the self-inflected atrocities of the Great Leap Forward
and the Cultural Revolution to which it sacrificed a generation.

The U.S. commanded about half the world's global output
(GDP), half its supply of gold. Today East Asia commands over 30
percent of a vastly expanded global GDP, exceeding the shrinking U.S.
share of about 25 percent. Consumer spending is increasing at roughly
twice the rate of ours and is unburdened by our debt. Savings are high in
East Asia. It commands over $3 trillion in foreign exchange reserves,
about 70 percent of the world's total, as of early 2008. Its rebirth was
led by governments, including Japan's, which were only nominally
democratic. The governments of the chopstick economies—the market
economies of Chinese origin or derivation, including Japan—had the
power to be rational and basically subordinate consumption to savings,

---

The policy related responsibilities, past and present, include President of the
U.S. Committee of the Pacific Economic Cooperation Council; Co Chairman, East
Asia Financial Markets Development Project; President and Chairman, Japan America
Society of Chicago; Chairman of the Midwest US Japan Association; Member, US
Korea Wisemen Council; Advisory Director, Korean Economic Institute; Chairman of
the Midwest US China Association. Honors include the Order of the Sacred Treasure
with Gold and Silver Star, Japan, and Honorary Professor, Renmin University, Beijing,
PR China.

investment in human and physical infrastructures, industrial production and exports. Japan's rebirth was led by General Douglas MacArthur in an unspoken alliance with the Emperor and twenty years of oligarchic one party rule. East Asians are not decoupled from conditions outside the region, but now the dragon is stirring within.

China is a vast and ancient land of contradictions. Confucianism is being revived as China modernizes. It is a land of many spoken languages, ethnic groups, religions and growing economic disparities. It is possible to travel in a pressurized, oxygen supplied high speed train, a miracle of modern engineering, from Xinjiang province in northwest China across the "roof of the world" to Tibet and back centuries to glimpse the dying embers of a feudal theocracy where monks still make butter tea and chant their mantras. China resolves its contradictions methodically. It crosses many seas, developing a rational blend of practices and policies from East and West, from past and present, from democracy and autocracy. Its rising meritocracy balances the claims of market and government—methodically developing a mix of administrative, structural and macroeconomic measures to sustain economic growth and distribute its benefits. The Party cracks down on corruption which in the traditional Chinese ethic undermines legitimacy. It experiments with elections at the village level while continuing an imperial tradition of demonstrated sensitivity to the wishes and interests of the Chinese people.

China's annual growth of about 9 percent won't be linear or immune to stresses in a global economy, but it looks sustainable. Its byproduct, inflation, caused largely by pressures on food and housing costs, is requiring macroeconomic and administrative actions by the government, including restraints on bank lending and appreciation of the currency. Weakness in foreign markets, especially the U.S., cause concern, but most of the growth is generated by savings and investment by companies which only started paying dividends in 2007, and increasingly by consumption. Exports contribute less to growth. China's trade with the world is typically in deficit, except for its huge surplus with the U.S. Its exports and imports have grown by roughly 24 percent each year. Its merchandise imports rose from $53 billion in 1990 to almost $800 billion in 2006. Other industrial countries run trade surpluses with China, and they have no soybeans to export. Germany, for example, runs a trade surplus; its officials are not overly unhappy with China's exchange rate regime, notwithstanding the strong Euro.

Congressmen blame China for the U.S. trade deficit. But China's exports are still about 60 percent re exports, imports to which value is added in China before they are exported. China's largest exporters are foreign companies. Wages and consumer spending are rising rapidly, albeit from a low base. The percentage of Chinese living on less than $1 per day fell from 33 percent in 1990 to below 10 percent in 2005. Productivity and profitability are soaring as it moves up the capital and technology intensity ladders. Government expenditures for scientific research are increasing at about 20 percent annually, for education about 45 percent. The Chinese are methodical. Their perspective is long term and immune to the political and budgetary cycles which dictate U.S. policy—making U.S. government funded civil research, for example, less efficient. Multinational corporations move research centers to China to be near the stream of talent emerging from its universities.

China is not the ominous, monolithic Communist power of Congressional perceptions and mass media depictions. Its challenges are profound. Income and wealth disparities are large and mounting. The environmental challenges are horrific. The iron rice bowl is broken and unreplaced by a seamless safety net and universal health care system. Provinces and municipalities can be difficult to control. Energy needs to be managed more efficiently. But step by step, China responds to challenges. Reason undergirds China's succession to the United States as a center of power in a world which accords less influence to military force and more to economic dynamism and traditional diplomacy.

China's priorities, like its diplomacy, are a rough mirror image of the new America's. China pursues a Westphalian policy of non-interference in the affairs of others. It does not wage preemptive or religious wars. With a fifth the world's population, long borders and sea lanes to patrol, at times challenged by a U.S. armed Taiwan agitated by separatists and the Bush Administration's perceived efforts to achieve a nuclear first strike capability, it spends perhaps an eighth of what the U.S. spends on the military while modernizing its forces. It supports old America's post World War II international order, including UN peacekeeping operations. It supports coexistence in the world. The Chinese are distrustful of ideology and religiosity, having suffered both. They resolve or defuse most of their territorial differences (some linger in the South China Sea and with India), invest strategically for the long term, trade the world, over and over time bestow and reap benefits of empire without being imperialists. China's foreign direct investment is increasing by about 40 percent annually and branching from sources of materials, energy and commodities into service industries. China sends engineers and doctors to Africa along with its capital. China's diplomacy in Sudan and North Korea is quiet. And the world beats a path to its door.

In Beijing, September 2004, I attended a banquet in the Great Hall of the People for four thousand guests of the government, including Ministers, the President and Premier, generals, leaders of Party and State, Governors and Mayors, Ambassadors from the world over. It was China's Liberation Day, a day to celebrate the communist triumph in 1948. Any security was out of sight. No metal detectors or weapons were visible. Admission required only an invitation —not even a passport. President Bush's 2005 martial inaugural celebrations funded by corporate interests and wealthy individuals, as well as taxpayers, took place four months later in a Washington under siege. Pennsylvania Avenue, the parade route, was sealed off, its man hole covers welded shut. The President and Vice President were inaugurated behind bullet proof glass.

For many Americans, including businessmen and Congressmen, seeing foreign countries from inside and America from outside is an unnatural experience. They tend to transpose their values and methods to countries which don't accept them. Europeans and Asians are more conditioned by history to the necessities of co existence. In the chopstick economies of East Asia, especially China, transactions are still based on relationships, on ethics and trust developed over time. In America they are based on contract, inferentially, on distrust. Lucian Pye, the eminent sinologist, dubbed traditional China a "virtuosity." It produces engineers in a ratio to lawyers roughly the inverse of America's ratio. A survey of Fortune 1000 companies indicates they are spending about $56 billion per year on law firms in addition to their expenditures for in house counsel, with the rate of expenditure increasing annually by about 20 percent. Chinese spend little money on lawyers, let alone golden parachutes and back-dated options. They invest the savings – and produce about two hundred fifty thousand engineers annually.

Relationships developed over many years in East Asia contributed to the first business career in the Black Book, though I hasten to assure my ancestral coauthors that business has never been more than an occasional distraction. I organized companies which provided advisory services to U.S. and Asian companies crossing the sea. These companies provided mergers and acquisitions advisory services to Japanese companies entering the U.S. in the 1980's. They offered Asian institutions alternative investment products in the 1990's.

In China, our first venture was a failure. With Professor John Lewis of Standford University, a renowned China scholar and consultant to the Department of Defense, we organized the HuaMei (China America) Telecommunications Company. I knew U.S. export control law, having written much of it. We explained to Chinese officials that U.S. export controls were aimed at China—not at foreign joint ventures in China, which we in Congress did not anticipate when re-writing the Export Administration Act. To HuaMei, a foreign joint venture in China, we could transfer U.S. technology for development of broad band networks—China's Internet. Though foreign investment in telecommunications companies was illegal in China, HuaMei's Chinese partners were the Ministry of Posts and Telecommunications, the Ministry of Electronics Industries, and the Commission for Science and Technology and Industry for National Defense (COSTIND), an industrial arm of the Peoples Liberation Army. The Chinese government owned half of HuaMei. Barriers can be lucrative if you know how to get behind them. AT&T was the principal supplier of equipment. The project was enthusiastically supported by senior officials in the National Economic Council (White House), the Departments of Defense, State and Commerce, and the intelligence community. HuaMei was a means of developing an American toehold in what would become the world's largest telecommunications market. Certain U.S. government agencies also saw it as a source of intelligence, but we never had to formally involve them. With much fanfare HuaMei rolled out and demonstrated a prototype broadband network in Guangzhou, China's first.

Barriers in China remained to be overcome, but this promising U.S. government supported opportunity to develop a huge market in China was killed by Members of Congress. HuaMei became a symbol of difficulties created by the American government for Americans attempting to do business in unfamiliar places. Republicans who seized control of the House of Representatives in 1995 excitedly complained that HuaMei was transferring high technology to the Chinese military and enhancing its battle field capabilities! Potential American strategic investors in HuaMei fled. These Republicans commissioned a General Accounting Office investigation which concluded that HuaMei's telecommunications equipment had mysteriously disappeared. No one consulted me, nor, so far as I know, my associates. We could have explained the project, its support in the U.S. government, and led investigators to the equipment. But the merits were not at issue. The Yellow Peril was returning. Fears are easily stirred and exploited by demagogues. America was shot in the foot again. By 2008, China had more Internet users than the U.S., and the number was increasing by 30 percent annually.

In early 2008, China's protection of Han Chinese from murder and looting in Tibet was misrepresented in the western media to depict a forceful suppression of peaceful protest and demands for "freedom." China was widely condemned in the West, the run up to the Olympics used to stage protests. Nepal's brutal suppression of peacefully protesting Tibetans was virtually ignored in this media. The Chinese people—and many knowledgeable westerners—were appalled by this reappearance of yellow journalism. Apart from the lack of journalistic integrity, the China bashing could make it more difficult for Chinese authorities to cease their outdated, Maoist rhetoric and engage in discussions with the Dalai Lama leading toward more autonomy for Tibet, a part of China, as is acknowledged by virtually all governments, the Dalai Lama, and the Tibetan Buddhist hierarchy. I have been to Tibet only once. Like others, I never saw nor have heard of Chinese restrictions on the practice by Tibetans of their religion. Damage has been caused to religious sites by economic activity, and clearly Han Chinese have moved into Tibet and seized many of the opportunities stemming from the economic development China is stimulating. But China is gradually raising living standards for poor Tibetans historically burdened by their theocracy and primitive agricultural economy.

In 2005, I founded and with Leo Melamed, former chairman of the Chicago Mercantile Exchange, organized the HuaMei (China-America) Capital Company to help Americans and Chinese cross the sea— do business with one another. HuaMei represents China's first investment in the U.S. financial service sector (leave aside two old Chinese bank branches). It is an intermediary for mergers and acquisitions, private equity investments and investment advisory services. We and our associates organized it after more than a year of research and discussion with friends and senior officials in China. We did business in China the Chinese way, proposing a partnership of equals, a sound business proposition, and a relationship based on mutual trust. We offered the Chinese an opportunity to acquire 50 percent of the new HuaMei, promising to increase the valuation for a U.S. strategic investor once the Chinese had committed. It was a proposition which all but two of the seventeen Chinese securities companies we selected for discussions wanted to accept. We won our first choice—the China Merchants Securities Company, a well managed, profitable member of the venerable Merchants group organized in the 1870's.

I circumvented my fellow American lawyers, a familiar practice by then, to document the transaction with China Merchants on one page and—with my Chinese associate communicating across the sea at night by phone closed the transaction. We increased the valuation of HuaMei and brought in a U.S. strategic investor with extensive mergers, acquisition and business development experience. The transaction was far more complicated, lawyer intensive and expensive on the U.S. side than the Chinese side.

HuaMei is organizing, as I write in early 2008. With capital and management from an additional U.S. investor it may not live up to its potential, but it already helps foreign companies find their way in China—and helps Chinese find their way as they branch out in the world. Another enterprise assists Chinese early stage companies develop and commercialize new technologies, including alternative energy sources and applications. Contrary to press reports, Chinese companies seek foreign investors (and advisors). My colleagues and I want to help them. We try to cross the sea which divides cultures and practices for mutual opportunity, Americans in China and Chinese in America respecting and trusting one another, adapting to each other's ways. The Chinese have learned a thing or two in the last two thousand years and even then they were the world's most inventive people. Many of the problems we encounter crossing the sea are made in America—and unnecessary. America is challenged less by China than by its own political and corporate governance. China is an opportunity which occurs at most once in a century. To paraphrase Ambassador Stapleton Roy, it will only be our enemy if that is what we want.

24: Epilogue

Livy, the historian, describing the decline of civic discipline and morals at the height of the Augustan Age, wrote (about 4 B.C.) that Rome had reached the point where "…we can neither endure our vices nor face their remedies."

The wit and humor of the Black Book is largely out of place in the new, rancorous poll and money driven American politics. Its jokes about politicians and politics have a new edge. The political center which crossed party lines and governed in my times faded and with it much of the civility Stevensons knew. Multi-billion dollar investments in federal elections increase with each cycle. According to public opinion polls, the new American "democracy" is more representative of the investors in politics than the American people. Most Americans favor more money for education, medical research, job training, renewable energy, the UN and peacekeeping —and cuts for the military and Iraq. Non-discretionary spending for Medicare, Social Security and debt service increases. Fiscal restraint is, therefore, exercised at the expense of the environment and natural resources, social services including health care and education, public broadcasting, foreign economic and humanitarian assistance —objects of public preference and importance to the security and standing of the country in the world. Ideologues and religious fundamentalists excite war fevers, intolerance toward immigrants and preach conservative "values," but polls indicate continuing public support for traditional values—not the values of the religious right wing base of the new Republican party, America's first religious party.

An American government suspended habeas corpus. Senior officials have sought to legitimize torture, kidnapping, and unauthorized electronic surveillance. Corruption acquired qualitative and quantitative dimensions unfamiliar to the Black Book, its roots in the first Gilded Age and Cook County notwithstanding. Wall Street scandals and executive compensation demonstrated a decadence—defined by the philosopher historian, Jacques Barzun, as self-indulgence—which is unfamiliar to most developed countries and many lesser developed, notably in East Asia. The robber barons of the first Gilded Age built great industries, often ruthlessly, but they often gave back to community and country, too.

4700 years ago this was written on an Assyrian tablet: "Our earth is degenerate in these latter days; there are signs that the world is speedily coming to an end; bribery and corruption are common; children no longer obey their parents; every man wants to write a book, and the end of the world is evidently approaching."

The end of the world is not approaching, but what of America? The U.S. shows symptoms of decline by the criteria and precedents elaborated in historical and philosophical works of note. Edward Gibbon in his literary masterpiece *History of the Decline and Fall of the Roman Empire,* demonstrates that the Empire crumbled from within, owing to the breakdown of the rule of law, the spirit of the people and an inability to comprehend and respond to challenges from within and without. For Gibbon the decline of Rome was the effect of "immoderate greatness," including hubris, imperial overstretch and the bloody "ecclesiastical discord" invoked by Christianity's efforts to gain souls for God and subjects for the Church, especially during and after the reign of Constantine I. Arnold Toynbee in his massive *Study of History,* which I read in the winter of 1953-4 when life was slow and cold for Marines dug in below Korea's Imjin River, elaborates his theory of empires and civilizations responding to challenge or failing to respond and then fading from history. Paul M. Kennedy in *The Rise and Fall of the Great Powers* attributes their decline to imperial overstretch and the increasing economic and political costs, the weight of their armaments and foreign entanglements. In *Empire* —his chronicle of the British Empire—Niall Ferguson opines that the "main problem" was economic policy in a government subject to "democratic principles." He writes: "Investors could no longer be confident that already indebted governments would have the will to cut spending and put up taxes; nor could they be sure that in the event of a gold outflow interest rates would be raised to maintain convertibility, regardless of the domestic squeeze that implied." The British Empire collapsed. The great creditor had become a debtor. Late in the life cycle of nations, Kevin Phillips in *American Theocracy* opines that their economies enter a "financialization" phase already mentioned which is often accompanied by militarism and decadence. In *Decline of the West,* Oswald Spengler describes an organic development of civilizations over successive stages of birth, blossoming, maturity and decline. The driving forces of civilizations are the fundamental principles which gave them birth. The end phases are often associated with materialistic, militaristic and ideological aims replacing those fundamental principles. In *Day of Empire,* Amy Chua, cites the breakdown of tolerance and inclusivity. Judging by the criteria and precedents cited in these works, America is far along in the life cycle of nations and empires.

In September 2007, economists at German's Allianz and Dresdner Bank announced results of a study of "sustainability of fiscal and ecological development" in eighteen countries. It used indicators similar to those used by the European Union's Lisbon Agenda to assess economic competitiveness. The U.S. came in 17th. Owing largely to its fiscal prudence, current account surplus and energy resources, Russia ranked higher. China was more "sustainable" than the U.S. Sweden ranked first.

At the peak of American triumphalism after the Soviet Union had collapsed, one prominent neo-conservative theorist, Francis Fukuyama, proclaimed the "end of history" and the ultimate triumph of Western liberalism, free market ideals and democracy. (He is having second thoughts.) The Bush II Administration reflects this triumphalism but is caught up in a conflict between reality and its illusions. It propounds a Wilsonian faith in freedom, democracy and free markets for all peoples while pursuing oil and global hegemony or a Pax Americana—the New American Century— based on military power, technology and collaboration with governments which are at best nominally democratic.

Neo-conservative ideology collides with reality. Hamas wins in Palestine, Hezbollah in Lebanon; the Muslim Brotherhood gains ground in Egypt. Pakistan is destabilized. Iran's influence spreads. Friendly Sunni states are endangered. U.S. influence and authority shrink virtually everywhere outside the old Soviet bloc, a handful of sub-Sahara republics in Africa and Albania. The venerable London-based International Institute for Strategic Studies' annual survey in 2007 concluded that one of the most significant developments was the continuing decline of U.S. influence and authority in the world. In Spain, Argentina, Germany, South Korea, Bolivia, Nicaragua and Venezuela, candidates have won elections by distancing themselves from the America of George Bush. Prime Minister Blair of Britain was wounded by proximity, and Aznar in Spain. In Australia, a friendly nation, 57 percent of the people were reported in 2005 to believe the democracy of George Bush was as dangerous as the fundamentalism of Islam. His ally, Prime Minister Howard, bit the political dust in 2007.

In a poll of sixteen countries by the Pew Foundation, all but three reported a higher public opinion of China than the U.S. though many still distinguish between the U.S. and the Bush Administration. In Turkey, 9 percent of the people were reported in 2007 with a favorable opinion of the U.S. Governments of the Western Hemisphere distance themselves from the U.S. In 2005, Latin American governments recognized China's "full market status" and rejected the Bush Administration's candidates for Secretary General of the Organization of American States. They denied it observer status at the conference of Arab and South American governments in Brazil, and endorsed the "land for peace" formula in Palestine of the UN and the old America. East Asian leaders exclude the U.S. as an observer from their annual meeting. Africa's leaders convene in Beijing.

Neo-liberal economic ideology is defied by experience in the real world. Ideology conflicts with ideology, religious fundamentalism with religious fundamentalism, spurring conflict which feeds upon itself. Clyde Prestowitz and Kevin Phillips are long time observers of the U.S. government, and they are not liberals in the contemporary usage of that maligned word. Some of the most trenchant critics of neo-conservative ideology are traditional conservatives. Patrick Buchanan complains of the international adventurism. Traditional, moderate Republicans like former Commerce Secretary Peter Peterson are appalled by the fiscal irresponsibility of the neo-conservatives and an undisciplined Congress. In *Rogue Nation,* Prestowitz describes "vices" burdening the new America. For one, it wages war for oil but fails to conserve it. (The U.S. consumes half the world's oil production with 5 percent of the world's population.) The other industrial nations decrease dependence on imported oil and reduce its cost to their economies through conservation, appreciating currencies and development of renewable sources. They face up to remedies, albeit imperfectly but rationally. Many of our remedies were repealed or stalled in the 1980's. The fuel efficiency requirements I coauthored when I was chairman of the Senate Subcommittee on Oil and Gas Production may be upgraded thirty years later to fleet standards already achieved by Honda, but what else is within our political competence? Clearly not a gas tax increase to decrease energy consumption and dependence on foreign sources while producing needed public revenues and promoting public transportation. Programs supported by lobbies are more likely, like subsidizing the conversion of corn to ethanol at the expense of taxpayers and poor the world over, for whom food costs are increased —and without producing more energy than is consumed in ethanol's production.

Within the global economy with infinite possibilities, America retreats. The human and physical infrastructures essential for effective global competition are undermined. It shifts resources to armaments and homeland security while propagating terrorism. The President has urged Americans to spend money, have a good time and wage war. Long gone is the draft which summoned the citizen soldier, and the stern Uncle Sam who challenged Americans to save. Job growth languishes. Real incomes stagnate for most Americans as some drop out of the work force, and incomes of the wealthiest rise. Incomes of investment bankers, lawyers and accountants soar even as scientific research and the creation of real wealth is outsourced. The American Empire is losing comparative advantage to nations more pragmatic and rational in a highly competitive post industrial era and global economy—to nations more like the old America than the new.

As empires and nations decline, others rise. Europe is consolidating and expanding, hesitantly developing its own military and foreign policy. Its economy is as large as the American economy. Per capita growth and hourly productivity are already comparable. Health care is universal. Education through the university is at little or no cost. Soon Europe may have a vast financial market. The capitalization of its financial markets is already larger than that of the U.S. It faces demographic challenges, including the assimilation of immigrants to maintain its aging work force. Unemployment is higher than in the U.S., though employment has caught up.

"Old" Europeans have created a secular, humane community of nations with strong social safety nets and an aversion to unprovoked war. Their spending on the military as a percentage of GDP is roughly 2 percent as opposed to 4 percent and rising for the U.S. Their fiscal and monetary policies are prudent by global standards. Turkey and central Europe will align with Europe. That's where their markets, capital and security lie. Russia will supply oil and gas. Albeit excessively dependent on energy and a declining population, Russia is recovering its patrimony from the ravages of neoliberal orthodoxy and its American apostles, some with sticky fingers, learning from the experience of East Asia, including the new China. It will not leave its oil and gas resources to the caprice of multinational oil companies. Russia ebbs and flows over more than four centuries. It is prone to corruption but its oil and gas will be a wealth creating source of national authority and security.

Its potentials for the production of food in a hungry world are impressive.

Europe's expansion and consolidation is clouded by defeat of its proposed "constitution," but it may succeed on the next round. Europe may haltingly consolidate and take up reins of global leadership dropped by the new America, "backing into the future," as one observer puts it, because it must. Russia, like East Asians and Arabs, ponders new monetary regimes and currencies to immunize themselves against the vicissitudes of the dollar and an International Monetary Fund influenced by the U.S., even as central banks and fund managers threaten to diversify out of the unsound dollar. Russia and China join the host of pragmatic countries with high savings and sovereign wealth funds.

Americans preach democracy to the world. President Bush claims it produces peace and freedom which he also favors. It's a politically opportunistic message. But he is treading in the failed footsteps of Leninists who, also, sought empire in the guise of ideology. In the old, empirical America of the Black Book, democracy, for all its imperfections, was not a means to an end. It was an end in itself —a process by which the people were informed by their politics and made rational decisions. Better to lose than prove oneself unworthy of winning, Adlai II said. The old America propagated democracy by example with a decent respect for the opinions of mankind. From Woodrow Wilson to John F. Kennedy, its Presidents were hailed the world over. Democracy was spread to the world by its first functioning example, the old America.

The Black Book reflects no ideology. Its politics was both pragmatic and idealistic. It reflects a rational politics born of the Enlightenment and values which included intelligence (of the cerebral sort), tolerance, respect for evidence and science —Reason. It recognizes that for democracy to succeed, the people must be informed by truth—to repeat, "all the truth"—and shielded by truth from the distempers excited in democracies by fools and demagogues seeking power. Its values are not those of neo-conservative ideologues who manifest little respect for evidence or the opinions of mankind, and in their lives reflect little experience "on the ground" in a pluralistic, rapidly changing world, none in the military on which they depend for "coercive" outcomes. Neo-conservative ideology has a likeness, not in secular Europe or East Asia or the American century of the Black Book, but in the fundamentalism it excites in the Islamic world.

Where is the American response to challenge? To Empire? To another Gilded Age? To unprovoked war? Senators debate Social Security, and immigration, and struggle to block the nomination of ideologues to the judiciary and UN. But where is the response to this ideological challenge to our social values, our interests and our fundamental principles of government? The challenge is from within. War is easy. Peace is hard.

The American people began to perceive President Bush's failure in 2005, according to polls. Republicans lost the elections in 2006. But where is the Democratic Party of the Black Book? Congress has never been capable of comprehensive, rational policy making except by supporting a President. But where is the world wise, courageous Presidential candidate, or titular Democratic leader, who after the defeats of 1952 and 1956, appointed the Democratic national chairmen and advisory councils, developed and articulated policy for the Democratic Party and its partisans waiting out the Eisenhower interregnum? He won in losing.

The system has changed. The titular leader is gone. The Democratic National Committee is a fundraising enterprise. Self-appointed advisory groups reflect prevailing orthodoxies. Their leaders are more likely to have roots in Wall Street than in Main Street and the real world. We hear pledges of faith, hope, unity, experience and change from Presidential candidates. Democrats were realists. Harry Truman was a fighter. Democrats had agendas for America. John F. Kennedy offered America a New Frontier based on the New America of Adlai II. Lyndon Johnson followed with the Great Society, including the expansion of civil liberties and a war against poverty. By 1973, the percentage of American people living in poverty was halved. It is not clear what Democrats of the new era stand for. For some Democrats, "winning is everything." That is the Nixon way. Who has the courage to be right? And lose, if need be?

In the politics of the Black Book and the old America, governing is everything. It would be right and more effective to remember that politics—and embrace the truth, wherever it may lie on that hypothetical spectrum of political philosophy contrived for its convenience by the media, even if it means being labeled a liberal—or made a target of The Lobby. It would be better to articulate the Old Deal of the Black Book and respond to challenge and restore to American politics values which made the country great, secure and the world's first successful democracy.

The Old Deal requires a return to Reason—leaving ideology and superstition to the Republicans. It restores U.S. authority and security in the world by supporting the UN and all its fragile institutions for peace, strategic arms control and development, addressing causes of terrorism, above all the conflict in Palestine, while waging war as a defensive last resort. It demonstrates the courage to wage peace by restoring and renewing the international order established with American leadership after World War II. It restores the country's civil authority and civil liberties. The Old Deal of the Black Book restores the social compact and addresses the needs of a competitive economy. It defends the global commons and atmosphere, ratifies the Kyoto Protocol and Comprehensive Test Ban Treaty, joins the International Court of Criminal Justice, supports an open, non-discriminatory world trading system, limits strategic arms and nuclear proliferation. It attacks citadels of corporate corruption, oligopoly and exploitation, and seeks in the world to close the gap between the haves and have-nots.

> We travel together, passengers in a little spaceship, dependent upon its vulnerable resources of air and soil, committed for our safety to its security and peace, preserved from annihilation only by the care, the work, and I will say, the love we give our fragile craft. We cannot maintain it half fortunate, half miserable, half confident, half despairing, half slave to the ancient enemies of mankind, half free in a liberation of resources undreamed of until this day. No craft, no crew, can travel safely with such vast contradictions; upon their resolution depends the survival of us all.
> *Adlai II*

Or are the systemic changes underlying America's retreat from its past so entrenched that our politics is no longer capable of response? It cannot respond to its unresponsiveness and restore the fundamental principles cited by Spengler. Decay within may be undermining its ability to respond to challenge from without. Perhaps America can endure neither its vices nor their remedies. Such possibilities are not contemplated in the Black Book. Cleveland, Bryan, the LaFollettes, Theodore Roosevelt—the progressive leaders of the first Gilded Age were rationalists and men of uncompromising principles, not afraid to take on the bosses (usually winning their support afterwards) and the industrial interests. In 1888, a young William Jennings Bryan wrote

Grover Cleveland saying, "I would rather fall with you fighting on and for a principle than succeed with a party representing nothing but an organized appetite." Cleveland lost to Harrison, resisting a protective tariff for industrial interests. Wilson followed. And Franklin Roosevelt. Truth was determinable and worth dying for.

In 1970, I commiserated with Senator Albert Gore Sr. of Tennessee, a principled Senator defeated for his support of civil rights. He reflected the old Democratic party when he replied, "We who live by the sword die by the sword." He is gone. Political parties are become "organized appetites" beyond the imaginings of William Jennings Bryan, a neglected figure in America's history. The Black Book's lessons are about Reason, the good fight, life as a learning experience, the human spirit and human family—abhorrence of absolutism and dogma. It is a metaphor, but its values have been better exemplified in other countries recently—and far from the U.S. Senate in which I once proudly served.

The next Stevenson generation has understandably demonstrated little appetite for the new politics. It includes a teacher and school administrator, doctor, rancher, communications expert and investment banker becoming a China expert. They are good citizens but not politicians or lawyers. They are, however, producing another generation. The grandchildren cannot drive up to the entrance of the White House with their parents or stroll beneath the great chestnut trees which shaded the lawn east of the American Capitol as their ancestors did. Pennsylvania Avenue is barricaded. Much of what remains of that lawn lies behind a wall.

Guided by their grandparents, little Katie, Anna and Adlai V maneuvered the subterranean corridors and metal detectors in early 2005 to reach the U.S. Capitol where, after a lengthy search and with much friendly assistance, they discovered the marble bust of Adlai I in a corridor to which it had been transferred from its former place of honor at the main entrance to the Senate chamber. They have been overheard discussing with more than passing interest, it seems, what it would be like to be a United States Senator. They are studying history and planning to learn Chinese. Their travels in the world have begun.

The Black Book spanned the American Century, an Age of Reason. It beckons Americans. It beckons an American President to follow in 2009.

The Ever-growing Tree

All great movements, every vigorous impulse that a community may feel, becomes perverted and distorted as time passes, and the atmosphere of the earth seems fatal to the noble aspirations of its peoples. A wide humanitarian sympathy in a nation easily degenerates into hysteria. A military spirit tends toward brutality. Liberty leads to licence, restraint to tyranny. The pride of race is distended to blustering arrogance. The fear of God produces bigotry and superstition. There appears no exception to the mournful rule, and the best efforts of men, however glorious their early results, have dismal endings, like plants which shoot and bud and put forth beautiful flowers, and then grow rank and coarse and are withered by the winter. It is only when we reflect that the decay gives birth to fresh life, and that new enthusiasms spring up to take places of those that die, as the acorn is nourished by the dead leaves of the oak, the hope strengthens that the rise and fall of men and their movements are only the changing foliage of the ever-growing tree of life, while underneath a greater revolution goes on continually.

Winston Churchill,
His Wit and Wisdom

Part II

Afterwords

The Readers employed in schools utilized passages from histories, the Bible and literature, heroic and patriotic declamations, to animate, educate and inform the young (as has been mentioned in the Chapter on Education). Politicians, notably Lincoln, also Adlai I were shaped by this pedagogy and the realities of communication in their time, and utilized the technique in their continuing education and development as citizens and politicians, also in their discourse, assiduously collecting bits of wit and wisdom as they went—and thus began the Black Book. The excerpts in the Afterwords also include many sent by supporters for encouragement, inspiration and, at times, consolation. They were sources of strength and comfort, as well as wisdom. But they are too diverse and numerous to fit comfortably in the material on politics, law, religion, economics, government— found in Part I. Their overflow begins with Humorous Recitations and Laugh Lines and ends with Temperance and Intemperance. The Black Book makes few claims to logic.

An ounce of history is worth a pound of logic.
Oliver Wendell Holmes

I: Humorous Recitations and Laugh Lines

A boy in the Kentucky mountains described his family: "My father is in jail for killing the butcher; my mother run off with the butcher; one sister is in the poor house; another is in the insane asylum; my brother is at Harvard." "What is he studying?" "Oh, he ain't studying; he was born with two heads and is in a bottle."

Lincoln told of a man who defended himself against an attacking boar with a pitchfork, killing the animal. When asked by the angry owner of the boar why he had not used the blunt end of the pitchfork, the man replied that the boar had not attacked with his blunt end.

Lincoln was told of a prominent historian, "It may be doubted whether any man of our generation has plunged more deeply into the sacred fount of learning." "Yes, or come up drier," Lincoln replied.

A condemned man put his foot on the first step to the gallows. It was unsteady, and he shrank back, asking, "Is this thing safe?"

The small daughter of a famous divine was busy with her crayon and pencil, and her mother asked her whose picture she was drawing. "God's," she replied. "But, dear, nobody knows how He looks," her mother admonished. "They will when I'm finished," said the child.

A preacher came across a parishioner working on a stony field to clear it. "Why, Jess, you and the Lord sure have done a wonderful job of clearing this field." To which Jess replied, "You should've seen it when the Lord had it all to hisself."

A minister was trying to talk his fund-raising committee into buying new chandeliers for the church. A committee member was opposed, saying: "In the first place I don't know how to spell it, in the second place there's nobody in the church who knows how to play them, and in the third place, we need more light."

A small boy's prayer in England during the War: "God bless Mummy and Daddy, my brother and sister, and save the King! And, Oh God, do take care of yourself, because if anything happens to you we're all sunk."

I'm like the little boy who asked his mother if we all come from dust. "Yes," she said, "That's what the Bible says." And do we return to dust?" "Yes, that's right." "Well," says the little boy, "I've just looked under the bed and there's somebody there, but I can't tell whether he's coming or going."

An old Quaker had retired for the night. He heard a noise downstairs. Rising, he took his shotgun from the wall, and tiptoed very quietly down the steps. Sure enough, there was a burglar looting the family silverware. In quiet tones, the Quaker addressed the burglar: "My friend, I would not harm thee for the world, but thee is standing where I am about to shoot."

A little boy jumbled his Biblical quotation and said: "A lie is an abomination unto the Lord and a very present help in trouble."

An Evangelist preacher was worried about the reputation of a certain lady in the congregation. One Sunday morning after the service, he greeted her by saying: "Oh, Mrs. Jones, I stayed up three hours last night praying for you." She replied, "Why, Reverend, if you had just picked up the phone, I would have come right over."

During a furious theological debate, Dean Swift lost his temper and asked a stranger: "On which side are you? Are you an atheist or a Deist?" "Oh neither, Sir," came the reply, "I am a dentist."

A man on the death row made one last polite, yet urgent appeal. "Dear Governor," he wrote, "They are fixin' to hang me Friday and here it is Tuesday. Hope to hear from you soon."

A prisoner to his cellmate: "I'm going to study and improve myself and when you're still a common thief, I'll be an embezzler."

A young man asked Dr. S. Parkes Cadman, "Can I lead a good Christian life in New York on $15 dollars a week?" "My boy that's all you can do."

Sydney Smith, the theologian, replied to an antagonist who, casting a slur on his vocation, charged, "If I had a son who was an idiot, I would make him a parson." The reply: "Your father was of a different opinion."

232

A minister, raising his eyes from the pulpit during his Sunday sermon, was horrified to see his young son in the balcony pelting the parishioners in the pews with a pea gun. While he was trying to gather his wits, the youngster shouted: "You 'tend to your preaching, Pa. I'll keep 'em awake."

A minister returned wearily from church and explained in response to his worried wife's inquiry that he had just attempted to persuade his congregation that it was the duty of the rich members to help the poor. "And," asked his wife, "did you convince them?" "I was half successful," replied the minister. "I convinced the poor."

The Protestant churches in America today are made up of conventional people who are addressed once a week by a conventional little man who asks them to be more conventional.

The Bishop sent a young priest off to a remote post in the tundra of northern Alaska. After a six months absence and no word of the young priest, the bishop decided to journey to Alaska to discover his whereabouts and welfare. He hired dog sleds and pushed through the tundra for days and finally encountered the young father in a shack on a northern river. He asked the young priest how he fared, and the priest replied he'd go crazy if were not for his martinis and his rosary. He then asked the bishop if he would like a martini. To which the bishop responded affirmatively. The young priest then called into an adjoining room, "Get the bishop a martini, Rosary."

When his friends heard that Mike was on his way out and knew that he had led a worldly life, they were concerned about what would happen to him in the hereafter. So they called on Mike and broke the news to him. "Yes," he said, "I know I am on the way out." So they said, "Well, Mike, you know how you have lived. We wonder if you wouldn't permit the Father to come over and talk with you." The Father came over and talked to Mike and finally he said, "Mike you know what the future holds for you. Before you pass into the great beyond, won't you embrace the good Lord and renounce the Devil?" Mike replied: "Father, I'll be happy to embrace the good Lord, but don't ask me to renounce the Devil. In the position I'm in I don't want to antagonize anybody."

The Duke of Wellington was hunting in Ireland when a peasant girl, one of the beaters, was shot in the rear end. An equerry ran forward to hush her howls: "Stop your caterwauling, you foolish girl, and think of the supreme honor you have this day enjoyed of being in contact, however remotely, with the heroic conqueror of Waterloo."

As told by Luns, Foreign Minister
of Holland

Never underestimate a woman unless you are talking about her age or her weight.

Apropos clubs for women: W.C.Fields said he approved of them when all other means fail.

If you come to a fork in the road, take it.
Yogi Berra

A little Irish boy and a girl changed bathing suits by the sea. Afterwards the little girl ran to her mother and exclaimed that she had not known there was such a difference between Catholics and Protestants.

Gambler leaving for the race track: " I hope I break even, I need the money."

One man is as good as another—to which the Irishman replied, "Yes, and sometimes a hell of a lot better."

Two Irishmen were lost in a snowstorm. Frozen, tired and discouraged, they were at the end of their rope when a St. Bernard dog appeared, wearing the usual cask of brandy around his neck…"Faith," exclaimed one, "look what's coming – man's best friend." "Sure," replied the other, "and look what's bringing it – a dog."

President Truman was asked, "Mr. President, do the people where you come from say 'a hen lays' or 'a hen lies'?" The president hesitated only a second and replied, "The people where I come from don't say 'a hen lays' or 'a hen lies'; they lift up the hen to see."

Adlai III's Senate seatmate, Edmund Muskie, told of a road fork in Maine where a tourist found signs pointing each way, both of which said, "Portland." He beckoned to a farmer leaning on a hoe and inquired, "Doesn't it make any difference which road I take to Portland?" Came the terse reply, "Not to me, it don't."

There was a terrible family feud in Kentucky. Adlai I pleaded with the families to bury the hatchet and get together. To which one of the feuders replied, "Git together! Why we were so close together at the last meeting that it took ten deputy sheriffs to separate us."

A New Jersey Congressman once brought two citizens of that state to visit President Lincoln. Seeking to impress the President, he introduced them as among "the weightiest men in southern New Jersey." After their departure, Lincoln remarked to an aide, "I wonder that end of the state did not tip up when they got off."

A lady complained to the police that her ring had been stolen. Asked when she last remembered it, she replied, "Why, come to think of it, it was just before I shook hands with Governor Stevenson."

A traveler lost during a thunder storm blundered his way through a forest in thick darkness, except when vivid lightening flashes showed him the way. The heavens were rent asunder by lightening and thunder. At last a flash and a crash more terrible than all the rest brought him to his knees. He was not a praying man. His petition was short and to the point. "O Lord," he gasped, "if it's all the same to you, please give us a little more light and a little less noise."

A troubled man asked the porter if it were possible to find a priest on the train. The porter replied that the whole Notre Dame team was aboard and that there were several priests – but they wanted to know did he want an offensive or defensive priest.

A motorist ran over a hog on the highway and tried to calm down the irate farmer. "Don't worry, I will replace your pig." "Replace him!" the farmer shouted. "You can't. You ain't fat enough."

This clash reminds me of the farmer back home who was asked what he'd do if he saw two trains speeding at each other from opposite directions. "I'd run and get my brother George," said the farmer, "'cause he ain't never seen a wreck."

An eight-year-old horse ran for the first time. The odds were a hundred to one. He won by twenty lengths going away. Asked why the horse had not raced before, the owner said: "I wanted to race him, but I couldn't catch him until yesterday."

An Indian in New Mexico was sending love messages to his sweetheart by smoke signal when an atomic bomb test went off, covering the sky with smoke for miles. "Gosh," the Indian uttered enviously, "I wish I'd said that."

George Bernard Shaw to Oscar Wilde, sarcastically: "Please come to the opening of my play with a friend—if any." Wilde to Shaw: "I'll come the second night—if any."

Mrs. Karl Marx, at the end of a long and bleak life, remarked: "How good it would have been if Karl had made some capital instead of writing so much about it."

A settler in early Illinois heard about the phenomenal memory of an Indian. He decided to test the famous memory and asked the Indian what he had for breakfast on the morning of August 12, 1852. The Indian answered without hesitation, "Eggs." The white man mumbled under his breath about the perfidy of redskins. "Eggs, indeed." Twenty years later he encountered the same Indian. Being civil, he greeted the Indian with the traditional, "How" to which the Indian replied, "Scrambled."

An Indian fighter, wounded, an arrow in his back, was asked if he was in terrible agony. He responded, "Not so bad, exceptn' when I laugh."

A man fell off a roof and was asked if the fall had hurt him. "The falling didn't hurt me, but the stopping nearly killed me."

"Officer, where am I?" "You're at the corner of 4th and Main." "Cut out the details – what I want to know is what city I'm in."

A chicken and a pig were walking down the street and came to a ham and egg stand. The chicken said: "Isn't it wonderful what our cooperation has done for the world?" To which the pig replied, "Yes, but for you it's only a contribution and for me it's a total commitment."

On the lesson of two evils: "Rastus," said his friend who had been reading in the paper about a number of fatal accidents, "If you had to take your choice 'twixt one or t'other, which would you ruther be in, a collision or an explosion?" "Man, a collision," said Rastus. "How come?" "Why, man, if you's in a collision, thar you is, but if you's in an explosion, whar is you?"

Adlai I

II. Fame, Greatness

If any man seeks for greatness, let him forget greatness
and ask for truth, and he will find both.
Horace Mann

Fame and greatness bear to each other little relationship in the
Black Book, the former sometimes acquired by persons more deserving
of oblivion. Fame and infamy are at times not far separated. Greatness,
in the Black Book, is worthy and won by virtue, unlike fame.

Fame is like a river, that beareth up things light and swollen, and
drowns things weighty and solid.
Sir Francis Bacon

Happy is the man who hath never known what it is to taste
fame—to have it is a purgatory, to want it is a hell.
Bulwyer Litton

Fame is proof that the people are gullible.
Emerson

Fame: "The last infirmity of noble minds."
Milton

Fame is not grounded on success
Though victories were Caesar's glory,
Lost battles made not Pompey less
But left him styled great in story.
Malicious fate doth oft devise
To beat the brave and fool the wise.
Lord Rochester, 18th century
(from a toast by J.C Masterman,
Vice Chancellor of Oxford
University to Adlai II, May 24,
1957)

The thirst for fame is much greater than the thirst for virtue.
Juvenal

Born of the sun he traveled a short while towards the sun

And left the vivid air signed with his honor.
Stephen Spender

What is the fame of men compared to their happiness?
Horace Walpole

Fame is but a slow decay. Even this shall pass away.
Theodore Tilton

He lives in fame that died in virtue's cause.
Shakespeare, Titus Andronicus

The greatest man is he who chooses right with the most invincible resolution; who resists the sorest temptation from within and without; who bears the heaviest burdens cheerfully; who is calmest in storms, and most fearless under menace and frowns; whose reliance on truth, on virtue, and on God is most unfaltering.
Seneca The Younger

To endure is greater than to dare; to tire out hostile fortune; to be daunted by no difficulty; to keep heart when all have lost it; to go through intrigue spotless; to forego even ambition when the end is gained — who can say that this is not greatness?
Thackery, The Virginian

Erasmus said one should see great men at a distance as one looks at tapestries.

No man need care for power or strive for it.
If you be wise and good, it will follow you
Though you may not desire it.
Alfred the Great

Senator Zebulon 'Zeb' B. Vance of North Carolina remarked that his fame for one generation, at least, was secure, inasmuch as one half the freckled faced boys and two thirds of the "yaller" dogs in North Carolina had been named in his honor.
Adlai I

III: Friends

In the Black Book, "the best of one's life is one's friends." A friend is a friend for life. Friends, more so than words of exhortation and inspiration, are a source of levity in good times, consolation in others, fortitude in all.

I don't wish to treat friendships daintily, but with the roughest courage. When they are real they are not glass threads, or frost work, but the solidest things we know.
Emerson

It is more shameful to distrust one's friends than to be deceived by them.
La Rochefoucauld, Maximes

Tell me, ye knowing and discerning few,
where I can find a friend that's firm and true,
who dares to stand by me in deep distress,
and then his love and friendship most express.

A friend in power is a friend at last.
Henry Adams

Why do you dislike me? I have never done anything to help you.
Confucius

I am thinking of you today because it is Christmas, and I wish you happiness—and tomorrow, because it will be the day after Christmas, I shall wish you happiness and so on throughout the year. I may not be able to tell you about it every day, but that makes no difference, the thought and the wish will be there just the same. Whenever joy and happiness come to you it will make me glad.
Henry Van Dyke

Chapel and fireside, country road and bay,
Have something of their friendliness resigned;
Another, if I would, I could not find,

And I am grown much older in a day.

> *George Santayana's* lament for a friend

IV: Aging

The wise never grow old, their minds are nursed
by living, by the bold light of day.
Southley

Life was to be lived to the full, every woken moment plumbed
for its lessons, none wasted in amusements. Humor, rarely repressed for
long in the Black Book, resurfaces.

What a man knows at fifty that he did not know at twenty is, for
the most part, incommunicable. It boils down to something like this:
The knowledge he has acquired with age is not the knowledge of
formulas, or forms of words, but of people, places, actions— a
knowledge not gained by words but by touch, sight, sound, victories,
failures, sleeplessness, devotion, love —the human experiences and
emotions of this earth, of oneself and other men, and perhaps, too, a
little faith, and a little reverence for the things you cannot see.
Adlai II

When Justice Oliver Wendell Holmes was almost ninety, several
of his brethren decided to find out what impact he had made on the man
in the street. So, during a luncheon recess several of them approached a
man in overalls on a park bench and asked him whether he knew who
Oliver Wendell Holmes was. "Holmes, why sure, he's that young fella
who is always disagreeing with the old fogeys on the Supreme Court."

"If you ask how I know that my youth it is spent,
My get-up-and-go, it has got up and went.
But sometimes I grin when I think where it has been."
Ogden Nash

A gentleman was interviewed on his 100th anniversary, and after
congratulating him, the reporter asked, "To what do you attribute your
longevity?" The centenarian thought for a moment and responded,
ticking off the items on his fingers, "I never smoke; I never drank liquor
and I never over ate; and I always rise at six in the morning." To which
the young reporter replied: "I had an uncle who acted the same way, but
he only lived to be eighty. How do you account for that?" "He didn't
keep it up for long enough," came the reply.

An elderly gentleman was telling his young lady friend of the difficulty he was having finding a gift for her. "Oh," she said, "I think the nicest gift is always something you've made yourself, like money."

A cluster of small fry were taken to visit the family patriarch on his 100th birthday. One youngster spoke up and asked: "Great granddaddy, can you still remember the first girl you kissed?" The old man piped in reply, "You don't get the picture at all, Johnny. I can't even remember the last."

> I get up in the morning and brush off my wits,
> I pick up the paper and read the obits,
> If my name is not there I know I'm not dead,
> So I eat a big breakfast and go back to bed.

If what is wanted is that deep wisdom expected of the old and wise, then on me you should not count. Mine is the kind possessed by a Kentucky mountain man who was sought out for his wisdom. One young fellow asked him, "Uncle Zeke, how come you are so wise, seein' you never went to school, none to speak of?" The old man answered: "Son, it's because I got good judgment. Good judgment comes from experience. And experience— well, that comes from poor judgment."

A man went to his doctor for a physical on his 65th birthday. He told the doctor that nothing was wrong with him, that he was in fine fettle and after examining him, the doctor detected no symptoms of anything wrong. He congratulated the patient on his good health and asked about the family history. The patient said his father was 85 years old and even healthier, had never missed a day of work, etc. What's more, he had a grandfather who was 105 years old and in better shape than both of them. "As a matter of fact," he said, "my grandfather is about to be married." The doctor asked, "Why does he want to get married?" To which the 65-year-old replied, "Who said he wanted to get married?"

When Mozart was my age he'd been dead for ten years.
Tom Lehrer

Old age is no such uncomfortable thing if one gives oneself up to it with a good grace and doesn't drag it about to midnight dances and the public show.

Horace Walpole

That we make a stand upon the ancient way, and then look upon us, and discover what is the straight and right way, and so walk in it.

Sir Francis Bacon, quoting from
Scriptures

A lady told Cicero she was thirty years of age to which he replied: "It must be true, for I have heard it these twenty years."

Oliver Wendell Holmes admired a beautiful young woman and turned to Justice Brandeis, sighing: "Oh! What I wouldn't give to be seventy again."

V: Inspiration and Exhortation

Times such as these have always bred defeatism and despair. But there remain, nonetheless, some few among us who believe man has within him the capacity to meet and overcome even the greatest challenges of this time. If we want to avoid defeat, we must wish to know the truth and be courageous enough to act upon it. If we get to know the truth and have the courage, we need not despair.

Albert Einstein

The Black Book's bits of wit, wisdom and whimsy include many about the good fight, conscience and truth, human spirit and the meaning of life. Some were messages of support and encouragement for the recipient. They were rarely used to enliven speeches or articles. Several found their way into the annual Christmas messages of Adlai II and III. In the main, they rejoice in life and its challenges and look beyond the next turn. Tucked away in the Black Book, they have been gentle sources of comfort in adversity, humility in triumph. In today's political environment, some will sound affected, but they were for the most part exhortations of concerned and engaged Americans, from constituents and supporters the world over.

One may long, as I do, for a gentler flame, a respite, a pause for musing. But perhaps there is no other peace for the artist than what he finds in the heat of combat. . .Great ideas, it has been said, come into the world as gently as doves. Perhaps then, if we listen attentively, we shall hear, amid the uproar of empires and nations, a faint flutter of wings, the gentle stirring of life and hope. Some will say that this hope lies in a nation; others, in a man. I believe rather that it is awakened, revived, nourished by millions of solitary individuals whose deeds and works every day negate frontiers and the crudest implications of history. As a result, there shines forth fleetingly the ever threatened truth that each and every man, on the foundation of his own sufferings and joys, builds for all.

Albert Camus

God gives every man the choice between trust and repose. Choose which you will. You can never have both.

Emerson

Whoever could make two ears of corn, or two blades of grass, to grow upon a spot of ground where only one grew before, would deserve better of mankind, and do more essential service to his country, than the whole race of politicians.

Jonathan Swift

Let me be a citizen of the world, a friend of all mankind.

Erasmus

What I must do is all that concerns me, not what the people think. This rule, equally arduous in actual and in intellectual life, may serve for the whole distinction between greatness and meanness. It is the harder because there will always be those who think they know what is your duty better than you know it. It is easy in the world to live after the world's opinion; it is easy in solitude to live after our own; but the great man is he who in the midst of the crowd keeps with perfect sweetness the independence of solitude.

Emerson

We are met on the broad pathway of good faith and good will so that no advantage is to be taken of either side but all to be openness, brotherhood, and love....

William Penn

No ray of sunlight is ever lost, but the green which it wakes in existence needs time to sprout, and it is not always granted to the sower to live to see the harvest. All work that is worth anything is done in faith.

Albert Schweitzer, Memoirs of Childhood

Tis not in mortals to command success, but we'll do more, Sempronius; we'll deserve it.

Addison, (Cited at an Oxford University Convocation honoring Adlai II)

Go placidly amid the noise and the haste and remember what peace there may be in silence. As far as possible without surrender, be on good terms with all persons. Speak your truth quietly and clearly, and listen to others, even to the dull and ignorant; they too have their

246

story. You are a child of the Universe no less than the trees and the stars; you have a right to be here. Therefore, be at peace with God, whatever you conceive Him to be, and, whatever your labors and aspirations in the noisy confusion of life, keep peace with your soul. With all its sham, drudgery and broken dreams, it is still a beautiful world.

From Desiderata, Old Saint Paul's
Church, Baltimore, 1692

Do all the good you can
By all the means you can
In all the ways you can
In all the places you can
At all the times you can
To all the people you can
As long as ever you can.
John Wesley

I cannot praise a fugitive and cloistered virtue, unexercised and unbreathed, that never sallies out and seeks her adversary, but slinks out of the race, where that immortal garland is to be run for, not without dust and heat.
Milton

Ah! When shall all men's good
Be each man's rule, a universal peace
Lie like a shaft of light across the land,
And like a lane of beams athwart the sea,
Thro' all the circle or the golden year?
Tennyson

Let us develop the resources of our land, call forth its power, build up all its institutions and see whether we in our day and generation may not perform something to be remembered.
Daniel Webster

Build on resolve and not upon regret
The structure of the future.
Do not grope among the shadows of the old
But let thy soul's delight shine on the path of hope,
And dissipate the darkness.

But the mind that has ranged the universe must now itself
control,
For the force in the mighty atom is less than the human soul;
And simpler than any equation are the words forever true:
Do ye unto others as ye would they do to you.

James T. Shotwell, from The Way

If there is any period one would desire to be born in – is it not
the era of revolution when the old and the new stand side by side, and
admit of being compared; when all the energies of man are searched by
fear and hope; when the historic glories of the old can be compensated
by the rich possibilities of the new era? This time, like all times, is a
very good one if one but knows what to do with it.

Emerson

All that is necessary for the triumph of evil is that good men do
nothing.

Edmund Burke

We make a living by what we get; we make a life by what we
do.

Winston Churchill

If we had a keen vision and feeling of all ordinary human life, it
would be like hearing the grass grow and the squirrel's heart beat, and
we should die of that roar which lies on the other side of silence.

George Eliot, Middlemarch

Let us not be weary in well doing, for in due season we shall
reap, if we faint not.

Galatians

The coward dies a thousand deaths, and a brave man dies just
once. Where there is no vision, the people perish.

Nothing is to be feared except fear itself.

Sir Francis Bacon

I do not know beneath what sky
Nor on what seas shall be thy fate;

I only know it shall be high,
I only know it shall be great.
Richard Hovey

The only limit to our realization of tomorrow will be our doubts of today. Let us move forward with strong and active faith.
Franklin D. Roosevelt, shortly before his death

On the plains of hesitation bleach the bones of countless millions who on the eve of rested, and resting, died.
Ingersoll

Fear not that life should come to an end, but rather, fear that it shall never have a beginning.
Cardinal Newman

There is no sorrow I have thought more about than that—to love what is great, and try to reach it, and yet to fail.
George Eliot

Advice to Andrew Jackson from his Mother:

In 1781 Andrew Jackson, then fourteen years of age, enlisted in the American army; was captured and thrown into prison where he contracted smallpox. His mother, Elizabeth Hutchinson Jackson, arranged for his release and nursed him back to health.

Responding to an urgent appeal, she left him to go to Charleston to nurse sick neighbors confined there on a British hospital ship. This errand of mercy cost her life. She caught yellow fever and died. Almost her last words to her son were:

"Andrew, if I should not see you again, I wish you to remember and treasure some things I have already said to you. In this world you will have to make your own way. To do that, you must have friends. You can make friends by being honest, and you can keep them by being steadfast. You must keep in mind that friends worth having will in the long run expect as much from you as they give you. To forget an obligation or to be ungrateful for a kindness is a base crime —not merely a fault or a sin, but an actual crime. Men guilty of it sooner or later must suffer the penalty. In personal conduct be always polite but never obsequious. None will respect you more than you respect yourself. Avoid quarrels as long as you can without yielding to imposition. But sustain your manhood always. Never bring a suit in law for assault and battery or for defamation. The law affords no remedy for such outrages that can satisfy the feelings of a true man. Never wound the feelings of others. Never brook wanton outrage upon your own feelings. If ever you have to vindicate your feelings or defend your honor, do it calmly. If angry at first, wait until your wrath cools before you proceed."

These words were repeated by General Jackson on his birthday, March 15, 1815, at New Orleans, to three members of his military family. "Gentlemen," said General Jackson, "I wish she could have lived to see this day. There never was a woman like her. She was gentle as a dove and as brave as a lioness. Her last words have been the law of my life."

He took counsel ever of his courage —never of his fears.

Keep your head cool, your heart warm, your backbone stiff and your feet on the ground.

> O for a living man to lead!
> That will not babble when we bleed;
> O for the silent doer of the deed!
> One that is happy in his height,
> And one that in a nation's night,
> Hath solitary certitude of light.
> *Stephen Phillips,* (English poet)

> Have communion with few
> Be familiar with one
> Deal justly with all
> Speak evil of none.

Faith means believing what is incredible, or it is no virtue at all. Hope means hoping when things are hopeless, or it is no virtue at all. And charity means pardoning what is unpardonable, or it is no virtue at all.
G.K. Chesterton

The only guide to a man is his conscience; the only shield to his memory is the sincerity and rectitude of his actions.
Winston Churchill

Thou hast faith, and I have works; show me thy faith without thy works, and I shall show thee my faith by my works.
Henry James

If another person treats me unreasonably, I will say: "I must have been wanting in kindness or propriety. How else should this have happened? Then I will mend my ways. If the other continues to be perverse, I must be selfless enough to say, 'I must have failed to do my best.' If all this is vain, I will say, 'Why vex myself about a wild beast?'" Thus the wise man has lifelong vigilance but not one moment's serious trouble.
Mencius

A merry heart doeth good like a medicine; but a broken spirit drieth up the bones.

Do not hope you are to gain the victory in a day, it may take months, it may take years. Inch by inch and step by step the battle must be fought. Over and over again you will be worsted and give ground, but do not therefore yield. Resolve never to be driven back quite so far as you have advanced.
Whyte Melville

One cannot behave so as to obtain the Esteem of the Wise and Good, without drawing on one's self at the same time the Envy and Malice of the Foolish and Wicked, and the latter is a Testimony of the former.
Benjamin Franklin, from a letter to
his sister who was troubled by
attacks against him.

Three things are necessary for the salvation of man: to know what he ought to believe; to know what he ought to desire; to know what he ought to do.
St. Thomas Aquinas

Emiliano Zapata, the illiterate Mexican revolutionary, said on being warned that he would be assassinated: "Then that's the way it must be and perhaps better, for some men find their real and permanent strength there. I think of Benito Juarez, of Abraham Lincoln, of Jesus Christ. Death only kills little men."

> I have loved the stars too fondly to be fearful of the night.
> *Sarah William*, (American poet)

> Nothing matters at last, but the integrity of your own mind.
> *Emerson*

> No man is an island, entire of itself; every man is a piece of the continent, a part of the main.... Any man's death diminishes me, because I am involved in mankind; and therefore never send to know for whom the bell tolls; it tolls for thee.
> *John Donne*

> Faith is the substance of things hoped for; the evidence of things not seen.
> *Hebrews*

> I did not come to condemn the world but to save the world.
> *Jesus*, (according to the Black Book)

> Cry if you can cry, but don't complain. Your path chose you. And you shall say thank you.
> *Dag Hammarskjold* shortly before his death.

> I salute you. There is nothing I can give you which you have not, but there is much, that while I cannot give you, you can take. No heaven can come to us unless our hearts find rest in today—take heaven —no peace lies in the future which is not hidden in the present—take peace —the gloom of the world is but a shadow, behind it, yet within our reach, is joy—take joy—and so at Christmas time I greet you with the prayer that for you now and forever the day breaks and the shadows flee away.
> *Fra. Giovanni*, 1513

> There are many echoes in the world, but only a few voices.
> *Goethe*

The hottest places in Hell are reserved for those who, during a time of moral crisis, preserve their neutrality.

Dante

Where there is patience and humility there is neither anger nor worry.

St. Francis

It is better to light candles than curse the darkness.

Chinese proverb (quoted by Adlai
II at observances for Eleanor
Roosevelt)

A great effort may be made in a moment of excitement, but continual little efforts can only be made on principle.

Goulburn

Build on resolve and not upon regret
The structure of the future.
Waste no tears upon the blotted record of last years
But turn the leaf, and smile.
Oh, smile to see the fair white pages
That remain to thee —and me.

This much I know of the sport (mountaineering), that the abilities it requires are just those which I feel we all need today: perseverance and patience, a firm grip on realities, careful but imaginative planning, a clear awareness of the dangers but also of the fact that fate is what we make it and the safest climber is he who never questions his ability to overcome all difficulties.

Dag Hammarskjold, from an
interview on his arrival at the
United Nations, April, 1953

Man will not attain the possible unless time and again he reaches for the impossible.

Max Weber

Let us not be weary in well doing, for in due season we shall reap, if we faint not.

Galatians

Bliss in possession will not last;
Remembered joys are never past;
At once the fountain, stream and sea
They were, they are, they yet shall be.

On the plains of hesitation bleach the bones
of countless millions who on the eve of
victory rested, and resting, died.
Ingersoll

The challenge to all of us is to prove that a free society can remain free, humane and creative, even when it is under heavy and ruthless fire; that it can combat poverty, injustice and intolerance in its own midst, even while resisting a monstrous foreign despotism; and that it can give men a glimpse of serenity and hope, even while its calls on them for sacrifice.
Adlai II

The future will be better tomorrow.
George W. Bush

VI: War and Peace

A Latin proverb volunteered by Lester Pearson, former Prime Minister of Canada: "If you want peace, prepare for peace."

Burmese proverbs volunteered by U Thant, former Secretary General of the United Nations:
"Unity comes before peace."
"He who is afraid knows no peace."
"Whenever there is love there is peace."

"...I do not believe that it is for the advantage of this country or any country in the world that any one nation should pride itself upon what it terms supremacy of the sea; and I hope the time is coming—I believe the hour is hastening —when we shall find that law and justice shall guide the councils, and shall direct the policy of the Christian nations of the world.

John Bright, House of Commons, 1865

Two contending kings: Charles V and his cousin Francis I. Charles summed up the situation with admirable candor: "My cousin and I are in complete agreement: we both want Milan."

A lion and an ox quarreled at a water-hole as to which would drink first. There was plenty of room for them to drink together, none the less they quarreled about precedence and were preparing to fight it out when, looking up, they saw the vultures wheeling low above them, waiting for the battle and its aftermath. So they decided to drink together.

Aesop's Fables

In Swahili (East Africa): When the elephants make war, the grass is crushed. Koreans employ a similar metaphor to make a larger point: When the whales make war, the shrimp are crushed. When the whales make love, the shrimp are crushed.

...A good general has no need of genius, nor of any great qualities; on the contrary, he is the better for the absence of the finest and highest of human qualities – love, poetry, tenderness, philosophic and inquiring doubt. He should be limited, firmly convinced that what he is doing is of great importance or he would never have patience to go through with it, and only then will he be a gallant general. God forbid he should be humane, should feel love and compassion, should pause to think what is right and wrong....

Tolstoy, War and Peace

To Secretary of the Navy Frank Knox and his assistant, Adlai II, in the Pacific during World War II, General Douglas MacArthur likened the death of a Chinese soldier to a dove which quietly and without a struggle folds its wings and dies.

There never was any party, faction, sect or cabal whatsoever, in which the most ignorant were not the most violent; for a bee is not a busier animal than a blockhead.

Alexander Pope

Ez for war, I call it murder
Ef you take a sword an'dror it,
There you hev it plain an' flat;
An go stick a feller thru,
I don't want to go no further
Guv'ment ain't to answer for it,
Than my testament fer that.
God'll send the bill to you.

James Russell Lowell, Bigelow
Papers, 1846

We have at last grasped the hardest of all truths this nation has had to learn; however remote the aggression, however distant the social or economic disasters that afflict other peoples, sooner or later we ourselves will feel their impact.

Sumner Welles

The human race is a family. Men are brothers. All wars are civil wars. All killing is fratricidal— as the poet Owen put it, 'I am the enemy you killed, my friend.'

Adlai II

The world is now too dangerous for anything but truth, too small for anything but brotherhood.

A.P.Davies

As one winter after another left the work of the Assyrian army in Mesopotamia still unfinished, the political tension in Judah must have relaxed. The government—for King Hezekiah seems at last to have been brought around to believe in Egypt—pursued their negotiations no longer with that decision and real patriotism, which the sense of near danger rouses in even the most selfish and mistaken of politicians, but rather with the heedlessness of principle, the desire to show their own cleverness and the passion for intrigue which run riot among statesmen, when danger is near enough to give an excuse for doing something, but too far away to oblige anything to be done in earnest.

On the Book of Isaiah

VII: Human Nature

The Black Book's comments on human nature are difficult to categorize, humorous as usual, and for the most part of universal applicability. I separate them from comments about the environment which conditions human nature—the "human condition"—which follow in the next chapter. Again, the dividing line is thin.

A confirmed optimist had the misfortune to fall from the roof of a skyscraper. His friends wondered what he could possibly say that would throw any cheerful light on the catastrophe, but he rose to the occasion. As he passed the fourth floor, he was heard to mutter: "So far, so good."

He is a self made man and worships his creator.

Depend on it, when a man knows he's to be hanged in a fortnight, it concentrates his mind wonderfully.
Dr. Johnson

The devil can quote Scripture for his purpose. An evil soul producing holy witness is like a villain with a smiling heart.
Shakespeare, The Merchant of Venice

We judge ourselves by our motives, others judge us by our actions.
Dwight Morrow

An opportunist is a man, who, finding himself in hot water, decides he needs a bath anyway.

The louder he talked of his honor, the faster we counted our spoons.
Emerson

Plato's definition of a man: "A man," he said, "is a two legged animal without feathers." Soon afterwards, one of his followers presented a plucked rooster for Plato's examination. "In such a situation," Plato reflected, "wise men reconsider."

Everyone said it couldn't be done,
But he with a grin replied:
How do you know it can't be done,
Leastwise, if you haven't tried?
And he went right to it and at it.
He tackled the thing that couldn't be done
And he couldn't do it!

I'd rather flunk my Wasserman test
than read the poems of Edgar Guest.
                              Dorothy Parker

"It appears that it does not appear to me now as it appeared to
have appeared to me then."
                              Justice Felix Frankfurter,
                              explaining a change of position

A farmer's pigs were all washed away by a flood. "How about
Johnson's pigs?" the farmer asked. "They're gone, too," he was told.
"And Larson's?" "All lost." "Humh," said the farmer, cheering up,
"Tain't as bad as I thought."

All the wise men were lined up on one side. And all the damned
fools on the other. And, by God, Sir, the damned fools were right.
                              Duke of Wellington

Sir, you are expressing a consternation you do not feel for a
calamity that has not occurred.
                              Dr. Johnson, cited by Croswell
                              Bowen

We see all sights from pole to pole
And glance and nod and bustle by
And never once possess our soul
Before we die.
                              Matthew Arnold

There is so much good in the worst of us
And so much bad in the best of us
That it hardly becomes any of us
To talk about the rest of us.

Self righteousness is the hallmark of inner guilt.

He was "a self centered little clod of ailments and grievances, complaining that the world would not devote itself to making him happy."

George Bernard Shaw

Of a metaphorical water beetle:
Who glided on the water's face
With ease, celerity and grace,
But if he stopped to try and think
Of how he did it, he would sink.

Hillaire Belloc

Two people who share the same bed may dream different dreams.

A Chinese maxim

You can put a curl in a pig's tail but it doesn't increase his weight.

The trouble with death bed conversions is that sometimes the patient doesn't die.

The young man who has not wept is a savage. The old man who will not laugh is a fool.

Fanaticism consists in redoubling your efforts when you have forgotten your aim.

George Santayana

A Roman felt sorry for himself because he did not have a shoe—until he saw a man who did not have a foot.

A wise man who stands firm is a statesman; a fool who stands firm is a catastrophe.

Many things have been revealed to the humble which are hidden from the great.

Give me the benefit of your convictions if you have any, but keep your doubts to yourself, for I have enough of my own.

Goethe

The royal crown cures not the headache.

Benjamin Franklin

A person who buries his head in the sand offers an engaging target.

Adlai II

An expert is like a eunuch in a harem—someone who knows all about it but can't do anything about it.

Dean Acheson

Anybody who would go to a psychoanalyst ought to have his head examined.

Sam Goldwyn

What time he could spare from the advancement of his person he devoted to the neglect of his duties.

Provided a man is not mad he can be cured of every folly but vanity.

Rousseau

If a man will begin with certainties, he shall end in doubts; but if he will be content to begin with doubts, he shall end in certainties.

Sir Francis Bacon

No man who is correctly informed as to the past will be disposed to take a morose or desponding view of the present.

Macauley

It is amazing how late life starts. I am afraid I shall only be born after I am dead.

A pessimist is one who makes difficulties of his opportunities; an optimist is one who makes opportunities of his difficulties.

I would never accept membership in the kind of club that would accept me as a member.

Groucho Marx

No one has ever gone bankrupt by underestimating the taste of the American public.

H.L. Mencken

John Randolph of Roanoke was told that a certain man had been denouncing him. "Denouncing me," replied Randolph with astonishment, "that's strange, I never did him a favor."

There are only three things in the world that can hiss: a goose, a serpent and a man.

Senator Ben 'Pitchfork' Tillman

VIII: The Human Condition

Man is the only creature that laughs and weeps; for he is the only
animal that is struck with the difference between what things are and
what they could be.

Hazlitt

This Chapter records aphorisms and anecdotes loosely depicting
the human condition or environment, as opposed to human nature in the
preceding chapter. It begins with a tale from Adlai I which implies that
the human condition improved in material respects during the span of
the Black Book. Though the family doctor who called upon his patients
is by now largely departed, and the profession of medicine shows
familiar signs of commercialization, there can be little doubt that the
human condition is the beneficiary of a better regulated medical
profession and much advanced medical science.

Residing with Adlai I in the old tavern at Metamora, Illinois
during its "palmy days" in the 1850's, was Doctor John—familiarly
known as Doc, "except upon state occasions." "Standing six feet six in
his number elevens, without an ounce of superfluous flesh, a neck
somewhat elongated and set off to great advantage by an immense
Adam's apple which appeared to be constantly on duty, head large and
features a trifle exaggerated, and with iron gray locks hanging
gracefully over his slightly stooped shoulders, the Doctor would have
given pause to McGregor, even with foot upon his native heather."

He claimed to be a son of "the real old Virginny" and
descendant of one of its "first families," and "there lingered about him
in very truth much of the chivalric bearing of the old cavalier stock. No
man living could possibly have invited a gentleman to partake of some
spirits or to participate in a glass of beer in a loftier manner."

However, the intellectual attainments of the Doctor were not of
the highest order. "He had journeyed little along the flowery paths of
literature. He never gave a 'local habitation or name to the particular
Medical College which had honored him with its degree. He was, as he
often asserted, of the 'epleptic' school of medicine. . . he solemnly
asseverated that it was the only school which permitted its practitioners
to accept all that was good, and reject all that was bad, of the other
schools. In his practice he had a supreme contempt for what he called
'written proscriptions,' and often boasted that he never let one of them
to go out of his office. He infinitely preferred to compound his own

medicines, which, with the aid of mortar and pestle, he did in unstinted measure in his office. . . . In administering his 'doses' his generous spirit manifested itself as clearly as along other lines. . . .It has been many times asserted, and with apparent confidence, that no patient of his ever complained of not receiving his full measure.

"It was a singular fact in the professional experience of this eminent practitioner, that his patients, regardless of age or sex, were all afflicted with a like malady. Many a time as he returned from a professional visit, mounted on his old roan, with his bushel measure medicine bag thrown across his saddle, in answer to my casual inquiry as to the ailment of his patient, he gave in oracular tones, the one all sufficient reply, *'only a slight derangement of the nervous system'*. . .He never quite forgave Mr. Lincoln the reply he once made to an ill advised interruption of the Doctor during a political speech. 'Well, well, Doctor,' replied Mr. Lincoln, good-humoredly, 'I will take anything from you *except your medicines.'*

The Doctor was a bachelor, and his 'May of life' had fallen into the sear and yellow leaf at the time of which we write. He was still, however, as he more than once assured me, an ardent admirer of the 'opposing sect'. . . . The Doctor was much given at times to what he denominated 'low down talks' such as are our wont when kindred souls hold close converse.

"Seated in my office on one occasion, at the hour when churchyards yawn, and being as he candidly admitted in a somewhat 'reminiscent' mood, he unwittingly gave expression to thoughts beyond the reaches of our souls, when I made earnest inquiry, 'Doctor, what in your judgment as a medical man is to be the final destination of the human soul?' "The solemn hour of midnight, together with the no less solemn inquiry, at once plunged the Doctor into deep thought. First carefully changing his quid from the right to the left jaw, he slowly and as if thoughtfully measuring his words, replied: 'Brother Stevenson, the solar system are one of which I have given very little reflection.'"

It's time for the human race to enter the solar system.
George W. Bush

All of us know that space and time have been annihilated on this small, small spaceship we call "planet earth." We can blow it up. We can annihilate the thin envelope of soil on which our nourishment depends, and contaminate the thin layer of air we breathe. This apocalyptic risk exists simply because our modern means of science have made neighbors of us all.

> *Adlai II* , 1965, three weeks before
> his death

No greater calamity can happen to a people than to break utterly with its past.

> *Gladstone*

History shows that great economic and social forces flow like a tide over communities only half conscious of what is befalling them.

> *John Stuart Mill*

Man is flying too fast for a world that is round. Soon he will catch up with himself, in a great rear end collision, and Man will never know that what hit Man from behind was Man.

> *James Thurber*

The world is not respectable;
It is mortal, tormented, confused, deluded forever;
But it is shot through with beauty, with love,
With glints of courage and laughter,
And struggles to the light among the thorns.

> *George Santayana*

The trouble with the world is that the good people get tired of being good before the bad people get tired of being bad.

Wandering between two worlds, one dead, the other powerless to be born.

> *Matthew Arnold*, Dover Beach

Men are so constituted that every one undertakes what he sees another successful in, whether he has aptitude for it or not.

> *Goethe*

This age knows the price of everything and the value of nothing.

> *Oscar Wilde*

It was then that falsehood came into our Russian land. The great misfortune, the root of all the evil to come, was the loss of faith in the value of personal opinions. People imagined that it was out of date to follow their own moral sense, that they must all sing the same tune in chorus, and live by other people's opinions, the notions of which were being crammed down everybody's throats. And there arose the power of the glittering phrase.

Boris Pasternak, Dr. Zhivago

Ah! When shall all men's good
Be each man's rule, and universal peace
Be like a shaft of light across the land,
And like a love of heaven athwart the sea,
Through all the circle of the golden year?
Tennyson

Two centuries ago when a great man appeared, people looked for God's purpose: today we look for his press agent.
Daniel Boorstin

He censures God who quarrels with the imperfections of man.
Thomas Burke

The more things change the more they remain the same.
French proverb

Anthropologists have discovered evidence of the missing link between prehistoric animal and civilized man: we are it.
South American sociologist

Behold the turtle. To make progress it must stick out its neck.
Benjamin Franklin

Them's as hunts treasures must go alone by night and when they find it they have to leave a little of their blood behind them.
Loren Eiseley, Scientist, quoting a woman of Bimini, from The Night Country

The acids of modernity are eating at the foundations of the old culture.

Those who can't remember the past are condemned to repeat it.
George Santayana

The cure for materialism is to have enough for everybody and some to spare. When people are sure of having what they need they cease to think about it.
Henry Ford

I do not know what comfort other people find in considering the weakness of great men, but 'tis always a mortification to me to observe that there is no perfection in humanity.
S. Montague

Every civilization rests on a set of promises. . . .If the promises are broken too often, the civilization dies, no matter how rich it may be, or how mechanically clever. Hope and faith depend on the promises: if hope and faith go, everything goes.
Herbert Agar

What man will not alter for the better, time, the great innovator, will alter for the worse.

Life is merely a bridge; ye are to pass over it and not build your dwelling upon it.
Agrapha of Jesus

A Greek definition of happiness: the full exercise of vital powers in a life giving them scope.

Bliss in possession will not last;
Remembered joys are never past;
At once the fountain, stream and sea
They were, they are, they yet shall be.
James Montgomery

The French Ambassador to Spain complimented Cervantes on his famous Don Quixote. Cervantes whispered, "Had it not been for the Inquisition I should have made it much more entertaining."

Man can always see further than he can reach — dream more than he can achieve.

The vigor of civilized societies is preserved by the widespread sense that high aims are worthwhile.

A.N. Whitehead

Russian during Cold War: "In the United States, man exploits man; in the Communist states it's the other way around."

IX: Prayers and Proverbs

Lord make me an instrument of Thy peace; where there is hatred, let me sow love; where there is injury, pardon; where there is doubt, faith; where there is despair, hope; where there is darkness, light, and where there is sadness, joy.

O Divine Master, grant that I may not so much seek to be consoled as to console; to be understood, as to understand; to be loved, as to love; for it is in giving that we receive, it is in pardoning that we are pardoned, and it is in dying that we are born to eternal life.

St. Francis of Assisi (found by Adlai II's bedside
after his death)

Religion, as revealed in the in the Black Book, is a Christian message of virtue, service, peace and love. Prayers offer comfort and a moral compass. They reflect little ritual, no intolerance or fundamentalism. The Black Book brings in prayers from foreign and ancient sources as if to underscore a universality of its ethic, discordant notes, too, as in all things. Though God is ever present, the message is never dogmatic, let alone messianic. Much of the Black Book's revealed religion is in the form of prayer and Scripture which, being familiar, is not recorded here.

THE FIRST PRAYER IN CONGRESS
December 17, 1777
Rev. J Duche, Chaplain

O Lord, our heavenly Father, High and Mighty, King of Kings and Lord of Lords, who doest from the Throne behold all the dwellers on earth and reignest with power supreme and uncontrolled over all kingdoms, empires and governments; look down in mercy we beseech Thee on these American States, who have fled to Thee from the rod of the oppressor, and thrown themselves on Thy gracious protection desiring henceforth to be dependent only on Thee.

To Thee they have appealed for the righteousness of their cause. To Thee do they look up for that countenance and support which Thou alone canst give. Take them therefore Heavenly Father under Thy nurturing care. Give them wisdom in counsel and valor in the field. Defeat the malicious designs of our cruel adversaries. Convince them of the unrighteousness of their cause, and if they perish in their sanguinary purpose, O, let the voice of thine own unerring justice, sounding in their hearts, constrain them to drop their weapons of war from their unnerved hands in the day of battle.

Be Thou present, O God of wisdom and direct the counsels of this honorable Assembly. Enable them to settle things on the best and surest foundation; that the scent of blood may speedily be closed, that order, harmony and peace may be effectually restored, and truth and just religion and piety may prevail and flourish among thy people. Preserve the health of their bodies, and the vigor of their minds; shower down on them and the millions they represent such temporal blessings as thou seest expedient for them in this world, and crown them with everlasting glory in the world to come. All this we ask in the name and through the merits of Jesus Christ, Thy Son, our Saviour.

> O God,
> Give me the serenity to accept
> what cannot be changed.
> Give me the courage to change
> what can be changed.
> And give me the wisdom
> To know one from the other
> *Reinhold Niebhur*

More things are wrought by prayer than this world dreams of....For so the whole round earth is every way bound by gold chains about the feet of God.

Tennyson, The Passing of Arthur

> Give me, Lord, a little light,
> Be it no more than a glow worm giveth,
> Which goeth about by night,
> To guide me through this life,
> This dream which lasteth but a day,
> Wherein are many things on which to stumble,
> And many things at which to laugh,
> And others like unto a stony path,
> Along which one goes leaping.
> *Prayer of an Aztec Chief*

Listen to the Exhortation of the Dawn!

Look to this Day!
For it is life, the very life of life.
In its brief course lie all the
Verities and Realities of your Existence:
The Bliss of Growth,
The Glory of Action,
The Splendor of Beauty,
For Yesterday is but a dream,
And tomorrow is only a Vision,
But Today well lived makes
Every Yesterday a Dream of Happiness,
And every Tomorrow a vision of Hope.
Look well therefore to this Day!
Such is the Salutation of the Dawn!

Salutation of the Dawn, Sanskrit,
c. 1200 BC

Oh Lord, support us all the day long, until the shadows lengthen
and the evening comes, and the busy world is hushed, and the fever of
life is over, and our work is done. Then in Thy mercy, grant us a safe
lodging and a holy rest, and peace at the last.

The Book of Common Prayer

Where there is patience and humility there is neither anger nor
worry.

St. Francis

Lord, we thank Thee for this place in which we dwell; for the
love that unites us; for the peace accorded us this day; for the hope with
which we expect tomorrow; for the health, the work, the food, and the
bright skies that make our lives delightful for our friends in all parts of
the earth.

Give us grace and strength to persevere. Give us courage, gaiety,
and the quiet mind; spare to us our friends; soften to us our enemies.
Bless us, if it may be, in all our innocent endeavors. If it may not be,
then give us the strength to encounter that which is to come, that we
may be brave in peril, constant in tribulation, temperate in wrath, and in
all changes of fortune and down to the gates of death, loyal and loving
to one another.

Robert Louis Stevenson

I (an Islamist) pray the prayer as the easterners (Christians) do:
May the peace of Allah abide with you
Wherever you stay, wherever you go,
May the beautiful palms of Allah grow;
Through days of labor and nights of rest,
The love of good Allah make you blest.
So I touch my heart as the Easterners do,
May the peace of Allah abide with you.

I (a Christian) asked God for strength, that I might achieve…
I was made weak, that I might learn humbly to obey.
I asked for health, that I might do greater things…
I was given infirmity, that I might do better things.
I asked for riches, that I might be happy…
I was given poverty that I might be wise.
I asked for power, that I might have the praise of men…
I was given weakness, that I might feel the need of God.
I asked for all things, that I might enjoy life…
I was given life, that I might enjoy all things.
I got nothing that I asked for—but everything I had hoped
for.
Almost despite myself, my unspoken prayers were answered.
I am among all men, most richly blessed!

Unknown Confederate soldier —
and a creed for the disabled

He hath showed thee, O man, what is good; and what doth the Lord require of thee, but to do justly, and to love mercy, and to walk humbly with thy God.

Micah, Ch. 6, Verse 8

History is the track of God's footsteps through time. It is in his dealings with our forefathers that we may expect to find the laws by which He will deal with us.

Kingsley

A Benediction:
God keep thee in the busy day
And in night's lonely hour;

though storms may gather 'round thy way
Trust His protecting power.
God guide thee; May his wisdom shine
Unclouded o'er thy soul
And lead thee by its light divine
To the eternal goal.
God Bless thee! On this earth below
And in the world above
A rich inheritance bestow
His everlasting love.

Let us confess our many sins, and beseech Him to give us a
higher courage, a purer patriotism, and more determination in our will;
that He will convert the hearts of our enemies, that He will hasten the
time when war shall cease.

Robert E. Lee, Orders of the Day,
August 13, 1863

God himself, the father and fashioner of all there is, older than
the sun or the sky, greater than time and eternity and all the flow of
being, is unutterable by any lawgiver, unutterable by any voice, not to
be seen by any eye. But we, being unable to apprehend his essence, use
the help of sounds and names and pictures, of beaten gold and ivory and
silver, of plants and rivers, mountain peaks and torrents, yearning for
the knowledge of him, and in our weakness naming all that is beautiful
in this world after his nature —just as happens to earthly lovers. To
them the most beautiful sight will be the actual lineaments of the
beloved, but for remembrance' sake they will be happy in the site of a
lyre, a little spear, a chair perhaps, or a running ground, or anything in
the world that wakens the memory of the beloved. Why should I further
examine and pass judgment about images? Let men know what is
divine. Let them know: that is all. If a Greek is stirred to the
remembrance of God by the art of Pheidias, an Egyptian by paying
worship to animals, another man by a river, another by fire....I have no
anger for their divergences; only let them know, let them love, let them
remember.

Maximus of Tyre, Dissertatio

A discordant Prayer contributed by a Member of the Alabama
House of Representatives in the mid 1950's: "ON FIRE FOR GOD"

Be not forgetful to entertain strangers, for thereby some have entertained angels unawares.

Hebrews XIII, 2, c. 65

An old Negro preacher of the deep south who never had to worry about empty pews always preceded his sermon with this prayer:

"Oh, Lawd, give thy servant dis mawnin 'de eye of de eagle and de wisdom of de owl; connect his soul with the gospel telephone in de central skies; 'luminate his brow with de sun of heaven; saturate his heart with love for de people; turpentine his 'magination, grease his lips with possum, loosen him with the sledge hammer of they power; 'lectrify his brain with de lightning of thy word; put 'petual motion in his arms, fill him plum full of de dynamite of glory; 'noint him all over with de kerosene oil of salvation and set him a-fire."

Just now the Sun was rising
Then He said, "His candles shineth on my head,
and by His light I go through darkness."
Bunyan

Judge not the Lord by feeble sense
But trust him for his grace
Behind a frowning providence
He hides a smiling face.
William Cowper

X: Marriage, Romance

Unlike the Chapter XII, Love, this one has nothing solemn to record from the Black Book about marriage, romance and the family—from which, I trust, no conclusions will be drawn.

A young man approached the father of his intended and asked his approval of the marriage. The father was skeptical. "I doubt very much," he said," that you can support my daughter—I can hardly do it myself." To which the young suitor offered the bright suggestion: "We'll just have to pool our resources."

A young bridegroom said that every time he was about to make ends meet, his wife moved the ends.

A man asked the judge for a divorce because his wife talked to much. The judge asked what she said. The poor man thought awhile and replied: "Well, Judge, she don't say."

Nothing upsets a woman like somebody's getting married she didn't even know had a beau.

A husband, told his mother-in-law was coming for a visit and asked for a comment, replied: "I refuse to answer on grounds it might tend to eliminate me."

Farmer Jones asked how he felt about his ailing wife, said: "Seems like Sadie's been awful slow about it. Danged if I don't wish as how she'd hurry up and git well—or something."

A waiter at one of the candlelight restaurants in Washington rushed up to a table the other evening and said, "Madam, your husband just slid under the table." "No," the woman replied, "he just came in the door."

Mixed emotions: The feeling you have when you see your mother-in-law drive over a cliff in your new Cadillac.

An English bishop received the following note from the Vicar of a village in his diocese: "My Lord, I regret to inform you of the death of my wife. Can you possibly send me a substitute for the weekend?"

Larry: "What do they call a man who is lucky in love?" Brad: "A bachelor."

A farmer and his wife went to a picnic. The wife carried the basket four miles to the park gate where he relieved her of the burden. "I think I'd better carry the basket now, my dear, we might get separated."

Proposal of a young farmer: "Marry me and I'll paint the house and the barn, inside and out; I'll put in electricity. I'll buy a brand new stove and a refrigerator – will you marry me?" She said, "Honey, let's leave it this way: you do all those things and then ask me again."

She is a fabulous first lady. I was a lucky man when she said, "Yes, I agree to marry you." I love her dearly, and I am proud of the job she is doing on behalf of all Americans. Just like I love my brother.

George W. Bush, September 9, 2003, Jacksonville, Florida

And I am glad Laura is here tonight. In my book, she's a fabulous first lady. And I love her a lot and I hope she loves me a lot for dragging her out of Texas.

George W. Bush, July 18, 2003, Dallas, Texas

276

XI: Youth, Children

I love these little people; and it is not a slight thing,
when they who are so fresh from God, and love us.
Charles Dickens

Dickens' moving comment about children expressed a universal
sentiment, but the affection for children expressed in the Black Book
was unaffected by such sobriety. Its comments are characteristically
humorous, often making a point.

As soon as his brother was born, little Willie hurried to spread
the news. He told his friend, Johnny: "We have a new baby, and it cost
$100." Johnny replied: "Gee, that's a lot of money just for a baby."
"Yes," Willie agreed, "But think how long they last."

Boy Scouts reported to the Scout Master the good deeds for the
day. First boy: "I helped a lady across the street at 4th and Main."
Second boy: "I helped a lady across the street at 4th and Main." Third
boy, conscious of his pledge to tell the truth: "Of course, it was the same
old lady. She didn't want to cross the street, and it took all three of us to
get the job done."

Youth is a wonderful state. It's a shame it has to be wasted on
young people.
George Bernard Shaw

Mrs. Oscar Hammerstein tells the story of the baby boy who was
perfect in every way, except his speech. He couldn't talk. At the age of
two, his parents began to worry. When he was three they hustled him off
to a child psychologist, whose efforts were fruitless. At six the boy was
still mute. But finally one morning at breakfast with his parents, the boy
blurted out, "This cocoa is no darn good." Both parents leaped with joy.
"Son," they exclaimed joyously, "you can talk! You've uttered a
complete sentence. But tell us, how come you haven't talked up to
now?" "Because," he replied, "up to now everything was all right."

A law student wrote at the bottom of a paper: "Professor Hayes,
I know this is not up to my standard. I'm sorry I haven't done well on
this examination. But I was up all night. At six this morning my wife

gave birth to a six pound baby girl. I was disappointed. I hoped it would be a boy. I wanted to name him after you."

Overheard in the high school locker room: "Well, the fight started when he hit me back."

A teacher asked children studying the Crusades, "Who was Saladin? Who was Richard the Lion Hearted? And what happened to Frederick Barbarossa?" No response to the former. As to Barbarossa, an eager pupil said, "Oh, he was suspended last week for smoking."

A family is moving to New York, and the little daughter is saying her last bedtime prayer in the old home: "Bless Daddy. Bless Mommy. Bless Freddy. And now dear Lord, I have to say good-bye. We are moving to New York."

Robert Taft was appointed Ambassador to Ireland by President Eisenhower where he enrolled his young daughter in school. On her first day in school, she was asked to rise and say something about herself. She responded, 'my great grandfather was President of the United States. My Grandfather was a United States Senator. My father is the American Ambassador. My name is Martha, and I am a Brownie.'

A tale often recited in opening
remarks of Adlai III

In the name of welfare reform, President Clinton signed a law repealing the Aid to Dependent Children program. Mothers on welfare were given five years to find work before their aid was ended. One and a half million children were thrust deeper into poverty, the five years of welfare had been exhausted.

XII: Love

Little of romantic love is recorded in the Black Book. The love of which it speaks is of humanity — and life.

Someday, after we have mastered the winds, the waves, the tides and gravity, we will harness for God the energies of Love: and then, for the second time in the history of the World, Man will have discovered Fire.

Pierre Teilhard de Chardin

Nor can that endure which has not its foundation upon love. For love alone diminishes not, but shines with its own light; makes an end of discord, softens the fires of hate, restores peace in the world, brings together the sundered, and redresses wrongs, aids all and injures none; and who so invokes its aid will find peace and safety and have no fear of future ill.

From the Act of Horodlo, 1413
AD

Love is the purest form of vital energy.
Pasternak

To love is not to look at one another but to look together in the same direction.
Saint-Exupery

Give smiles to those who love you less, but keep your tears for me.
Thomas Moore

No wonder you love him, he, too, was mad.
Nietsche

She bid me take love lightly.
As the leaves grown on the tree
But I was one and twenty
And with her did not agree.
From *Sally Garden, Irish song*

Not where I breathe, but where I love, I live.
Southwell

XIII: Temperance and Intemperance

A doctor advised his patient to stop drinking. He later saw the patient inebriated and berated him: "I told you that if you wanted to see and hear, you'd have to stop drinking." "Doc, what I've been drinking is so much better than what I've been seeing and hearing lately that I've decided to keep it up."

In the early days reflected in the Black Book, temperance is an object of intense commitment by many and, therefore, a politically sensitive subject. As times pass, intemperance becomes a subject of humor —and greater tolerance.

From Adlai I:
Alfred W. Arrington started as a circuit riding preacher, became a circuit riding lawyer, politician and venerable Judge—following a by now familiar path. He became an advocate of renown with an attractive appearance and "to crown all, a massive Websterian forehead, needing no seal to give the world assurance of a man." In addition to his judicial labors, Arrington, wrote vivid sketches from an early part of his life spent in Texas, including a piece on Paul Denton, an early Methodist circuit rider, who had been "announced" to preach at a famous Spring where "plenty of good liquor" was promised to all who attended.

During the ensuing sermon, a "desperado" demanded: "Mr. Denton, where is the liquor you promised?". . . . "There!" answered the preacher in tones of thunder and pointing his motionless finger at a spring gushing up in two columns from the bosom of the earth with a sound like a shout of joy, "There," he repeated, "there is the liquor which God the Eternal brews for all his children. Not in the simmering still over the smoky fires choked with poisonous gases, surrounded with stench of sickening odors and corruptions, doth your father in heaven prepare the precious essence of life—pure cold water; but in the green glade and grassy dell, where the red deer wanders and the child loves to play, there God brews it; and down, low down, in the deepest valleys, where the fountains murmur, and the rills sigh, and high upon the mountain tops where the naked granite glitters like gold in the sun, where the storm cloud broods and the thunder storms crash; and far out on the wide, wild sea, where the hurricane howls music and the big waves roll the chorus, sweeping the march of God — there he brews it, the beverage of life, health giving water. And everywhere it is a thing of life and beauty — gleaming in the dew drop; singing in the summer rain; shining in the ice gem till the trees all seem turned to living jewels; spreading a golden veil over the sun or a white gauze around the midnight moon; sporting in the glacier; folding its bright snow curtain softly about the wintry world; and weaving the many colored bow whose warp is the rain drops of earth, whose woof is the sunbeam of heaven, all checkered over with the mystic hand of refraction. . . .Still it is beautiful, that blessed life-water. No poisonous bubbles are on its brink; its foam brings not murder and madness; no blood stains its liquid glass; pale widows and starving orphans weep not burning tears into its depths; no drunkard's shrieking ghost from the grave curses it in the world of eternal despair. Beautiful, pure, blessed, and glorious. Speak out, my friends, would you exchange it for the demon's drink, alcohol?" Pity the thirsty desperado.

Also from Adlai I:

One Duncan was a candidate for the Legislature in ante bellum days when the temperance question was giving much trouble to aspirants for public office. In the midst of his speech in the old McLean County (Illinois) courthouse, the candidate was interrupted by one of the inquisitive type who appear when least wanted, with the question:

'Mr. Duncan, are you in favor of the Maine law (which established prohibition for that state)?'

'Yes, yes, I am coming to that very soon.'

Shying off to the tariff, the improvement of Western rivers, and the necessity of rigid economy in all public expenditures, our candidate was about to close when the same troublesome inquiry, 'Mr. Duncan, *are you in favor* of the Maine Law?' again greeted his unwilling ears.

'Oh yes,' exclaimed the orator, in tone and manner indicating much thankfulness: 'I am glad you called my attention to this subject; I know I was about to forget it. My fellow-citizens have a right to know my views upon all public question, and I have nothing to conceal. I have no respect for candidates who attempt to dodge any of these great questions. I have given you fully, my views upon the tariff, upon a general system of internal improvements, and something of my own services in the past; and now thanking you for your attention, will —'

'Mr. Duncan, are you *in favor of the Maine Law?'* were the words that again escaped the lips of the importunate inquisitor.

Fully appreciating his dilemma —with constituents about evenly divided upon the dangerous question —the candidate at once nerved himself for the answer upon which hung his fears, and boldly replied:

Yes, sir, I am in favor of the law, but everlastingly opposed to its enforcement!'

A temperance lady orator concluded her peroration: "I would rather commit adultery than take a glass of beer." Voice from the audience: "Who wouldn't?"

Brooks Hayes

A drunk kept calling the hotel switchboard all night to ask what time the bar opened and finally was informed that in his condition he would not be admitted. He shouted in reply: "I don't want in, I want out."

Winston Churchill, according to legend, received a group of temperance ladies at his country home. They were concerned about his moral, as well as his physical, well being. "Mr. Prime Minister," said their spokesman, "if all the brandy you have drunk in the past five years was poured into this room, it would reach up to here." As she indicated a point almost half way up the wall, the Prime Minister looked at her and then into her eyes, "Ah, madam," he said wistfully, "so little done, so much to do."

Lady Astor, the peppery Virginian wife of Lord Astor—with whom in 1945-6 we spent weekends at their famous estate, Cliveden, outside London, also a weekend retreat for Churchill—was reputed to have approached Churchill at a party and said, "You are drunk." Sir Winston replied, "Madam, you are ugly. But in the morning I will be sober."

An Irishman went to a particularly boisterous wake. He drank too much, passed out and was placed in a coffin by his friends. Upon wakening he was startled to find himself in such circumstances and said to himself, "If I'm alive then why am I in this coffin—and if I'm dead why do I have to go to the bathroom so badly."

Acknowledgements

Many are our benefactors in this enterprise stretching back more than a century and a half. Without Jesse Fell and his protégé, David Davis, there might never have been a President Abraham Lincoln—or the Black Book. Too many are the benefactors over the Black Book's span for recognition. Carol Evans aided Adlai II with many years of faithful service in government and out. Phyllis Gustafson served with him and followed with me for more than thirty years until her death. She left her modest savings to a neighbor and to favorite causes of the Stevensons. Carol and Phyllis, never married, faithful and diligent, little recognized, were keepers of the Black Book. In helping organize and edit it for publication, Barbara Ascher brought order to a product of disorderly habits and contributed a detached perspective, succeeding Joy Johannsen whose generous editorial efforts were sadly cut short by illness. Mary Trimble rescued the Black Book from my typing while contributing valuable editorial suggestions and needed encouragement. Frances Mautner-Markhof, Director of the Austrian Center for International Studies, encouraged me during many moments of weariness in recent years, and contributed to the historical perspective, sharpening dull memories of Gibbon, Spengler and Clausewitz. Greg Koos, President of the McLean County Historical Museum, contributed valuable recollections of my family and its roots in that County. Phyllis Wender a literary agent who offered sound editorial comments and was a source of encouragement with an evident interest in recording history for its lessons. Paul Dillon offered many helpful comments. Terry Stephan gave me and son Warwick invaluable copy editing and assistance and advice. Nancy is a member of the Black Book's cast and my partner, the mother to our family. Her faithful, near life-long support, even as she wrote her own books, made the effort possible for me. She aided Adlai II in his later years.

In pulling together the bits of wit and wisdom which comprise the Black Book, I came across a copy of Thesaurus of Anecdotes by Edmund Fuller, Crown Publishers, 1942, inscribed by Adlai II. It includes some anecdotes also recorded in the Black Book — many of them Lincoln stories. Provenance is at times difficult to establish. Mr. Fuller prefaces his Thesaurus with a message which encouraged me to persevere:

"Anecdotes are stories with points. They are tools — nail-sinkers to drive home arguments firmly.

They are the origin of all thinking. In their old form they are known as parables. By means of them, Jesus Christ taught. The prophets and sages of all ancient religions and wisdom employed the simple, effective parable.

Thus, stories with points were made to embody profound teachings. So the Greek slave, Aesop, sagely propounded his fables. Today the true anecdote is still the counterpart of the parable and fable. Time has tended to shorten it somewhat and, as an attribute of our temperament, we have made it often funny....

All prove something. The thing to remember is, many jokes are anecdotes but not all anecdotes are funny."

I would disappoint my coauthors, if, in the end, we failed to acknowledge the indebtedness of an American family to the America of the Black Book. It was our privilege to have served it— and by this modest means to recall it.

Index

Taft, Robert 181, 277
Taft, William H. 152
Tagge, George 128
Talleyrand 78, 105
Talmadge, Herman 89
Teilhard de Chardin, Pierre 278
Tennyson, Alfred 246, 265, 269
Thackery 238
Thailand 158
Thant, U 254
The International Monetary Fund 157
Thompson, James 205
Thoreau, Henry David 201
Thurber, James 264
Thurmond, Strom 27
Tillman, Ben 'Pitchfork' 261
Tilton, Theodore 238
Tolstoy 255
Toynbee, Arnold 34, 162, 220
Trueblood, Elton 124
Truman, Harry 27, 64, 85, 176, 181, 225
Turkey 92, 168, 222, 223
Twain, Mark 24, 84, 95, 101, 102, 103, 107, 134
Tyler, Alexander 80
Tyler, Patrick 173
Urqhart, Brian 169
Van Dyke, Henry 239
Vance, Cyrus 44
Vance, Zebulon 'Zeb' 119, 238
Venezuela 221
Vietnam 42, 43, 44, 49, 50, 93, 171, 180, 182, 185, 193
Volcker, Paul 154
Voltaire 105, 117, 123
von Clausewitz, Carl 5, 174, 183
Vrydolyak, Edward 207
Walker, Dan 43
Walker, Kenneth 48
Walpole, Horace 238, 243
Walt, Stephen 202
Warren, Charles 99
Washington, George 186, 206